D1714823

Jewish Souls,
Bureaucratic Minds

Jewish Souls, Bureaucratic Minds

Jewish Bureaucracy and Policymaking in Late Imperial Russia, 1850–1917

VASSILI SCHEDRIN

Wayne State University Press
Detroit

20 19 18 17 16   5 4 3 2 1

ISBN 978-0-8143-4042-4 (cloth); ISBN 978-0-8143-4043-1 (ebook)
Library of Congress Cataloging Number: 2016954100

Typeset by Keata Brewer, E.T. Lowe Publishing
Composed in Adobe Caslon Pro

Wayne State University Press
Leonard N. Simons Building
4809 Woodward Avenue
Detroit, Michigan 48201-1309

Visit us online at wsupress.wayne.edu

For my wife,
Elena Karavannykh

For my children,
Nadya, Vera, Denis, Mikhail, and Timofey

In loving memory of my parents,
Liudmila Naumkina and Albert Schedrin

Contents

Acknowledgments

The research and writing of the dissertation on which this book is based was a life-changing experience for me. As I lived through many challenges, choices, changes, losses and gains in my personal life, I was also living during a great turning point of world history: the end of the Cold War, the fall of the Soviet Union, and the emergence of a new Russia. In the midst of these unprecedented political, social and economic shifts, I was privileged to take part in the effort to reclaim Russia's forgotten and forbidden past, rediscovering hidden archives and rethinking neglected historical experience. Now that my book is being published, I want to express immense gratitude to my teachers, colleagues, and friends who instructed, challenged, criticized, advised, helped in many ways, and simply believed in me all along.

It all started in late 1980s Moscow. I was initiated as a student of history in the uniquely stimulating atmosphere of the Historical Archives Institute (now the Russian State University for the Humanities) headed by the late Iurii Afanas'ev. Leading Russian historians, such as Nataliia Basovskaia, Mikhail Davydov, and the late Aleksandr Stepanskii, taught me the craft of working with archival sources and the art of writing history. At the same time, I was lucky to be the student of world-renowned experts in Jewish studies, Jewish history, literature, and languages from the United States and Israel, including Menachem Ben-Sasson, Robert Chazan, David Fishman, Pesach Fiszman, Samuel Kassow, Dov-Ber Kerler, and David Roskies, while Marek Web of the YIVO Institute for Jewish Research introduced me to the archival collections in Russian Jewish history.

My intellectual and professional growth continued overseas in the Near Eastern and Judaic Studies Department at Brandeis University.

Acknowledgments

My teachers at Brandeis and at other universities in the greater Boston area shaped me as a scholar and teacher of Jewish history, fostering my understanding of scholarship and teaching as a calling, not only as a career. Antony Polonsky was and is much more than a principal academic advisor to me during my years at graduate school. He sets the standard of professionalism and humanity for me, along with my other teachers, including Gregory Freeze, Reuven Kimelman, Benjamin Ravid, Jonathan Sarna, and Ruth Wisse.

The writing of my dissertation and the reshaping of it into a book greatly benefited from the criticism and invaluable advice of my mentors and colleagues, foremost among them ChaeRan Freeze, Yohanan Petrovsky-Shtern, and Steven Zipperstein. I am grateful to many more, including Eugene Avrutin, Valerii Dymshits, Brian Horowits, Viktor Kelner, the late John Klier, Mikhail Krutikov, Benjamin Nathans, Moshe Rosman, and Shaul Stampfer, who kindly read and rigorously commented on my writing and generously shared their expertise and insight.

I very much appreciate the warm atmosphere and intellectual support that I found at the Center for Jewish Studies at the University of Florida in Gainesville, where I did most of my work on this book. My colleagues and friends, including Norman Goda, Eric Kligerman, Jack Kugelmass, Dragan Kujundzic, and Tamir Sorek, helped make my time in Florida most productive.

My current appointment as the Alfred and Isabel Bader Post-Doctoral Fellow in Jewish Studies at Queen's University has generously afforded me the precious time needed at the final stages of this book project.

Two essential contributors to this book are Nataliia Grinchenko of the National Library of Russia, who facilitated my archival and library research in St. Petersburg, and Annette Ezekiel Kogan, my editor. To them I am greatly indebted for the accuracy of facts and the clarity of the argument presented in this book.

Kathryn Wildfong of Wayne State University Press made my manuscript's preparation, editing, and production a hassle-free and efficient process, from which this book and its author greatly benefited.

The Howard Sachar Travel Fellowship and Provost's Dissertation Expense Award from Brandeis University facilitated my dissertation research and writing. The Research Expense Award for Faculty from

Franklin and Marshall College provided support for reshaping and expanding my PhD dissertation into a book manuscript.

My love for my wife, Elena Karavannykh, and my children, Nadya, Vera, Denis, Mikhail, and Timofey, as well as their love, which I feel and appreciate, truly propelled my writing. This love continues to propel my life and work. I dedicate this book to my loved ones.

Introduction

The only ones who pretended to understand nothing [of genuine Jewish interest], who toadied more than ever to the government and tried to induce the Jewish population to adopt the same tactics, were . . . Jews . . . who claimed to speak in the name of their people. . . . They trembled lest any word . . . of theirs should reflect on the quality of their patriotism, and when the most sensitive interests of the Jewish people were in balance, it was the patriotism . . . that turned the scale. . . . The iron course of history has passed over them. They refused to reckon with the soul of the people and the future does not reckon with them. Even their names are forgotten.

—*Shmarya Levin, Forward from Exile*

This book focuses on the Russian Jewish bureaucrats known as *uchenye evrei* (lit., learned Jews or expert Jews).[1] They have never been the subject of a historical study, by their contemporaries nor by later scholars. However, the fictional expert Jew became a stereotype in Russian language, culture, politics, and literature. What can we learn about expert Jews and how can we reconcile the stereotype with the reality?

There are three perspectives on expert Jews: Russian, Jewish, and that of the expert Jews themselves.

In Russian culture, the "expert Jew" was a symbol of the hypocritical humanism, goodwill, and civility of the Russian imperial authorities. Thus, a fictional governor claims that he is not an antisemite because he works side by side with an expert Jew on his staff. However, this governor

1

uses the expertise of his expert Jew to justify essentially antisemitic policies: "In order to persecute the Jews, the governor made the expert Jew his closest aide."[2] In the world of Russian bureaucracy, such proximity to one's superiors meant full compliance with their policies and unquestioning obedience to their orders, even those that went against basic morals, ethical norms, and social conventions.[3] Thus, the term "expert Jew" was also used to describe corrupt intellectuals whose service can be bought by the authorities and who is invested with some authority himself. As a Russian official, the expert Jew served the tsar and the tsarist state. Therefore, the expert Jew's service ethos was founded on the official (*kazennyi*) understanding of progress and the public good. Furthermore, the fictional Jewish officials found in Russian literature are called "lackeys of the official good" (*lakei kazennogo dobra*).[4]

Jews expected nothing but trouble from any Russian official. However, Russian officials were not bad because they were immoral or simply mean. They caused trouble for Jews in their capacity as state official. As the Russian saying goes, "Sergeant is his rank, not his fault" (*uriadnik—chin, a ne vina*).[5] However, as the Jewish saying goes, "A Jewish governor is [as unthinkable] as a Jewish drunkard" (*evrei-gubernator, chto evrei-p'ianitsa*).[6] In the Jewish popular imagination, the very idea of a Jewish official was immoral and un-Jewish. By accepting an official rank, a Jewish official rejected Judaism and Jewish identity. Betraying his people, he opened a virtual "store full of [Jewish] vices for the empire," selling or exposing Jewish sins against the government to the Russian authorities.[7] Jewish officials sifted meticulously through their "merchandise," making inventory of Jews and their vices, giving a proper name to every item, because "anonymity is suspicious, and there should be order in the empire."[8] Jewish officials explained Judaism to the Russian authorities in order to make sure that the Jewish faith fully supported, and by no means undermined, the autocratic throne.[9]

For Jewish officials themselves, the choice of a bureaucratic career was a difficult moral and ethical decision. This choice and the resulting successful career were paid for dearly by a constant and inescapable syndrome of split personality. The fictional Russian attorney Miron Dorskii (né Meilakh Vainshtein) "was split into two, three, [even] four [parts]. His heart was stuck there, in the Pale of Settlement . . . however, his mind, though living on sufferance (*na ptich'ikh pravakh*), had settled beyond the Pale. Well, not on the very top [of the social ladder], but not on the lowest rung."[10]

In striking contrast to popular perceptions and literary accounts, archival documents reveal a very different, much brighter, and broader picture: a more attractive and nuanced portrait of the actual historical expert Jews. Reports by their Russian superiors—governors and other top imperial officials—testify that expert Jews were instrumental and even essential for building mutual trust between the Russian government and Russian Jews, allowing them to work together. In some cases, the intervention of expert Jews even prevented bloody incidents of antisemitic violence in the cities of the Pale of Settlement. The voluminous official memoranda of expert Jews reveal their genuine care about Jewish communal and religious life. Expert Jews in great measure shaped the policies of the Russian state, which allowed and even supported key traditional Jewish institutions, such as the religious courts (*batei din*), and key regulations of Jewish religious law (*halacha*), such as the ban on taking oaths in between the holidays of Rosh Hashana and Yom Kippur. The unofficial pursuits of expert Jews, such as their original works of historiography, contributed a great deal to the building of modern Jewish identity through the discovery and research of Jewish history in Russia. In the modern Russian state, only official perceptions and opinions about political and social problems really mattered in policymaking. Piles of bureaucratic paperwork compellingly show that the voices of expert Jews, expressing their true concern with the improvement of the social and economic status of Russian Jews, were often the only Jewish voices heard and taken into account by the government.

In fact, the actual historical Jewish officials—the expert Jews—who lived and worked in late imperial Russia loyally and eagerly served the tsar and the empire. Thoroughly bureaucratic in their mindset, they were still genuinely Jewish in their souls. The combination of a bureaucratic mentality and a Jewish identity was integral to the service and everyday life of expert Jews. Their personal integrity helped give integrity and continuity to the official policies toward Russian Jews, which expert Jews helped make. This book represents a discovery of the real expert Jews: Russian officials with Jewish souls and bureaucratic minds.

In this book, we examine the phenomenon of Jewish bureaucracy in the Russian empire—its institutions, personnel, and policies—from 1850 to 1917. In particular, we focus on the institution of expert Jews, the mid-level Jewish bureaucrats who served the Russian state both in the Pale of Settlement and in the central offices of the Ministry of Internal Affairs in St. Petersburg.

The Russian government created the bureaucratic institution of expert Jews in the mid-nineteenth century as a means of realizing its ambitious program of social transformation and integration of imperial minorities, including Jews. Since the early nineteenth century, Russian imperial policies toward ethnic and religious minorities were increasingly based on a *mission civilisatrice*. They did not target the religious confessions themselves, but the traditional way of life of the minorities. The modern Russian state generally upheld the policies of religious tolerance of premodern Russia, but at the same time it sought the social transformation of the national minorities it had inherited.[11] To this end, the imperial government invested enormous effort into the transformation and standardization of the diverse lifestyles of minorities by means of paternalistic bureaucratic policies based on *raison d'état* and inspired by the Western culture of the Enlightenment. Certain minority groups such as Poles, Ukrainians, Muslims, and Jews were considered the least loyal segment of the minority population and thus received the most attention from the authorities. In the case of the Russian Jews, government policies targeted their perceived traditional "wandering," their "unsettled" lifestyle (as compared to that of the surrounding Russian peasants, firmly settled and historically bound to the land on which they toiled),[12] and were aimed at cultivating patterns of firm settlement, modern education, and social transformation of traditional Jewish society.

The government initially formed a Jewish bureaucracy as a clerical institution responsible for the regulation of religious aspects of Jewish life. This institution, however, ended up playing a far greater role than that of religious regulation: it was central to the administration of the Jews, providing crucial support for government policies encouraging Jewish conformity to imperial social and legal standards. The Jewish bureaucracy's "moral exhortation" of the Jews promoted the authority of the government and legitimized its administrative measures.[13]

The creation of the Jewish clerical bureaucracy, such as government rabbis and expert Jews, was by no means a unique phenomenon in the context of Russian imperial policy toward other religious minorities, including Muslims and non-Orthodox Christians. Because of the acute shortage of adequate Russian bureaucratic personnel, the government often incorporated traditional indigenous non-Russian elites into the imperial bureaucracy, which, historically and culturally, was completely alien to minority peoples. These elites were also assigned bureaucratic functions that bound them to the government and significantly weakened their ties to their native social and political environment.[14] Thus, non-Russian officials effectively joined the ranks of Russian bureaucracy, adopting the culture and mission of imperial officialdom.

The bureaucracy of late imperial Russia assumed responsibility for two major tasks: preserving the political integrity and upholding the technical modernization of the autocratic regime. In taking on these tasks, Russian ministries and other bureaucratic organs attempted to redirect the backward agrarian Russian society along the path of historical progress. The largest Russian bureaucratic agency, the Ministry of Internal Affairs, which included the Jewish clerical bureaucracy, embodied this mission and effectively represented a quasi-state for the tens of millions of imperial subjects of all classes, races, and religions under its bureaucratic control. In actuality, these bureaucratic institutions supplanted autocracy in everyday political and administrative practice. Thus, the ever-expanding bureaucratic institutes of the Russian ministerial system consolidated and wielded much of the real political power in late imperial Russia. The bureaucrats themselves remodeled their mission and status of humble servitors of the tsar, and emerged as a powerful social elite in Russian society.[15]

In the sphere of official policymaking toward the Jews, bureaucratic institutions and procedures in most cases prevailed over the antisemitic attitudes and actions of Russian officials. Jewish advocates of integration into Russian society such as Mikhail Morgulis believed that the emergence of the Jewish bureaucratic sector, including the office of expert Jew, could "emancipate a whole class of the population [the Jews] from personal whim [of individual officials]."[16] In this sense, Jewish bureaucracy would create an institutional buffer between official policymakers and the Jews affected by those policies. Thus, the bureaucratization of all aspects of Russian Jewish life could help neutralize the notorious judeophobia of the tsars and individual bureaucrats.[17]

The emergence of Russian Jewish bureaucracy paralleled and in many key aspects emulated similar processes in modern European states such as Prussia, Austria-Hungary, and France.[18] According to Robert Crews, the design of bureaucratized religious authority rested on the proposition, elaborated by Enlightenment thinkers throughout Europe, that religions everywhere display certain common characteristics. Tolerated faiths, essentially elaborate systems of discipline, could prove valuable to "enlightened" rulers. Thus, recourse to religious authority might contribute to the making of loyal and disciplined subjects.[19] This vision shaped the initial design of the Russian Jewish clerical bureaucracy, modeled on the French Jewish consistories, bureaucratized representative institutions linking Jewish communities with the French state. However, in the end Russian Jewish bureaucracy, especially expert Jews, became an integral part of imperial Russian officialdom, complete with its paternalistic attitude toward society. Thus, while Jewish bureaucracies in Europe represented the Jews in affairs of state, Russian Jewish bureaucracy represented the state in Jewish affairs.

In contrast with other Jewish state servitors within Russian Jewish bureaucracy, such as government rabbis (*kazennye ravviny*) and members of the Rabbinical Commission (*chleny Ravvinskoi komissii*), expert Jews (*uchenye evrei*) were the most integrated group within the world of Russian officialdom. This unique social group was a bureaucratic elite and an important state institution. Their lives and careers were vivid examples of what Michael Stanislawski has called the "institutionalization of the Russian Haskalah."[20] They were maskilim (adherents of the Haskalah, the Jewish enlightenment) not only by confession, but also by profession. Educated in the official Jewish school system set up by the government and rising through the ranks of government service, they ultimately represented the fulfillment of the imperial integrationist political vision.

The main contribution of expert Jews was in the sphere of policy-making and implementation. Unlike the traditional intercession of *shtadlanim* (Jewish lobbyists) in the high courts of power, expert Jews employed highly routinized bureaucratic procedures, including daily communications with both the provincial and central bureaucracies.[21] This book illustrates how, at the local level, expert Jews advised the state, influenced decision making, negotiated power, and shaped Russian state policy toward the Jews. We examine the complex interactions between the Russian state, the modern Jewish elites, and traditional Jewish society.

Based on extensive new archival data from the former Soviet archives, this book is a new look at the secluded world of Russian bureaucracy where Jews shared policymaking and administrative tasks with their Russian colleagues. The new sources show that these Russian Jewish bureaucrats were competent, full participants in official Russian politics.

In this book, Russian Jewish bureaucracy is seen as a phenomenon that grew out of very different concepts, including Western political strategies of Jewish modernization and integration, Russian imperial policies toward ethnic and religious minorities, and the Russian bureaucratic milieu. Several important questions arise: What was the political agenda of the Russian Jewish bureaucracy? How did this agenda compare with that of traditional Jewish politics (i.e., *shtadlanut*), modern Jewish politics (i.e., socialism and nationalism), and Russian government politics (i.e., integration vs. isolation of the Jews)? How did Jewish bureaucrats integrate their politics into the political milieu of the general Russian bureaucracy? What factors contributed to the political continuity and institutional endurance of Russian Jewish bureaucracy?

The introduction of expert Jews—an important elite group largely overlooked by scholars—substantially changed the political, social, and institutional map of modern Russian Jewry. The argument of this book is that expert Jews did not aim to exploit the power of the Russian state, as did Russian maskilim. Nor did these Jewish bureaucrats desire to dominate traditional communal Jewish politics, as did the maskilim's Orthodox opponents. Instead, Russian Jewish bureaucrats were motivated primarily by their unique bureaucratic service ethos, which combined a devotion to the Jewish people with a strong commitment to change through the bureaucratic transformation of the Jews.

In nineteenth-century western Europe, most modern states legally emancipated the Jews. European governments vigorously pursued the civil regeneration of the Jews, seeking a transformation of the wretched medieval Jew into a full member of the non-Jewish nation and a citizen of the state. By contrast, the modern Russian state never fully, in the European sense, emancipated its Jews.[22] Instead, the Russian government mainly sought to create order within the Jewish population, rather than civil improvement. The main argument of this book is that, in this context, the government's chief priority was the appropriation of traditional religious authority (by establishing a government rabbinate, the office of expert Jew, and the Rabbinical Commission) and of select traditional institutions (such as the rabbinical courts, *batei din*) under the bureaucratic control of the state. This bureaucratized authority integrated the Jews into the confessional structure of imperial society. Thus, government policymakers conceived of Jews and the other tolerated confessions (on par with non-Orthodox Christians, Muslims, and others) as an essential building block of the imperial state rather than as a burdensome and harmful minority.

We demonstrate how the bureaucratic mindset of expert Jews helped to shape state policies as well as, ultimately, a distinctively Russian Jewish modernity. Labeled by scholars as "modernity without emancipation or assimilation,"[23] it was driven by bureaucratization, the universal method of ordering the empire. Relying upon the support and insight of the Jewish bureaucratic corps, the government achieved a substantial degree of conformity of Russian Jews to the imperial standard through their bureaucratic integration in the established social, judicial, and confessional structures of the state. Initially inspired by western European enlightenment and committed to the regeneration of the Jews as part of its general *mission civilisatrice*, the Russian imperial state ended up instead pursuing a bureaucratic transformation of the Jews. Thus, the bureaucratic chancellery overshadowed the modern school as the principal locus of this transformation; bureaucratic solutions replaced civil regeneration as the primary means of modernization, and imperial loyalty and conformity surpassed enlightenment as the main objective of change.

This book builds upon the work of the original Russian Jewish historians and recent historiographical developments and focuses on the institution of expert Jew as a crucial factor in the development of official Jewish policy. We seek to uncover and analyze the broader motivations behind official Jewish policy, which were based on the political vision and policymaking contributions of Russian Jewish bureaucrats.

Russian Jewish historiography has a rich legacy going back more than a century. Over the decades, its focus shifted gradually from the Jews in Russia as the object of Russian policies and politics, to Russian Jews as a political subject in their own right. Initially, the development of state policies on Jews was seen as a one-sided process with the state exerting political and administrative pressure on Jewish communities. As a result, the earliest histories of Russian Jews portray an unbridgeable abyss between the Russian government and Russian Jews, without any positive mutual relationships.[24] Later, historians narrowed this abyss and established that there was a political connection between the government and the Jews. In their view, the Russian maskilim—the modernized vanguard of Russian Jewry—were the link between the empire's Jews and Russian bureaucracy. Maskilim developed special relationships with the government and closely collaborated with Russian bureaucrats on the social and cultural transformation of the Russian Jewish communities. In particular, the maskilim of the 1860s and 1870s proved to be the most zealous servants of the state, obsessed with bureaucratic procedure and possessing a blind faith in the benevolent Russian government.[25]

Further analysis of the Russian government institutions responsible for the administration of the Jews revealed other mechanisms of official policymaking and implementation. New scholarship demonstrated that even the harshest official policies toward the Jews, such as military conscription and compulsory education, ruthlessly implemented by the empire, were motivated by *raison d'état* rather than by the personal judeophobia of the tsar and the bureaucracy.[26] Scholars also attempted to create a more historically nuanced portrait of Russian bureaucratic policymakers and their maskilic advisors, and to understand the actual working relationships between these groups. The new picture of these relationships included the central figure of the expert Jew, the "visible and undeniable proof of the nexus between maskilim and the Russian government."[27] Most recent studies in the field point out the crucial role of the modern Russian state and its bureaucratic institutions in implementing policies of Jewish integration in late Russian empire. The analyses of the structure and routine operations of official institutions such as the Russian army, government rabbinate, and Jewish communal administration shed new light on the motivation, goals, and methods of official Russian policy toward the Jews.[28] This book brings out the key role of the Russian Jewish bureaucratic elite—expert Jews—in nineteenth-century Russian Jewish history, and thus makes a new contribution to historiography. Expert Jews are shown here to be a major official link between the government and the Jews as the bureaucratic driving force behind the transformation of Russian Jewry.

This book is, above all, an institutional history. Therefore, the Russian context—the history of imperial bureaucratic institutions and their staff—is given special attention. Analysis of historical developments within Russian bureaucracy provides a new perspective on state policies toward the Jews. Russian bureaucrats—ranging from top officials at the Ministry of Internal Affairs in St. Petersburg to provincial administrators in the Pale of Settlement—shaped their policies in close collaboration with Jewish bureaucrats—expert Jews. An examination of the institutional history of the late Russian empire also reveals the remarkable endurance of the imperial administration of Jewish religious affairs as a whole, including the Rabbinical Commission, expert Jews, and government rabbis. These offices provided indispensable institutional support to state policy and were actively used by Russian bureaucratic agencies until the final days of the empire. This book is also a prosopographical analysis of Jewish bureaucracy. Biographical materials on expert Jews, including information on their education, careers, economic status, families, and descendants, reveal the high social profile of Jewish officials, comparable to the status of their Russian bureaucratic counterparts. A prosopographic examination of expert Jews sheds light on their ethos and motivation, which shaped them as officials of the Russian state, as well as the policies they helped to develop.[29]

The rich literary output of expert Jews analyzed in this book places Jewish bureaucrats within the realm of the Russian Jewish intelligentsia.[30] The publications of expert Jews—journalism and scholarship, translations and public addresses that appeared mainly in Russian-language periodicals—expressed their loyal and moderate stance, supporting the government on all major issues of official Jewish policy. Their position was firm and consistent throughout their entire history. The historical writings of expert Jews are of special interest: the Russian Jewish bureaucrats conceived of and designed their semi-academic texts as reference material for the development of state policies toward the Jews. However, these works also reveal the distinct Jewish identity of the expert Jews and their sincere concern for the fate of Russian Jewry.

The enormous expansion of the historical source base due to the recent opening of the former Soviet archives had a great impact on the writing of this book. The archival materials of the Russian ministries and provincial chancelleries illustrate the close collaboration between Russian and Jewish bureaucrats at every level of imperial officialdom. Based on these materials, this book examines bureaucratic procedures related to official policies known as *sblizhenie* (rapprochement) between Jews and other imperial subjects. These policies were aimed at the social and civic conformity of Jews to the standards of imperial society, including its estate structure and legal norms. In fact, the Russian empire had no uniform policy of integration and ethnic unification of its minorities. The range of possible degrees and types of integration under various circumstances and toward various minorities is indicated by some of the terms used by Russian bureaucrats in addition to *sblizhenie*: *khristianizatsiia* (Christianization), *assimiliatsiia* (assimilation), *sliianie* (fusion), *tsivilizatsiia* (civilization), and *obrusenie* (Russification).[31] The government never subjected Russian Jews to the vigorous Russification imposed on Ukrainians, nor to the wide-ranging Christianization inflicted on the Muslim Tatars. However, the Jews never had the considerable degree of autonomy granted to the Baltic Germans, Finns, and Muslim peoples of Central Asia. For the relatively small, acculturated, and politically mobilized faction of Russian Jews, the policies of rapprochement resulted in selective integration within the elite segments of Russian society.[32] For the majority of Russian Jews, however, integration was indirect, represented by their eventual inclusion within the standardized systems of the judiciary, taxation, and universal military draft. Expert Jews, the focus of this book, were key in implementing and strengthening this indirect integration of Russian Jews.

The primary source base for this study encompasses voluminous archival and printed material on expert Jews in the archival and library depositories of the Russian Federation. The Russian State Historical Archive (*Rossiiskii gosudarstvennyi istoricheskii arkhiv* [RGIA]) and the Russian National Library (*Rossiiskaia natsional'naia biblioteka* [RNB]) in St. Petersburg provided the main primary source data. Important source materials on the early history of expert Jews in the 1850s and 1860s, unavailable at the archives due to a major fire that destroyed the offices of the Ministry of Internal Affairs in St. Petersburg in 1862, were recovered from publications of the period.[33] The very few available personal archives of expert Jews and literary accounts of their work complement the source base.[34]

These materials include Russian government documents on expert Jews (legislation, memoranda, and correspondence), the reactions of traditional Jewish communities to the administrative work of expert Jews (official and unofficial communications, petitions, and other kinds of responses), official paperwork produced by expert Jews related to their missions (investigations, surveys, revisions, and censuses), biographical material on expert Jews (information on their education, career, economic status, families, and descendants), and information on the extracurricular activities of expert Jews (literary works, public presentations and sermons, journalism, translations, and scholarship).

Nearly 10,000 pages of archival records were examined for this book. New source material is used here for the first time in a scholarly work. These bureaucratic narratives, dealing with the immediate realities of Jewish life, reveal obscured details of policy and decision making, which were ultimately of great consequence for the course of Russian Jewish history.[35] The new material is viewed here as the practical embodiment of Russian Jewish bureaucratic politics. It is an invaluable record of the routine bureaucratic handling of everyday problems of Jewish life in the Russian empire. From this material, a picture emerges of how state policies were formulated, debated, and adopted. It is this picture that this book attempts to reconstruct.

The book is made up of five chapters and an appendix.

The first chapter, "Jews and the Grasp of the Empire," introduces and contextualizes expert Jews as an important phenomenon of imperial Russian and modern Jewish history. This chapter explores the development of the Russian ministerial system in the nineteenth and early twentieth centuries as the framework for the analysis of official institutions of Jewish policy. Jewish policy is examined as an integral component within the general religious and confessional policy of the empire toward its non-Christian subjects, *inorodtsy* (aliens), which included Jews. The chapter also analyzes the Doctrine of Tolerated Faiths embodied in the structure of modern Jewish bureaucratic institutions in Europe and Russia. It describes how, in the 1840s, the Russian government turned to contemporary European models of administration of the Jewish population, and the proven success of the French consistorial system led the Russian government to adopt it as an institutional and administrative model.

The second chapter, "Bureaucratic Jews," focuses specifically on the office of expert Jew as an institution of imperial bureaucracy. From 1850 to 1917, the office of expert Jew was an indispensable feature of every provincial chancellery in the Pale of Settlement, and of the central offices of the Ministry of Internal Affairs in St. Petersburg. This chapter defines the institutional parameters of expert Jews based on their political mission. It also examines the bureaucratic agenda and operational framework of expert Jews as set by imperial legislation and departmental regulations. A survey of the institutional evolution of expert Jews and their changing roles within the imperial bureaucratic power structures concludes this chapter.

The third chapter, "Without Haste and Without Rest," traces the careers of individual expert Jews and examines their own path to modernization. This chapter demonstrates how their mission as servitors of the modern state along with their unique service ethos, acquired through specialized modern education, motivated their policymaking. Thus, in the end, expert Jews became a bureaucratic window through which Russian Jews and Russian bureaucrats could see and communicate with one another.

The fourth chapter, "Jews, Law, and Order," examines the service of expert Jews from 1850 to 1917. In the 1850s, expert Jews appeared as bureaucratic pioneers exploring the western and southern borderlands of the Russian empire, densely populated by Jews. They thus set the groundwork for possible solutions of the Jewish question in Russia. One such solution, the civil standardization of the Jews, was aimed at the disintegration of Jewish communal autonomy and the absorption of individual Jewish subjects of the Russian tsar into the imperial judicial system. This chapter shows how, with the help of expert Jews, the legal status of Russian Jews was significantly reconfigured to preserve and harmonize remnants of the old autonomous structures within the new imperial order. This chapter also examines the bureaucratic input of expert Jews regarding the social and cultural integration of Russian Jews into the greater imperial society. At the outset, in the mid-nineteenth century, Jewish bureaucracy was instituted by the modern Russian state in order to get rid of the social and cultural separation of the traditional Jewish community, defined by the government as the religious and social "fanaticism" of the Jews. However, by the end of the century, the government sought to compromise on this approach to Judaism in order to gain support among the traditional Jews and conservative religious leadership in order to uphold conservative domestic policy and contain radical political activity and revolution.

The fifth chapter, "Literature and the Table of Ranks," examines the non-bureaucratic pursuits of expert Jews. It focuses on the literary activity of Jewish bureaucrats, demonstrating that their official bureaucratic status determined their ideology and intellectual pursuits, which were essentially an extension of their service and a means of promoting official Jewish policy. This chapter also tackles the origins of "Russian Wissenschaft"—the semi-academic and academic study of Jewish history and literature in the Russian language. Unlike its German source and counterpart, Wissenschaft des Judentums, the Russian version was in large measure nurtured by the Russian government and by the needs of empire building. Russian Wissenschaft emerged in the early 1850s, when ambitious social—rather than religious, as was the case of the classical German Wissenschaft—reforms of traditional Jewish life made the Russian government a major sponsor as well as a major consumer of historical scholarship on the subject of Jewish past. We argue in this chapter that Russian Jewish bureaucrats serving the government in the office of expert Jew should be counted among the pioneers of Russian Jewish historiography. This chapter includes fragments of two of my articles: "Story within a Story: The First Russian-Language Jewish History Textbooks, 1880s–1890s," in *Polin: Studies in Polish Jewry, Volume 30: Jewish Education in Eastern Europe*, edited by Eliyana Adler and Antony Polonsky and to be published in 2017 by the Littman Library of Jewish Civilization on behalf of the Institute for Polish-Jewish Studies and the American Association for Polish-Jewish Studies; and "Wissenschaft des Judentums and the Emergence of Russian Jewish Historiography," in *Wissenschaft des Judentums in Europe: Comparative and Transnational Perspectives*, edited by Christian Wiese and Mirjam Thulin and to be published by De Gruyter in 2017. This material is used here with permission from editors and publishers of both volumes.

The appendix includes a list of expert Jews and their terms of service by province of the Pale of Settlement. It also provides details on expert Jews' lives and careers: lifespan, education, official rank, salaries, awards, social and family status, non-bureaucratic professions, other bureaucratic and non-bureaucratic appointments.

All dates prior to February 1918 are given according to the Old Style (Julian) Calendar in use in late imperial Russia. It was behind the Western (Gregorian) Calendar by twelve days in the nineteenth century and thirteen days in the twentieth century. Transliteration of Russian, Yiddish, and Hebrew words generally follows the Romanization systems used by the Library of Congress, with the exception of certain well-known names for which other transliterations (such as Simon Dubnow, Samuel Joseph Fuenn, and Abraham Harkavy) are commonly used. All translations are mine unless otherwise indicated.

1

Jews and the Grasp of the Empire

Jewish Bureaucratic Hierarchy

On May 17, 1840, the Russian Minister of Internal Affairs, General *Aide-de-Camp* Lev Perovskii, at the order of the emperor, issued a circular directive to the governor-generals to set up committees of provincial bureaucrats and trusted and educated Jews in order to establish the post of provincial rabbis (*gubernskie ravviny*) supplemented by religious boards (*dukhovnye pravleniia*) in Odessa, Kiev, Vitebsk, Poltava, and Mitava. The government conceived of the institution of *provincial rabbi* as an office that would supervise the district government rabbinate (*uezdnye kazennye ravviny*) and appeal its decisions in religious matters. In his directive, Perovskii emphasized the key role of this unprecedented Jewish clerical hierarchy within the system of the imperial administration, "so that the government with the help of this bureaucratic hierarchy (*chinonachalie*) could establish measures to lift up the fallen and disgraced Jewish religion to the purity of its teaching."[1] As the context of Perovskii's directive implies, the Jewish religion, plagued by the "false teachings" of rabbis and "perverted interpretations" of the Talmud, had degenerated to the point of "fanatical hatred towards Christians." The only way to repair the Jewish religion was through "true enlightenment," which would contribute to a rapprochement between the Jews and other subjects of the Empire, and make them "useful to the Fatherland."[2] To that end, the imperial government had already applied such powerful tools of social transformation as compulsory military service (1827), secular education (1840) for Jewish males, and engagement of Jews in the agricultural colonization of the imperial southern frontier (1807).[3] Nevertheless, the Minister of Internal Affairs considered the introduction of a Jewish "bureaucratic hierarchy" a matter of paramount importance. Jewish bureaucracy was thus envisioned and designed by the Russian government as a core institution for the support and implementation of official Jewish policy.

The focus of this chapter is the institutional history of Russian Jewish policy implemented through Russian Jewish bureaucracy. This chapter surveys the process of building and developing institutions in the Russian empire from the nineteenth through the beginning of the twentieth century, an essential context for analyzing the official institutions of Jewish policy. This policy is examined as an integral component within the general religious and confessional policy of the Empire toward its non-Christian subjects, *inorodtsy* (aliens).

The first encounter between Jews and Russian bureaucracy took place at the end of the eighteenth century. The Russian government made an ultimately unsuccessful attempt at co-opting the traditional Jewish institute of community representatives, *shtadlanim*, into the structure of the imperial administration. In the 1840s, the Russian government turned its attention toward contemporary European models for the administration of the Jewish population. The proven success of the French consistorial system in the integration and administration of the Jews motivated the Russian government to adopt it as an institutional and administrative model for Russian Jews. In 1848, the hierarchical administration of Jewish religious affairs was finally established in Russia. It included the district rabbinate (*uezdnye kazennye ravviny*) on the lower level, the provincial rabbinate (*gubernskie ravviny*) substituted by the temporary office of expert Jews (*uchenye evrei*) in the middle, and the Rabbinical Commission (*ravvinskaia komissia*) at the top. This bureaucratic hierarchy remained in place, intact and unchanged, until the Revolution of 1917.

The Russian Ministerial System

The Russian ministerial system—a vast bureaucratic apparatus comprising about a dozen ministries, the principal agencies of imperial administration—was built and consolidated during the nineteenth century. The imperial administration of Russian Jews (created in 1804) was an integral part of the Russian ministerial system (created in 1802) and paralleled its emergence and development from the outset. With the establishment of the ministerial system, the Russian monarchy sought to improve the effectiveness of the government by delegating significant portions of executive power to trusted representatives of the monarch, the ministers. The absolute authority of ministers within their departments would replace the administrative chaos of the collegiate system of the Russian government of the eighteenth century. The political mandate of the ministers included the improvement and modernization of every aspect of the Russian state and society, except the fundamental principles of the unlimited autocratic power of the tsar. The role of the ministerial system was twofold: the preservation of political traditions and the introduction of administrative innovations. This duality was inherent in the role of the ministers, who were at once loyal servants of the emperor and powerful principals in their branches of executive power.[4]

The Russian ministerial system was ideologically based on the doctrine of "ministerial power."[5] Ministerial power was administrative and police power. Its doctrine combined that of the premodern Muscovite administrative legacy, the early modern European tutelary state, and the modern administrative practices of the Napoleonic regime in France. The tradition of government intervention in the social sphere existed in premodern Russia since the fifteenth century. In the eighteenth century, this tradition was reinforced by Western imports, such as *polizeistaat* (a well-ordered "police" state), and the traditional state tutelage of society and government intervention grew exponentially. The goal of ministerial power in Russia was the "common welfare," that is, an absolute social good, the positivist ideal and ultimate goal of enlightened monarchs and their ministers who possessed the exclusive prerogative to define that goal and measure its progress. In other words, politics was the sole privilege of the monarch and the bureaucracy. Any politics beyond the confines of ministerial offices was considered at the least illegitimate and ultimately subversive. Through the lens of ministerial power, the authorities viewed Russian society as immature and not to be trusted with any political role. The political activities of the bureaucracy, such as legislation and reforms, were primarily designed as improvements of the institutional structure and bureaucratic procedures within the ministerial system.

The doctrine of ministerial power defined the ministerial system and permeated the bureaucratic ethos of imperial officialdom. However, within the ministerial system, the institutes of personal power (monarch's edicts, special and extraordinary committees appointed by the tsar) competed with the agencies of institutional power (the regular ministries and their departments).[6] This tension, along with the increased political role of the ministerial system and bureaucracy as a whole, was manifest in every branch of the imperial government, including the administration of Jewish affairs. Thus, in the early 1800s through the mid-1830s when the Russian ministerial system was still relatively weak, official Jewish policies were debated and adopted by special Jewish committees appointed by the emperor.[7] During the period of the Great Reforms in the mid-1850s–1870s, when the power of the ministerial system had considerably grown, the making of Jewish policy was the prerogative of the Department of Spiritual Affairs of Foreign Faiths (*Departament dukhovnykh del inostrannykh ispovedanii* [DDDII]) at the Ministry of Internal Affairs (*Ministerstvo vnutrennikh del* [MVD]). On the local, provincial, and district levels, these policies were implemented by the government rabbinate supervised by the Rabbinical Commission and subordinate to the DDDII, and by expert Jews, who were subordinate to local governors and reported directly to the Minister of Internal Affairs. In the late imperial period, from the 1880s to 1917, bureaucratic institutions dominated Russian politics, and the MVD assumed full control of official Jewish policy.

Ministry of Internal Affairs

In the late imperial period, from 1850 to 1917, the MVD was the largest and the most powerful institution among all Russian ministries. Its realm included key areas of imperial domestic policy: provincial and district administration, police, censorship, public health, administration of Christian sects and non-Christian religions, and much more. The MVD was essentially a government within the government. The enormous army of its bureaucrats regulated the lives of every class and stratum of the Russian and non-Russian subjects of the empire.

Its lack of specialization and broad police mandate distinguished the MVD among other ministries from its founding in 1802. The MVD was devised and developed as the principal administrative and police agency of the empire. In the 1820s to the 1830s the MVD gradually transferred many of its original economic and technical functions, including the postal service and state-controlled mining industry, to other ministries. At the same time, the institutional structure and personnel of the MVD came of age. In the 1840s, this structure and its cadres enabled the ministry to accumulate critical information about Russian society and the economy, and effectively transform this information into policy by developing legislation and reforms. Moreover, by the 1860s the MVD had transformed itself into the principal institutional base of political power in Russia.[8]

A strong connection between official institutions and their personnel was a permanent feature of the Russian administrative tradition. In eighteenth-century Russia, the essentially modern and progressive institutional apparatus of the State Colleges was still staffed mainly by incompetent and corrupt personnel of the old Muscovite administration. For this reason, Emperor Peter I appointed only the most loyal and trusted of his associates to head these institutions. In the nineteenth century, in similar fashion, Emperor Alexander I entrusted departments of the government to his ministers, many of whom were his close associates and personal friends. However, in the formative period of the ministerial system, compulsory education was introduced to the middle and lower levels of Russian officialdom as an essential component of their loyal service. The MVD and other Russian ministries motivated their personnel through faster promotion and more successful careers available to bureaucrats who completed their education in specialized schools, gymnasia, and universities. Educated bureaucrats gradually replaced the incompetent and corrupt officials in the central ministries and provincial administration. This development signified the overall professionalization of the civil service and bureaucracy in the Russian empire.

Specially trusted elite bureaucratic cadres continued to play an important role not only in the highest echelons of power but throughout the ministerial system. Their role was eventually institutionalized in the departmental structure of the MVD. Emperor Nicholas I did not fully trust regular bureaucratic institutions and their regular staff. In important administrative matters, he primarily relied on specially appointed committees of handpicked trusted officials, and on frequent inspection missions conducted by him personally or by his special emissaries. In the 1830s, under the minister Count Dmitrii Nikolaevich Bludov, the MVD co-opted such special emissaries into its formal structure as "officials for special missions" (*chinovniki dlia osobykh poruchenii*). Starting in 1836, these officials became a permanent feature of the MVD in the imperial capital and the Russian provinces.[9] As a rule, these positions were assigned to middle-ranking bureaucrats and came with a complete range of government service benefits. The head of the MVD was allowed a staff of up to fifteen such officials, whom he picked himself and who were fully at his disposal. Like the minister, every provincial governor had an allowance of up to five officials for special missions. These elite officials had the authority to breach hierarchical and departmental restrictions when on their missions. Thus they were in a powerful position, beyond that of regular bureaucratic institutions.

In 1839, Nicholas I approved the permanent organizational structure of ministries and departments. From this point on, the division of administrative functions within the ministerial system and the authority of Russian bureaucracy were defined by law and, therefore, were only nominally dependent on the will of the monarch.

Nicholas's legislation gave his ministers significant independence and power in matters of bureaucratic personnel, including their recruitment, promotion, and compensation. Many ministers took advantage of this institutional development to pursue their own political agenda. In the 1840s, the head of the MVD, Count Lev Alekseevich Perovskii, sought to attract members of the Russian intelligentsia to administrative work for his ministry. Perovskii's personnel policy transformed the MVD into an important bureaucratic link between the government and society. Under Perovskii, the lower and middle levels of the MVD were staffed by a new generation of Russian officialdom, "enlightened bureaucrats," who played a decisive role in the planning and implementation of the Great Reforms of the 1860s and 1870s.[10]

In 1837, Nicholas I eliminated the post of governor-general. Governor-generals, high-ranking military officers dispatched by the emperor to oversee the provinces, were directly subordinate to the monarch and operated outside the regular provincial administration subordinate to the MVD.[11] At the same time, a reform of the provincial administration took place across the empire. This reform firmly placed ultimate authority in the provinces with the MVD. The practice of circular directives (*tsirkuliary*) issued by the Minister of Internal Affairs also originated in the 1830s. These directives did not require the emperor's approval and were fully legal. Finally, the MVD assumed full control of the provinces and essentially became their surrogate government.[12]

Confessional Policy of the Russian Empire

The MVD was the principal government institution responsible for the shaping and implementation of the confessional policies of the Russian empire with regard to its non-Orthodox and non-Christian subjects. The first half of the nineteenth century, the formative period of the Russian ministerial system, coincided with a transitional period of the traditional confessional policy of the empire.

From the 1820s to the 1860s Russian imperial policy gradually moved from the classical model of a dynastic empire, generally tolerant of national and religious diversity, to that of a modern, unified, and centralized nation-state.[13] In reality, this transition was never fully accomplished. The confessional policy of the Russian empire, as a result, had characteristics of both models—the Russian empire, a conglomeration of nations under the rule of one dynasty, and imperial Russia, a multinational state with, at its core, the native dominant Russian nation surrounded by inferior and backward non-Russian minorities.

The concepts of dominant (*gospodstvuiushchaia*) and recognized (*priznavaemye*) religions formed the basis of the confessional policy of the Russian empire in the eighteenth and beginning of the nineteenth centuries.[14] Orthodox Christianity was the dominant religion, that of the ruling dynasty and the majority of the population. It was thus given the status of dominant religion with the exclusive privilege of conversion and proselytizing.

Institutionally, the Russian Orthodox Church also had special status. Besides maintaining a monopoly on religious matters of the Orthodox population, the church had an institutional structure that paralleled that of the Russian state, including religious courts, schools, and a clerical bureaucracy. Furthermore, the government widely used the institutional structures of the Orthodox Church in its purely secular policies. Even though the church had no legal means of independent administrative authority in secular matters, it was frequently asked to back various government policies. From 1797, the Orthodox parish clergy was assigned the "moral exhortation" of the peasants, to instill in them loyalty to the throne and obedience to the local administration.[15] Thus, the hierarchical organization of the Orthodox clergy and clerical institutions, parallel and complementary to that of the government, played a key role in the implementation of official Russian domestic policies.

In rural areas, in the absence of an adequate civil administration, Orthodox parish priests were made responsible for registering the population, instilling loyalty to the authorities, and spreading literacy and education. For many Russian bureaucrats, Orthodox Christianity seemed inherently connected to enlightenment, responsibility, loyalty, and other civic values that the government hoped to instill in its subjects. Thus, the spread of Orthodox Christianity was considered to be an important means of civilizing and improving the population of the empire.[16]

In the second half of the eighteenth century and the first half of the nineteenth, as a result of aggressive territorial expansion, the Russian empire acquired vast new regions with a tremendously religiously diverse population. Hundreds of thousands of new imperial subjects, including Catholic and Protestant Christians, Muslim and Jews, came under the scepter of the Russian emperor. The Russian government, unable to instill loyalty to the empire in its new subjects through its own inadequate administrative apparatus and the limited resources of the Orthodox institutions, granted these religions the semi-autonomous status of "recognized foreign faiths" (*priznavaemye inostrannye ispovedaniia*). The recognized faiths enjoyed rather broad religious freedoms. However, some limitations were instituted as well. Recognized religions were strictly forbidden from executing conversions and proselytizing, solely the privilege of the dominant religion, Orthodox Christianity. Official recognition of these religions also presumed considerable state intervention and government control over the everyday affairs of religious communities, and regulation of their religious lives. As a result, a new branch of the imperial government, "the administration of spiritual affairs of foreign faiths" (*upravlenie dukhovnymi delami inostrannykh ispovedanii*), emerged.

The essential agenda of imperial domestic policy, carried out through the administration of spiritual affairs of foreign faiths by the bureaucratic apparatus of the MVD, included registration of taxpayers and military recruits among *inorodtsy*; civil improvement (i.e., inculcation of loyalty and education) of imperial minorities; and maintenance of religious integrity and orthodoxy (seen as a principal guarantee of territorial integrity of the empire) of recognized faiths.[17]

The major agents of imperial confessional policy were the provincial clergy of foreign faiths. Due to the *maloliudstvo*, an endemic shortage of competent Russian administrators, the lower levels of the religious administration of imperial minorities were routinely staffed by indigenous clerical elites.[18] This official clergy was integrated into the Russian government bureaucracy through the hierarchical institutional structures of the foreign faiths, such as dioceses, episcopates, parishes, as well as those of the government, including consistories, spiritual boards, and school districts.

In complicated cases involving faiths without traditional clerical hierarchies and even without an established clergy, like Muslims and Jews, the government overrode the situation by creating artificial, essentially bureaucratic, clerical elites and hierarchical institutional frameworks integrated within Russian bureaucracy. This innovation had important consequences for imperial confessional policy.[19] The reasonably successful institutionalization of the religious administration of Russian Muslims and Jews and their demonstrated loyalty to and support of the government proved that the dominant Russian Orthodox religion and its institutions were not a necessity in this matter. There was thus an implicit acknowledgment by the imperial government of the moral qualities and civic values rooted within the recognized non-Christian religions, and of their ultimate key role in carrying out the goals of imperial domestic policy. Universal morals and values, including loyalty to the throne and religious conservatism, united the dominant and recognized religions as far as their political agenda was concerned. Thus, for imperial bureaucrats, these morals and values had the potential to unite non-Russian *inorodtsy* (aliens) with native Russians and create the basis of their eventual rapprochement.

Administration of the Spiritual Affairs of Foreign Faiths

Institution building within the administration of spiritual affairs of foreign faiths paralleled the expansion and state building of the empire, developing spontaneously on the basis of ad-hoc administrative decisions and without proper uniform legislation.

During the second half of the eighteenth century, several institutions administering foreign faiths, from animists to Protestants, emerged throughout the Russian provinces. These included the Orenburg Commission on Foreign Faiths (1751), provincial Roman-Catholic consistories (1783), provincial Lutheran consistories (1785), and the Muslim Spiritual Assembly in Ufa (1788). At the same time, the government attempted to centralize the administration of foreign faiths and integrate it within the framework of the imperial bureaucracy. Thus, in 1754, the spiritual affairs of Lutherans were placed under the authority of the College of Justice, a judicial organ of the Russian government in St. Petersburg. In 1797, the College of Justice also incorporated the Department of Spiritual Affairs of Catholics.[20]

In the next stage of its institutional development, the imperial administration of foreign faiths was absorbed by the newly established Russian ministerial system. On July 25, 1810, the Main Directorate of Spiritual Affairs of Foreign Faiths (*Glavnoe upravlenie dukhovnykh del inostrannykh ispovedanii* [GUDDII]) was created as an independent agency within the ministerial system. GUDDII was charged with "all matters related to the clergy of various foreign religions and faiths, excluding their court cases, still under jurisdiction of the Senate."[21] GUDDII oversaw the following non-Orthodox Christian and non-Christian religions: Armenian Gregorian, Roman Catholicism, Greek Uniate, Evangelical Lutheran, Judaism, and Islam.

According to the official historian of the MVD, Nikolai Varadinov, GUDDII's formative years from 1810 to 1816 "lacked events worthy of historical record."[22] The Directorate's structure was not fully established and its head, Prince Aleksandr Nikolaevich Golitsyn (1773–1844), was just "getting acquainted" with the vague subject of spiritual affairs of foreign faiths.[23] In Varadinov's view, this bleak beginning could not have been otherwise. The administrative scope of the GUDDII was not yet clearly defined. Moreover, its field, the spiritual affairs of foreign faiths, was equally foreign and new to Russian bureaucrats. As a result, during its early years the GUDDII existed mainly on paper, awaiting the time when official "views and directions would be elaborated, and goals and requirements would be defined," to start its actual work.[24]

On October 24, 1817, the GUDDII merged with two other previously independent institutions, the Ministry of National Enlightenment and the Holy Synod, to form the new Ministry of National Enlightenment and Spiritual Affairs (*Ministerstvo narodnogo prosveshcheniia i dukhovnykh del* [MNPDD]). The emperor's manifesto on the establishment of the new ministry made it clear that this institutional centralization was necessitated by the monarch's desire "that Christian piety be the basis of true enlightenment."[25] The manifesto also put the Minister of Spiritual Affairs and National Enlightenment in "the same position in relation to the Holy Synod that the Minister of Justice occupied in relation to the Senate."[26] Therefore, the new minister was made head of the highest clerical authority of Russian Orthodoxy, the Synod, similar to the Minister of Justice who was head of the highest imperial court of appeals, the Senate. Thus, through the MNPDD, the state assumed full administrative control over the dominant as well as the recognized religions of the empire.

The establishment of the MNPDD brought unprecedented change in imperial confessional policy. An attitude of "spiritual cosmopolitanism," dominant among the highest Russian officials including the minister Prince Golitsyn, was developed and translated into a policy of "religious indifference."[27] This policy, based on the theories of "universal Christianity," rejected principal differences among the major Christian beliefs, such as Catholicism, Protestantism, and Orthodoxy, and approached non-Christian religions, including Islam and Judaism, with equal respect. The policy of "religious indifference" sought to eliminate the fundamental inequality between the dominant and recognized religions and ultimately level them in subordination to the secular state, not associated with any religion.

When launched, this policy immediately violated the basic privilege of the dominant religion: the exclusive right to proselytize among imperial subjects. The violation was institutionalized by the emperor's decree establishing the Russian Bible Society (*Russkoe Bibleiskoe obshchestvo* [RBO]) in St. Petersburg on December 6, 1812. The RBO published and distributed the Old and New Testaments in foreign languages, including modern Russian, and operated under the patronage of the GUDDII and MNPDD.[28] The RBO quickly grew and expanded into the provinces. In 1819 it had 49 provincial branches and 124 district associations.[29] Thus, the RBO evolved into an influential institution, firmly established and backed by solid bureaucratic support, pursuing a missionary agenda and intervening in the realm of the dominant religion beyond the control of its institutions.[30] The Orthodox Holy Synod, the central institution of the dominant religion, was reduced to a department within the MNPDD on par with the RBO and the new Department of Spiritual Affairs (*Departament dukhovnykh del* [DDD]), which replaced the former GUDDII and eventually included the Synod.

With the creation of the MNPDD, its head Prince Aleksandr Golitsyn acquired enough power[31] to realize his doctrine of "religious indifference" through institutional policy. Under his guidance, the administration of foreign faiths finally took shape and defined its long-awaited directions and goals.

The new Department of Spiritual Affairs (DDD) was a basic bureaucratic unit of the MNPDD. The DDD comprised four sections. The first "Greco-Russian" section administered the affairs and institutions of the Russian Orthodox Church. This section was, moreover, the supreme organ of the Holy Synod, and thus further integrated the Synod within the ministerial system.[32] The other three sections administered to the non-Orthodox religions of the empire. The second section was in charge of the Roman Catholic, Greek Uniate, and Armenian Gregorian faiths. The third section oversaw the Protestants. The fourth section dealt with the Jews, the Muslims, and the rest of the non-Christian religions. The sections were divided into *stoly* ("desks" or chancelleries). The chancelleries directly handled the whole spectrum of spiritual affairs, including clergy appointments and salaries, control of routine proceedings of religious institutions such as religious boards, monasteries, educational and charitable organizations, control of clerical assets and properties, and collection of population statistics provided by the parish clergy.

Nine elaborate paragraphs of the founding statute of the MNPDD described the structure and responsibilities of the DDD in great detail.[33] The degree of specificity obviously correlated with such factors as the level of familiarity of the Russian bureaucracy with a particular non-Orthodox religion, the level of bureaucratic intervention into its spiritual affairs, and the level of bureaucratic integration of its clergy into imperial official-dom. Thus, the administration of Catholics was defined in thirty-seven articles of the Statute, Protestants in twenty-six, and non-Christians in seven, six of which concerned Muslims and only one the Jews. In the case of the Jews, the statute laconically put the DDD in charge of "all matters concerning Jewish religious law, excluding criminal cases and property disputes, which are subject to the Minister's decision."[34]

Ultimately, the doctrine of "religious indifference" failed to transform the traditional confessional policy of the Russian empire. As was often the case, Russian reforms, based on a special relationship between the emperor and a particular minister, were doomed even in the short term.[35] Thus, when Golitsyn's fortunes changed in 1824, his revolutionary policy came to an end. In May 1824 Prince Golitsyn was removed from the leadership of the MNPDD, the RBO, and the Synod, and his minis-try was dismantled. The Ministry of National Enlightenment, the Holy Synod, and the Main Directorate of Spiritual Affairs of Foreign Faiths (GUDDII) were reestablished as independent agencies.[36] The RBO was shut down in 1826. The Holy Synod was granted official confirmation of its missionary privileges in 1828.[37] The institutional base of Golitsyn's policy therefore collapsed, and the traditional balance between dominant and recognized religions prevailed.

However, Golitsyn's vision significantly influenced the imperial ad-ministration of religious affairs in the long term. The most important result was the firm integration of confessional policy within the bureau-cratic structures of the ministerial system. The principal agency for the administration of spiritual affairs of foreign faiths was also established and developed on the basis of Golitsyn's legacy.

The considerable institutional power of the newly independent GUDDII and its important role in domestic policy were soon claimed by the growing Ministry of Internal Affairs (MVD). On February 2, 1832, the emperor's decree placed the GUDDII within the departmental structure of the MVD, where it was transformed into the Department of Spiritual Affairs of Foreign Faiths (*Departament dukhovnykh del inostrannykh ispovedanii* [DDDII]). The new institutional structure of the DDDII reflected its status as an integral part of the ministerial system. The DDDII included three sections, two of which administered the religious affairs of foreign faiths: the first section was put in charge of Roman Catholics, the second dealt with the rest of the non-Orthodox religious spectrum, including the Jews. The third section coordinated the MVD's work on religious matters of recognized faiths with other ministries and the Senate.[38]

From 1832 to 1917, the DDDII underwent several reorganizations. At the beginning of the twentieth century, its structure took its final shape. It grew to include six sections, four of which administered the religious affairs of non-Orthodox faiths and Orthodox sectarians. The first section administered Roman and Armenian Catholics, the second Armenian Gregorian Christians and all non-Christians including Jews, the fourth Protestants. The fifth section, added in 1909, administered various Orthodox sects including old-believers. Two sections handled general economic and administrative issues: the third section managed clerical assets including properties and finances; the sixth section conducted audits and administrative inspections.[39]

The DDDII staff and its budget were reassessed by the MVD in 1834, 1896, and 1907. However, in terms of budget, these reassessments did not result in considerable change. While the annual budget of the MVD was increased from 9 million rubles in 1855 to 40 million rubles in 1881,[40] the DDDII budget was always a minuscule share, a tiny proportion of one percent of these moneys. From 1834 to 1896, its annual budget was the meager sum of 50,000–70,000 rubles.[41]

However, in the 1830s as part of the MVD, the DDDII gained its share of the vast array of powerful instruments to be used in its confessional policy: statutes, regulations, circular directives, and institutional infrastructure in the provinces. The DDDII started using its enhanced bureaucratic power through introduction of legislation and institutional frameworks in the administration of the recognized non-Orthodox and non-Christian religions: Protestantism (1832), Judaism (1835), Armenian Gregorian Christianity (1836), and Buddhism (1853).[42]

Thus, in the 1830s, institutional changes within the Russian ministerial system brought about a substantial shift in imperial confessional policy. The establishment of bureaucratic authority over recognized foreign faiths enabled the far-reaching intervention of the government, represented by the DDDII, into the religious and social lives of non-Orthodox subjects of the empire.

Early Jewish Bureaucracy: The Deputies of the Jewish People

The idea of a Jewish clerical bureaucracy had been on the minds of Russian statesmen since the early 1800s. It was then explored on paper in several unrealized institutional projects developed by the Russian government with some Jewish involvement. In its practical work at the turn of the nineteenth century, the government also sought the input of the Jewish communities, represented by the institute of the deputies of the Jewish people, in matters of official Jewish policy. In 1773, 1802, and 1807 the Russian government summoned elected representatives of the Jewish communities to a discussion on imperial legislation concerning the adjustment of the status of Jewish subjects within the political, social, and economic structures of the empire, such as their placement under the jurisdiction of the imperial Municipal Statute (*Gorodovoe polozhenie*) of 1773. However, the deputies were not yet sufficiently integrated into Russian bureaucracy: they only supplemented the regular power structures in charge of Jewish policy, and more importantly they were elected representatives of the Jews rather than professional and loyal bureaucrats appointed by the government.

The government started systematic institution building in the sphere of Jewish policy in 1802, when the major transformation of the general imperial bureaucracy and establishment of the ministerial system were still under way. The first blueprints of Jewish bureaucracy were designed by two members of the first Imperial Jewish Committee in 1802–1804. Both authors of the projects—the Russian senator, Minister of Justice, and full committee member Gavriil Derzhavin, and the Jewish entrepreneur and committee consultant Nota Notkin—focused on traditional Jewish communal and administrative autonomy as an issue of primary concern. However, they held fundamentally opposing views on the traditional power of the kahal administration and its future in the system of the bureaucratic administration of the empire.

Abolition of the kahals—elected Jewish communal councils, the principal authority of premodern autonomous Jewish communities—was the point of departure for Derzhavin. The traditional authority of the kahals, including their administrative, judicial, and fiscal powers, would be surrendered to the government institutions of administration and police. Derzhavin also proposed a centralized bureaucratic hierarchy for the administration of religious affairs of the Jews. Its lower level, *uezdnye shkoly* (district synagogues), would include district rabbis and their assistants, elected by the community and approved by the governor. District synagogues would conduct everyday religious rituals, keep the population registered, and arbitrate in religious disputes. The middle level, *gubernskie sinagogi* (provincial synagogues), would consist of five *sud'i* (judges), elected by the heads of the district synagogues and approved by the Protector. The judges would oversee the district synagogues and function as the court of appeals for their decisions in religious matters. Above the provincial synagogues would be the *sendarin* (Sanhedrin) composed of five *pistsy* (scribes), appointed by the Protector. The scribes would be the pool of candidates for the office of chief rabbi, elected by the leadership of district and provincial synagogues and approved by the emperor. The *sendarin* would have the highest authority in the administration of religious affairs of the Jews and be the highest court of appeals in religious matters. The entire hierarchy would be supervised and managed by the Protector, a Christian bureaucrat appointed by the emperor, endowed with a full range of religious and civil powers, a powerful "combination of the Chief Procurator of the [Holy] Synod and the governor-general."[43]

Notkin's project largely salvaged the structures of the kahal administration. He sought a balance between Jewish interests and the government's goals of implementing its reforms from above. He envisioned an institutional hierarchy incorporating government bureaucrats along with the kahal leadership, making and implementing Jewish policy in close collaboration. The lower level of this hierarchy would include provincial commissions of Jewish deputies controlled by the governors. On the higher level, all provincial commissions would be overseen by a *popechitel'* (curator), a Russian bureaucrat with direct access to the emperor. Thus, the Jewish deputies would be fully integrated into the Russian administration. For instance, Jewish taxes would be collected by the Russian administration and spent by the provincial commissions of Jewish deputies upon the curator's approval. Moreover, educated Jews with demonstrated proficiency in the Russian language would be appointed to bureaucratic institutions of the Russian administration and enjoy the full privileges and benefits of civil service. David Fishman, biographer of Notkin and his generation of modern Russian Jews, argued that if his project had been realized, it would have produced a whole new social class of privileged and acculturated Jews in Russia.[44]

Despite the different approaches to the future of the traditional kahal administration, both projects upheld the critical role of bureaucratic institutions as the essential basis for the administration of the Jews. Both Derzhavin and Notkin also envisioned the fundamental bureaucratization of Jewish officials.

Jews, like Notkin, participated in the proceedings of the first Imperial Jewish Committee in an official yet informal capacity. Emperor Alexander I granted his official permission for every committee member to have one Jewish aide for expert advising during the committee sessions. Thus, Nota Notkin provided his expertise to committee member Gavriil Derzhavin. These experts were mostly recruited from the tiny Jewish community in St. Petersburg, "the most enlightened among the Jews, also known for their honesty."[45] They included businessman and government contractor Abram Perets (with committee secretary Mikhail Speranskii), Koenigsberg University graduate Leon Elkan (with committee member Prince Severin Pototzki), and prominent Russian maskil Mordechai Lefin (with committee member Prince Adam Czartoryski).[46] The Jewish experts of the committee did not evolve into a permanent bureaucratic institution, mostly due to the fact that the committee itself was a special temporary advisory board for the coordination of Jewish policy rather than a permanent government agency with a firm structure and defined responsibilities.

The first regular bureaucratic institution in the field of Jewish policy, *deputaty evreiskogo naroda* (Deputies of the Jewish People), emerged in the Russian empire during the second decade of the nineteenth century.[47] In 1812, several Russian Jewish communities authorized Leizer Dillon and Zundel Zonnenberg, Jewish contractors for the Russian army well connected in the St. Petersburg bureaucratic chancelleries, to lobby for their interests in the imperial ministries as their official deputies.[48] In 1818, the institution of elected representatives of Russian Jewish communities,

Deputies of the Jewish People, was granted official status and placed within the administrative structure of the MNPDD under the direct authority of the minister. In the same year in Vilna, an assembly of eighteen communal representatives from all over the Pale of Settlement elected three deputies and a secretary, along with their emergency replacements. The elected deputies were subject to confirmation by the minister and approval by the emperor. They would reside in the capital city of St. Petersburg with the financial support of their communities, and contribute to official Jewish policy by collaborating with the government and transmitting the policies to the Jewish communities.

The MNPDD conceived of the Deputies of the Jewish People as the principal institution for supervision of the Jews. The deputies were charged with inculcating loyalty and civil responsibility in Jewish subjects of the empire, including proper registration, taxation, and obedience to the authorities and the law. They were also supposed to mediate bureaucratic communication between the government and the Jews, including the timely submission of correct population and fiscal statistics, official petitions, and transmission of government regulations and legislation. In contrast to the MNPDD, the Jewish communities did not view the deputies, elected and supported by communal vote and money, as agents of the government. They considered the deputies to be, first and foremost, representatives of Jewish interests, intercessors on behalf of the Jews, essentially *shtadlanim*—traditional Jewish lobbyists.[49] Thus, the Jewish communities officially conveyed to the deputies all communications with the government and restrained from petitioning the authorities without the consent of their representatives.

The Deputies of the Jewish People by and large acted as de facto *shtadlanim*. By means of corruption and personal connections within the bureaucracy, the deputies managed to postpone government policies on the social transformation of Russian Jews, including compulsory secular education, a ban on traditional Jewish dress, and expulsion of Jews from rural areas. However, they won the sympathy and support of minister Prince Golitsyn, who signed the remarkable MNPDD circular directive stipulating that popular belief alone was not sufficient reason for arrest and persecution on blood libel charges against Jews and must be accompanied by tangible criminal evidence and due process of investigation. Moreover, the deputies constantly leaked information about bureaucratic deliberations and initiatives on Jewish policy to the leadership of the Jewish communities. Allegedly, in some cases the deputies misled the Jews with falsified information about official threats in order to exert additional influence and to extract additional funding from the communal leadership.[50]

As a result, the government started doubting the purpose and political utility of the Deputies of the Jewish People. These doubts intensified in 1824 due to a major institutional change within the government: the dismantling of the MNPDD and the resignation of Prince Golitsyn, who personally promoted the institution of the deputies. Admiral Aleksandr Semenovich Shishkov (1754–1841), who became the new head of the GUDDII, the bureaucratic sponsor of the deputies, believed that the deputies were a superfluous and even detrimental institutional supplement. Instead of aiding the government, they only collected money from Jews and provided them with sensitive administrative information. Thus, the institution of the Deputies of the Jewish People was doomed and ultimately eliminated in 1825.

The whole era of corporate representation of the Jews in the Russian imperial administration came to an end with the demise of the institution of the deputies. The first encounter between the Jews and Russian bureaucracy took place during the formative period of vigorous state and institution building of the empire, which brought about significant institutional and political change and fundamentally transformed Russian bureaucracy itself. The Jews were perfect strangers in the midst of this institutional turmoil. Both the new, enlightened, and acculturated economic Jewish elite (Dillon, Zonnenberg, Notkin, Perets, and others) and the traditional kahal leadership (the Deputies of the Jewish People) sought incorporation into the imperial bureaucratic power structures, using traditional modus operandi of *shtadlanim*. When dealing with the Russian bureaucracy, they defended the interests of the Jews to the detriment of the government. When dealing with the Jewish communal leadership, they pursued their own interests. As a result, the government could not rely on them as its loyal servants and bureaucratic agents within the Jewish communities. The collaboration between them and Russian bureaucrats was too often based on personal connections and tutelage rather than on established bureaucratic procedures.

In the 1830s and 1840s the institution building of the imperial government apparatus moved toward centralization, unification, and the bureaucratization of power. The institution building of the imperial Jewish bureaucracy followed this same path. This turning point was a radical departure from the traditional ways of Jewish representation and intercession in the government administration.

The French Consistorial System

In 1840, the MVD charted a basic draft of the institutional structure of the imperial administration of Jewish religious affairs. At its core was an imported model of consistories, originally the French institutional framework for administration of the Jews, established in 1808. Building on French know-how, the MVD planned to develop its own institutional framework of provincial consistories and a provincial rabbinate subordinate to the central agency in St. Petersburg.[51]

Throughout the eighteenth and nineteenth centuries, the Russian government consistently based its administrative innovations on political theories and practices borrowed from western Europe. This was the case with its Jewish policies as well. Historians pointed out many parallels in the goals, means, and practical measures of official policy toward the Jews in the Russian empire and in European countries such as France, Prussia, and Austria-Hungary. Recent scholarship has examined the technical aspects and historical context of this remarkable parallel, including the study and practical application of the European experience by Russian bureaucracy.[52] Several Russian ministries and their high-ranking officials carefully studied European institutions and policies that had evidently succeeded in the political and social integration of the Jews into modern Western societies.

In the 1840s, the Minister of State Domains, Count Pavel Dmitrievich Kiselev, studied institutions and policies aimed at the social transformation and administration of the Jews in Austria, Baden, Bavaria, Prussia, and France. Based on his findings, Kiselev concluded that the Russian government should pursue the following crucial policies, modeled on European examples: dissolve the kahal, modernize (i.e., bureaucratize) the traditional rabbinate, and create a system of compulsory secular education for Jews.[53] According to Kiselev, the central role in the implementation of this ambitious agenda was to be played by the bureaucratic "Jewish clergy," modeled on contemporary French consistories, which were successfully "turned by the [French] government into an instrument for implementation of its policies."[54]

During the 1850s, Russian ministries routinely dispatched their officials to Europe for further study of Western policies toward the Jews. In 1857, the Ministry of Popular Enlightenment dispatched Professor Nikita Petrovich Giliarov-Platonov of the Moscow Orthodox Theological Academy to Prussia with the assignment of studying the German experience in organizing Jewish schools and rabbinical seminaries in particular.[55] In 1860, Aleksandr Borisovich Rikhter, Russian ambassador to Belgium, presented the Jewish Committee in St. Petersburg with his survey of Jewish policies of various European governments.[56] In 1858, Nikolai Gradovskii, head of the Jewish division at the DDDII and secretary of the Rabbinical Commission, visited France, Belgium, Prussia, and England. By the order of Emmanuil Karlovich Sivers, director of the DDDII, Gradovskii "while abroad, should closely study the following subjects: 1) the foundations of religious administration for the Jews; 2) the internal workings and procedures of such administration; 3) the cadres of such administration."[57]

Returning from abroad and reporting their findings, Russian officials by and large praised the achievements of European governments in integrating and emancipating their Jewish subjects. However, these reports clearly distinguished between full civic emancipation of the Jews as a distant goal of Russian policy and immediate routine bureaucratic policies aimed at gradual social integration and standardization. The authors of these reports observed that contemporary European governments "strive ... to amalgamate Jews in their rights and privileges into the general mass of their subjects."[58] Most of these officials also agreed that, in words of Nikolai Gradovskii, "the state where this goal is most successfully realized is France. Here, prejudices against the Jews are almost entirely extinct, not only among the members of the government, but among regular people. Jews are indistinguishable from the rest of the citizens, enjoy all private and public rights, and often occupy prestigious positions in government and public service."[59]

In sum, the study of contemporary European institutions and policies aimed at integration of the Jews was widely practiced by Russian officialdom. Moreover, the European experience was frequently, though selectively, incorporated into official Russian policy toward the Jews. However, transplantation of an entire foreign institutional framework to Russian soil was a rare and remarkable occurrence.

In the 1800s the original consistorial system was established in France as part of the realization of Napoleon's vision of a secular centralized state incorporating a religious administration within its bureaucratic structures. In the 1840s, this vision obviously resonated with the goals of the Russian ministerial system. Therefore, consistories, with three decades of successful practical implementation behind them, seemed attractive to Russian bureaucrats, who saw the great potential of the consistorial system to take root and thrive on Russian soil.

Since the French consistorial system, including its institutional structure and basic functions, was thoroughly replicated by the Russian government, an overview of its history and key features is appropriate here.

———

The French consistorial system had no parallels among the traditional institutions of Jewish communal organization. The consistorial system was an unprecedented project of social and political integration of the Jews, successfully realized by the modern European state using purely bureaucratic means. In the end, the consistories, essentially bureaucratic institutions fully controlled and funded by the government, virtually transformed French Jewry and French Judaism.

The conception and realization of the consistorial system in 1806–1809 came as part of Napoleon's broader vision of the balance of power between church and state. Negotiations between the French emperor and the pope resulted in granting Catholicism and Protestantism the status of official French religions, officially recognized by the French state. The leadership of French Jewry opted for a similar recognition of Judaism, which was granted by Napoleon in return for establishing comprehensive government control over Jewish religious matters. As a result, the Jewish consistories emerged, modeled upon the previously established Protestant institutions, fully funded (since 1831) by the French government.[60]

The consistorial system included a substantial hierarchy of institutions and officials, with the Central Consistory in Paris at the top. The Central Consistory comprised three rabbis and two lay members, originally appointed by the government and later on by the leadership of the consistories. The Central Consistory was charged with the general supervision and control of the French Jews and, above all, French rabbis. It was directly subordinate to the French Ministry of Cults. The lower level of the system included local departmental consistories that directly supervised Jewish communities (as many as a hundred per consistory) throughout the country. Each departmental consistory had five members: two rabbis and three lay members, elected by a college of twenty-five notables. The Ministry of Cults appointed notables among the local Jews on the basis of their political loyalty and economic wealth.

The French government did not ban such informal traditional institutes of the Jewish community as *chavurot* (voluntary societies) and independent *minyanim* (prayer assemblies), although these organizations were deprived of any legal power to represent the French Jews. The consistory was the single official channel of Jewish policy. The consistory, overseeing several dozens of communities, replaced the traditional Jewish community as the principal institutional and administrative entity.

The consistorial system was a quasi-governmental structure within French bureaucracy. In this institutional framework, consistories were engaged in government policymaking and implementation through routine bureaucratic procedures of communication and collaboration with each other and with other administrative structures, such as magistrates and police.

Overall, the political and administrative mandate of the consistories was based on the French version of the *quid pro quo* contract of Jewish emancipation in modern Europe. The French government guaranteed full citizenship rights to the Jews. The French Jewish economic elite largely in control of the consistorial apparatus guaranteed the civil responsibility and loyalty of the Jews to the government. Accordingly, Napoleon's *Règlement* (Statute on Jews) of 1806 and consequent French laws and regulations of the Ministry of Cults from 1823 to 1844 entrusted the consistories with the following responsibilities: administration of the Jews, including collection of special Jewish taxes (until 1831); overseeing the election and service of community officials; management of communal properties; overseeing religious ritual; appointment of supervision staff, *commissaires-surveillants*; "regeneration" of the Jews, including their secular education, civil enlightenment, and encouragement of productive labor among them; policing of the Jews, including registration of the population, recruits and taxpayers; and general overseeing of their political loyalty.[61]

The Jewish economic elite dominant in the consistories supplemented the bureaucratic mandate with its own essentially integrationist social and political agenda. It included the neutralization of any anti-Jewish attitudes and campaigns in French society, largely through legal action and intervention of the government; improvement of the image of the Jews in French public opinion; and formal religious reform of Judaism aimed at modeling the rabbinate and Jewish rites after modern Christian clergy and ritual.[62]

The religious policies of the consistories, including ousting the institutional authority of the rabbinate and replacing it with lay leadership and reforms of traditional ritual, were fundamentally anti-traditional. These policies were aimed at the integration of the Jews into French society, increasing their social conformity by means of structural transformation of French Judaism and its institutions and by the overall secularization of the Jewish lifestyle. French reformers of Judaism, unlike their German colleagues, were not particularly religious and did not produce any theological breakthroughs. Their reform platform was based on formal changes and general laicist attitudes pervading contemporary French bureaucracy and society. It included the modification of synagogue ritual after the Protestant model, secularization of Jewish education (from elementary schools to the rabbinical seminary), and establishment of secular control over the rabbinate.

In the 1840s, when the consistorial system caught the attention of Russian bureaucrats, its "ritual reform" had accomplished a great deal. In the 1820s, the consistories introduced substantial changes to French congregations, such as obligatory rabbinical sermons in French, choirs, and orderly worship. A government uniform, similar to that of the Protestant pastors, was prescribed for all rabbis and cantors. Traditional Jewish religious schools, *chadarim* and *yeshivot*, were banned across the country. A Jewish catechism replaced the *chumash* (Pentateuch) and other *sifrei kodesh* (biblical commentaries and talmudic literature) as the only official textbook for Jewish religious instruction. The rite of confirmation, based on an examination on the catechism, was established. In the 1840s, the traditional sale of *mitzvot* (lit., commandments; traditionally,

40

opportunities to perform such rituals as opening the Torah ark and raising the Torah scroll were bought by congregants, with proceeds usually going to charity) in the synagogue was banned in order to promote its status as a temple and holy place. Jewish funeral procedures came under strict government regulation. Circumcision was placed under control of public health officials to guarantee its compliance with contemporary hygienic norms. These ritual reforms secured the administrative monopoly of the consistories and their lay leadership, and established their control over the entire spectrum of Jewish religious life.

The French rabbinate of the nineteenth century depended on bureaucracy, both institutionally and ideologically, as the "spiritual," religious arm of the consistorial apparatus. The secondary role of the rabbinate, subordinate to the lay leadership, was inherent in the original design of the consistorial system. Napoleon and the French Ministry of Cults believed that the traditional rabbinate was the principal basis of perceived Jewish social and religious isolation. Thus, traditional rabbis could not be trusted and should be placed under the control of secular authorities. Consequently, after 1808 all rabbinical appointments in France were made by the Ministry of Cults based on the recommendations of the consistories and police approval. From 1808 to 1848, appointed rabbis swore allegiance to the government. Their official oath included a pledge to report any suspicious and anti-government activity of the Jews to the authorities. The *Règlement* of 1806 entrusted rabbis with the inculcation of loyalty to the country and the emperor including obedience to the law, military service, a daily prayer for the monarch, and proper official registration of births, deaths, marriages, and divorces.[63]

In 1829 a rabbinical seminary was set up in Metz under the control of the Central Consistory and the Ministry of Cults.[64] The seminary became the principal institution for the education and official accreditation of the modern French rabbinate. Its graduates did not boast extensive knowledge of both religious and secular subjects. Unlike their German colleagues, who, as a rule, combined substantial traditional Jewish education with university degrees, modern French rabbis only had to complete six years of study at the Metz seminary to be officially ordained. The compensation of French rabbis was as limited as their education, and was set at an annual rate of 300–600 francs as of 1843. As a rule, an official rabbinical career was pursued by Jewish youth of the humblest social background, who could not afford better education and subsequently better careers. By the 1880s the French rabbinate was entirely staffed by graduates of the rabbinical seminary.

Finally, in 1844, a government ordinance established an unprecedented hierarchical structure within the rabbinate. The ordinance instituted levels of subordination and control, including a chief rabbi at the Central Consistory in Paris, chief rabbis at the departmental consistories, and district rabbis. The chief rabbi in Paris, at the highest level of the hierarchy, was himself subordinate to the lay leadership of the Central Consistory and the bureaucratic authority of the Ministry of Cults.

As a result of these administrative and ritual reforms, the modern French rabbinate emerged. It was a semi-bureaucratic agency devoid of any social initiative and political ambition. Indistinguishable in its status and purpose from the official clergy of other religions recognized by the state, the French rabbinate was firmly integrated within the fundamentally secular bureaucratic power structures administering the religious affairs of French Jews: the consistorial system and the Ministry of Cults.

In the 1840s, the consistorial system took the shape that the Russian government used as a model of institution building for the religious administration of the Russian Jews. The consistorial system developed and successfully implemented institutions and policies that seemed to be a perfect match for the integrationist political goals and bureaucratic concerns of the Russian ministerial system. The consistories provided the prototype of a comprehensive bureaucratic institution affecting, directly or indirectly, all spheres of Jewish life. Its bureaucratic sprawl penetrated all strata of the Jewish population, from traditional and modern elites to plain village Jews. Its officials, including rabbis, *commissaires surveillants* (consistorial supervisors), and *ministres officiants* (population registrars), were salaried state servitors under oath to the government, with a broadly defined bureaucratic and police mandate.

The Russian government could see the remarkable success of the integration of the French Jews, including the rabbinate, its least loyal segment. Russian officialdom believed that the consistorial system had orchestrated this accomplishment, and therefore the MVD decided to apply this powerful solution to Russian Jews.

In the 1840s, the MVD initiated a large-scale institutional transformation of the administration of Jewish subjects, aimed at their social and cultural integration into the structures of the empire. The abolishment of the kahal, the ubiquitous institute of Jewish political and social isolation, was simultaneously the main objective and the means of the proposed change. Iulii Gessen's study of imperial policy toward the Jews defined the 1840s reforms as essentially an institutional reorganization of Jewish life. The government considered the kahal's fiscal powers and its alliance with the traditional rabbinate as the fundamental sources of institutional support for Jewish communal autonomy. This combination of social and religious authority enabled the traditional Jewish elite to rule the Jewish populace. Therefore, the government sought to establish its own bureaucratic control over taxation and administration of the Jews. The proposed reforms also targeted the rabbinate, whose religious authority would be reduced to exclusively "spiritual matters," and officially restricted issues of ritual and religious law, including worship, marriage, divorce, burial, etc., to be resolved by a specially instituted religious bureaucracy at the imperial, provincial, and district levels. By means of this reorganization, the kahal along with the isolationist thrust of its politics would be effectively dissolved.[65]

In 1886, forty years after the religious administration for the Jews was institutionalized in Russia, a DDDII memorandum reflected on the original goals of the government: "One of the incentives for the establishment of the Rabbinical Commission was the government's desire to form a highest agency of control for religious affairs of the Jews, which would supervise and guide the lowest echelon—the provincial and district rabbinate. With the aid of expert Jews [at the provincial level], the government sought to advance, among the ignorant Jewish masses, a rapprochement between the Jews and the native population."[66] In fact, the constituent institutions of Russian religious administration for the Jews performed quite independent functions. The Rabbinical Commission acted as a Jewish Supreme Court in religious matters. Provincial expert Jews were charged with helping the government identify and overcome "Jewish fanaticism," that is, social isolation. The district rabbinate took over police functions, including registration of Jewish taxpayers and recruits.

Thus, the realization of the ambitious government program of social transformation of Russian Jews necessitated fundamental rebuilding of the framework of traditional Jewish religious and communal institutions. In this process, the Jewish bureaucratic elite emerged as the principal institutional base for imperial Jewish policy.

2

Bureaucratic Jews

Establishment of the Office of Expert Jews

On August 1, 1840, as per an MVD circular directive, a committee on the establishment of the provincial rabbinate and provincial Jewish religious boards was set up in Odessa under the governor-general of Novorossiia and Bessarabiia, Prince Mikhail Semenovich Vorontsov.[1] The MVD directive also ordered that governor-generals should establish the same committees in the other major administrative centers of the Pale of Settlement, including Kiev, Vilna, Vitebsk, Poltava, and Mitava. The directive stipulated detailed instructions for the proceedings, and specified the MVD's vision of the general purpose of the rabbinate, its structure and functions in the context of the proposed system of religious administration for the Jews. Moreover, the MVD expected the committees to nominate "desirable" candidates for the provincial rabbinate from a pool of loyal Jews sympathetic to official policies.

The directive put forward the *chinonachalie* (bureaucratic hierarchy) as the fundamental principle of religious administration for the Jews. Incongruously, this bureaucratization of Jewish life was not aimed at the delegation of actual administrative authority to Jewish officialdom, but instead implied the establishment of Jewish echelons of bureaucratic control within the Russian administration, in order to help "discover and prevent any abuses" perpetrated by Jews. Thus, the directive considered the provincial rabbinate a supervisory agency that would only help implement Jewish policy by reporting infringements, rather than enforce it with full administrative power. The provincial rabbinate would only supervise the district rabbinate in matters of proper ceremonial conduct and interpretation of religious law. The provincial rabbis would report their findings (in secret, if necessary) to their superiors, the governor-generals, for further administrative action.

The directive envisioned the role of the provincial rabbis evenly split between inspection and arbitration. The governor-generals would dispatch the provincial rabbis to inspect the district rabbis and local religious and communal institutions, to audit the records of their bureaucratic and financial transactions, and to attest to the loyalty of district rabbis and other religious personnel. The provincial rabbis would also preside over the proceedings of the provincial Jewish religious boards examining cases and disputes of religious law, including divorces and proper ceremonial conduct. The provincial rabbis would also aid in official censorship of Jewish religious literature with examination, on their inspection missions, of "books used by the Jews for prayer and for study of religious doctrines" for any "secretive and malicious" content.[2] All official transactions of the provincial rabbis and provincial Jewish religious boards would be conducted in the Russian language.

The Odessa Committee met from August to November 1840. It included Major-General Dmitrii Akhlestyshev, the military governor of Odessa and chairman of the committee; Appolon Skal'kovskii, secretary of the Odessa commercial council and Odessa exchange and secretary of the committee; four Russian officials assigned to the committee by the provincial chancelleries of Novorossiia and Bessarabiia; and three deputies of the Odessa Jewish community—Betsalel Shtern, headmaster of the Jewish school, and merchants Khaim Efrusi and Moisei Likhtenshtadt.[3]

The Odessa Committee signified an important phase in the development of Jewish bureaucracy in the Russian empire. In contrast to the early forms of Jewish representation in the government administration, such as the experts of the Jewish Committee and the Deputies of the Jewish People, the Jewish members of the Odessa Committee were neither experts nor deputies in the full sense of the word.[4] They were selected and appointed by the provincial administration based on their qualifications (that is, "educated and loyal Jews"),[5] and collaborated on equal terms with the Russian officials, selected and appointed by the same administration. The chairman Akhlestyshev reported to Governor-general Vorontsov that both *pochetnyi grazhdanin* (honored citizen) Shtern and *nadvornyi sovetnik* (court counselor) Skal'kovskii proved to be "most resourceful members of the committee and provided crucial input to the drafting of legislation" proposed as a result of the committee's deliberations.[6] Moreover, wrote Akhlestyshev, "both *chinovniki* (officials) successfully combined their significant contribution to the committee with their principal jobs."[7] Thus, by recognizing the Jewish members of the committee as *chinovniki* (officials), the authorities no longer saw them as Jewish traditional deputies, representing the interests of the Jewish communities. Instead, in close bureaucratic collaboration with Russian officials, they ultimately represented the government, and performed "service assigned to the committee by imperial order," as Akhlestyshev put it.[8]

The Jewish members of the committee apparently got a taste of bureaucratic work and applied themselves as true bureaucrats, drafting extensive legislation on the provincial rabbinate, totaling more than two hundred paragraphs. The authors of the draft went far beyond their mandate stipulated by the MVD directive, presenting a comprehensive proposal entitled the "Statute on Jewish Clergy."[9] Thus, they did not limit their effort to listing ways to curb "anything detrimental" to the religious life of the Jews, but went on to propose a means for instilling "anything useful" in the Jews.[10] The new Jewish elite would emerge as a result of vigorous institution building proposed in the draft "Statute." The proposal pointed out the steps toward modernization of the traditional rabbinate, concerning its social makeup, institutional significance, and social and religious prestige. The steps included equality in status and privileges of the rabbinate and the clergy of recognized non-Orthodox Christian faiths; establishment of an official hierarchy of rabbinical ranks; and designation to the rabbinate of full control over Jewish religious ritual, religious education of Jewish youth, and general enlightenment of the Jews. Since the "Statute" draft treated the current Russian traditional rabbinate as a largely inadequate cadre base, it outlined another bureaucratic solution, recommending the establishment of a government-sponsored rabbinical seminary aimed at training and official certification of modern Russian rabbis. The committee member Betsalel Shtern designed a proposed curriculum for the seminary, which would include "subjects comprising the core of Jewish theology in the glory days of Judaism (at the time of the Spanish Caliphates)."[11]

The Odessa Committee was a turning point in the history of imperial Jewish bureaucracy. The Jewish members of the committee did not directly represent the interests of the Jews (whether of traditional or of maskilic background), but collaborated with Russian bureaucrats in their official capacity as Russian officials, entrusted by the government with an important bureaucratic mission. Their work culminated in the concept of a "Jewish clergy," a professionally trained Jewish bureaucracy carrying out the social and political agenda of the government.

In 1844, the government launched comprehensive institutional reforms aimed at the dismantling of the traditional framework of Jewish communal organizations, replacing them with the centralized bureaucratic institutions of the Russian empire. The reforms marked the all-encompassing intervention of state bureaucracy into every aspect of Jewish life, including administration (abolishment of the kahal), taxation (introduction of the *korobochnyi sbor*, a special Jewish poll tax), education (establishment of government-sponsored Jewish schools), occupation (promotion of productive labor), and lifestyle (prohibition of traditional Jewish dress, regulation of marital issues). To implement these policies, the government invented a Jewish bureaucracy modeled on the French consistories. It included the Rabbinical Commission and provincial rabbinate, above the district rabbinate, which was in the midst of the traditional Jewish masses. The authorities planned on eventually forming a "reserve of cadres educated in the spirit of the government" to staff the newly established Jewish bureaucracy.[12]

The replication of the French institutional prototype in the Russian Pale of Settlement inevitably ran into the problem of adequate cadres envisioned by the Odessa Committee. The governor-generals reported an acute scarcity of loyal and educated Jews at their disposal, resulting in their inability to staff the provincial rabbinate. To deal with the problem, on December 20, 1844, the State Council recommended a provisional solution to the Jewish Committee, which was in charge of coordinating the reforms. Instead of rabbis, the governor-generals would incorporate special inspectors into their chancelleries, recruited from among the *uchenye evrei* (educated [lit., learned] Jews), to oversee the proper ceremonial conduct and official transactions of the government district rabbis. On February 18, 1846, the Jewish Committee officially endorsed this initiative and received final approval from the emperor. Thus, the committee decreed that "1) in the provinces where Jews are officially granted residence, as a provisional measure, every governor-general may appoint two Jewish inspectors with the addition of a third if necessary; 2) without giving any special instructions to these inspectors, put them in full dependence on the governor-generals, who may use them in cases pertaining to religious matters, as directed by special secret regulation; 3) the appointment of these inspectors is provisional."[13] In the 1840s, the MVD referred to the novice Jewish bureaucrats as *inspektory iz uchenykh evreev* (inspectors from among the expert Jews). Eventually, "inspector" was dropped from the official title and the new bureaucratic office was incorporated by the imperial legislation under the rubric *uchenye evrei* (expert Jews).[14]

The same decree by the Jewish Committee stipulated that the MVD should develop an official statute on expert Jews and detailed instructions for their official use by the governor-generals. To that end, the MVD requested information from the governor-generals about Jewish *izuverstvo* (religious bigotry) in their provinces, and their opinions regarding the anticipated role of the Jewish bureaucrats in overcoming this bigotry.

The governor-generals promptly provided their feedback. The governor-general of Kiev, Podolia, and Volhyn, general *aide-de-camp* Dmitrii Gavrilovich Bibikov, looked forward to commissioning expert Jews with "various observational tasks, official scrutiny of secret information [regarding the Jews], exposure of any abuses [by the Jews], and examination of Jewish books and manuscripts."[15] The acting governor-general of Novorossiia and Bessarabiia, Lieutenant-general Pavel Ivanovich Fedorov, expressed his strong belief that the crucial task of "exposure of all kinds of religious fanaticism among the Jews" required the involvement of "virtuous Jews who accepted Christian teaching," and who, besides linguistic proficiency in Hebrew and Yiddish, possessed "significant knowledge of Jewish rituals and traditions."[16] The acting governor-general of Vitebsk, Mogilev, and Smolensk, Prince Sergei Alekseevich Dolgorukov, provided a broader vision of the role of expert Jews, who, besides supplying the authorities with expertise and accurate information on Jewish matters, would "exert their personal moral influence to instill in the Jews an ultimate trust in the government and its tutelage; to convince the Jews of the advantages of [modern] education; and to eradicate their ungrounded fear [of government policies]."[17]

These opinions amounted to a draft design of Russian Jewish bureaucracy, which incorporated the basic features of its French prototype such as its police and regeneration functions. The Russian administrators wanted the service of loyal and, ideally, baptized Jews commissioned with, in addition to their bureaucratic and police duties, a broad social mission of cultivating loyalty among the Jews and eradicating Jewish fanaticism by applying their moral influence. However, this design deliberately left another important function of the consistorial system—administration—outside the bureaucratic scope of the expert Jews.

Based on the decree of the Jewish Committee and the feedback of the provincial administrators, the MVD finalized the "statute on expert Jews." It stipulated that "1) every governor-general in the Pale of Settlement should appoint two, or, if necessary and approved by the Minister of Internal Affairs, three expert Jews for official assignments in matters which require special knowledge of rituals and regulations of Jewish religious law. During their term in office, expert Jews are exempt from residence restrictions established for the general Jewish population prohibiting them from settling in Kiev, Kharkov, and Riga; 2) governor-generals should recruit expert Jews primarily among the rabbis meriting the government's confidence and carrying authority with their communities; 3) expert Jews should be officially sworn into office in the provincial synagogue ... [expert Jews'] service term is indefinite; however, they can officially petition for resignation, and they can also be dismissed from office by the governor-general; 4) expert Jews are fully dependent on the governor-generals, who may use them at their discretion; expert Jews are absolutely prohibited from conducting any official transactions independently, without a special order from the governor-general, and they should only execute the commands of their superiors; 5) expert Jews are entitled to the following compensation: a) a salary funded by the *korobochnyi sbor* [special Jewish tax on kosher meat] and negotiated between the Minister of Internal Affairs and governor-general, not exceeding 900 silver rubles per annum; b) an exemption from all civil obligations, including taxes and military service, during their time in office; c) honorary citizenship, medals and other rewards for outstanding accomplishments and impeccable service of more than fifteen years in office."[18]

On July 3, 1850, the statute was signed into law by Emperor Nicholas I.[19] Thus, the former provisional status of expert Jews was upgraded to a permanent one, and the new bureaucratic position was launched. This position bore few similarities to its consistorial prototype. Unlike the consistories, expert Jews had no clear-cut bureaucratic agenda, since their only responsibility was the execution of the governor-general's orders. Furthermore, while the French consistories were the only legitimate institution representing Jews in their official communications with the government, Russian expert Jews could hardly represent themselves, since they were merely a bureaucratic extension of the provincial authorities. In sum, expert Jews emerged as state servants and yet another bureaucratic office within the provincial administration of the MVD. At the same time, the bureaucratic origins of expert Jews made them stand out among Jewish subjects of the empire as the officially recognized Jewish elite, distinguished by its proximity to the authorities and entitled to exclusive benefits and privileges. The MVD still sought the bureaucratic integration of the traditional Jewish elite, stipulating that expert Jews had to be recruited from rabbis loyal to the government and influential in their communities. At the outset, the traditional rabbinical elite demonstrated little interest in the office of expert Jew, deprived of any real power. However, the government's appeal gained ground in the 1890s in a very different political environment.[20]

Classification of Expert Jews

Official bureaucratic documents, including correspondence, memoranda, and draft legislation, were filled with contradictory and misleading usage of the term *uchenyi evrei* (expert Jew) and its variations, *uchenye ravviny* (expert rabbis), or simply *uchenyi* (a learned person or expert). The following perplexing selection of linguistic and bureaucratic puzzles exposes the challenging process of creating a Jewish bureaucratic elite.

In 1858, the head of the DDDII, Count Emmanuil Karlovich Sivers, in his official memorandum to the Minister of Internal Affairs, Sergei Stepanovich Lanskoi, reported that the original design of the imperial religious administration for the Jews included *uchenye ravviny* (learned rabbis), who could "successfully influence the minds of their co-religionists."[21]

In 1856, an anonymous memorandum received by the head of the MVD, Sergei Lanskoi, proposed raising the authority of the Rabbinical Commission by incorporating into its agenda "the most important issues in contemporary Jewish life," including "a most anticipated invitation to Russia for *uchenye ravviny* (expert rabbis) from abroad, the establishment of consistories, and the subsequent liberation of the Russian Jews from the so-called *uchenye evrei* (expert Jews), and their abuse and rapaciousness."[22]

In 1859, Iona Khaimovich Gurliand, the government rabbi of Poltava, in his official report to the Minister of National Enlightenment Evgraf Petrovich Kovalevskii, recommended placing the traditional Jewish teachers, melamdim, under government control. To this end, he suggested that under the authority of the headmasters of every provincial gymnasium in the Pale of Settlement, a position of "special *uchenyi evrei* (expert Jew), similar to the inspectors of parish schools, should be established to ensure that government regulations and decrees regarding Jewish education were properly executed even in the most distant localities; this official should report to the headmaster and to the *uchenyi evrei* (expert Jew) under the superintendent of the educational district."[23]

In 1861, a proposal submitted to the MVD by Avraam Gordon, a graduate of the Vilna Rabbinical Seminary and law student at St. Petersburg University, deemed the educational requirements for the position of district government rabbi to be too low. Gordon referred to the law, stipulating that "government rabbinical positions should only be occupied by *uchenye evrei* (expert Jews),"[24] and appealed to reason, stating that "three years in a gymnasium did not entitle anyone to the status of *uchenyi* (learned person or expert)."[25]

Paragraph 137 of the 1874 draft *Ustav o evreiakh* (Statute on Jews) stipulated that prayer rituals in officially established synagogues could be conducted "by any *uchenyi evrei* (expert Jew) elected by the community."[26] Paragraph 140 stated that proper divorce procedure between Jews required "the official permission of the [government] rabbi or of some other *uchenyi evrei* (expert Jew)."[27] Paragraph 158 obliged the Jews of every locality with one or more established synagogues "to elect and submit a *uchenyi i pochetnyi evrei* (learned and honored Jew) for approval by the provincial authorities, for the position of local [government] rabbi."[28]

These examples elicit more questions than explanations. What was the difference between an "expert Jew" and a "expert rabbi"? Were expert Jews elected by the Jewish communities or appointed by the government? What did the actual responsibilities of the expert Jews include: conducting religious rituals or overseeing the broader scope of Jewish religious life? What was meant by the "learning" and "expertise" of "learned" and "expert" Jews?

The definition of the term *uchenyi evrei* provided by the Russian Jewish encyclopedia brings some order to this discord of meanings.[29] The entry in the Encyclopedia is of particular significance since it was compiled by Moisei Lazarevich Kreps, himself the expert Jew at the DDDII from 1907 to 1917 and, in fact, the last expert Jew of the Russian empire. The entry, prepared by Kreps in 1913, surveyed five decades of the history of expert Jews. Its dry and detached style reveals the bureaucratic identity of its author. The entry, which lacks historical context and reads as a bureaucratic memorandum, presents an inventory of pertinent imperial legislation and ministerial regulations, and provides an unambiguous and comprehensive classification of expert Jews within the religious administration for the Jews.

Kreps's entry did not discuss the origins of this administration, including its French consistorial prototype and planned hierarchy of the rabbinate. According to his timeline, officials known as *uchenye evrei* (expert Jews) first appeared in the early 1840s at the Ministry of National Enlightenment, the locus of official Jewish policy at that time. When the government attempted to bring order to the traditional Jewish religious organization, the Jews "declared that they had no clergy to execute ecclesiastical authority among them, similar to the authority of the church among the Christians. However, they had learned experts proficient in theology and competent in religious matters. The principal expert in every Jewish community is the rabbi, a title that could be translated as *uchenyi* (a learned one). Thus, besides the rabbi, the law established several positions of *uchenye evrei* (learned or expert Jews) for various commissions."[30] Therefore, according to Kreps, the religious administration for Jews in Russia emerged as a non-hierarchical network of government officials, *uchenye evrei* (expert Jews), recruited among traditional experts in Jewish theology and law, including rabbis and other Jews with traditional learning.

A recent study by Verena Dohrn took Kreps's account of the origins of expert Jews at face value. Thus, she defined *uchenyi evrei* (expert Jew) as a traditional Jewish honorary status recognized by the government. This status allowed the traditional Jewish elite—rabbis—to serve as official experts and bureaucratic agents of the government. At the same time, according to Dohrn, the emerging secular Jewish elite of Russian maskilim vigorously sought the status of expert Jew to secure their official recognition and authority among the Jews. By changing the meaning of *uchenost'* (learning or expertise), implied in the status of expert Jew, from proficiency in religious matters to general secular education, Russian maskilim ultimately gained access to this office.[31] However, a detailed analysis of Kreps's definitions and documentary sources on expert Jews leads to different conclusions.

From the onset and throughout the history of the office, the learning and expertise of expert Jews was definitely based on their proficiency in Jewish religious matters.[32] At the same time, the title of expert Jew was a genuine product of the Russian language and its bureaucratic lingo. In contemporary Russian of the time the word *uchenyi* in similar combinations meant someone "trained" or "skilled," for example, *uchenyi plotnik*, literally a carpenter trained for his profession or skilled carpenter.[33] Thus, this word was used for the official definition of professional qualification. It was primarily a Russian bureaucratic classification of qualified Jewish officials incorporated within the religious administration for Jews in Russia, rather than a Jewish traditional honorary status. Moreover, their qualification alone, whether based on learning and expertise in Jewish religious matters or on secular education, did not entitle them, in the eyes of the government, to elite status among the Jews. Instead, it was their demonstrated political loyalty and formal contribution to official Jewish policy that made expert Jews the Jewish bureaucratic elite.

In the Encyclopedia entry, Kreps based his classification of expert Jews on their specialized bureaucratic commissions and the degree of their bureaucratic integration within the provincial religious administration for Jews in Russia, and within the central agencies of the Russian ministerial system. His schema included the following categories of Jewish bureaucrats.

Expert Jews at synagogues and prayer houses were members of the *dukhovnye pravleniia* (religious boards) of Jewish prayer assemblies elected by the Jewish communities. The religious boards, under the authority of the district government rabbis, were governing bodies attached to every synagogue in the empire, and included *uchenyi* or *more-horaa* (expert Jew), *starosta* or *gabai* (warden), and *kaznachei* or *neeman* (treasurer).[34] As stipulated by law, unofficial, "spiritual" rabbis were allowed to run for this office. Expert Jews at synagogues and prayer houses could resolve "any contradictory issues regarding prayers and other rituals of the Jewish faith."[35] In their absence, only the local government rabbi was permitted by law to assume the mandate of expert Jew on a temporary basis.

Expert Jews under the superintendents of educational districts were the Jewish officials of the Ministry of National Enlightenment (*Ministerstvo narodnogo prosveshcheniia* [MNP]) appointed by the government. This position, established in 1844, was that of ensuring "expertise in Jewish matters and inspection of the curriculum of government-sponsored Jewish schools under the close supervision of specially appointed Russian officials."[36] These expert Jews were meant to provide support to government policy aimed at the integration of the Jews through modern education. To ensure successful implementation of this policy among traditional Russian Jews and to overcome their general distrust of Russian officialdom, expert Jews would provide the government with guidance based on their "Jewish theological learning and special knowledge of the rules and procedures of Jewish religious law."[37]

The post of expert Jew under the Minister of National Enlightenment was established "at the same time and for the same purpose as expert Jews under the superintendents of educational districts. However, the incumbent should possess educational qualifications at least at the level of the gymnasium."[38] In fact, this expert Jew served as the special assistant to the Minister of National Enlightenment in the field of government policy on Jewish education. The first expert Jews in this office, Rabbi Max Lilienthal (1841–1844) and Leon Mandel'shtam (1846–1857), were direct protégés of the Minister Count Sergei Uvarov, and were granted broad authority in matters of secular Jewish education. When the institutional role of the Ministry in Jewish policy shrank, the significance of the expert Jew decreased accordingly. Upon the retirement of Leon Mandel'shtam in 1857, the position of expert Jew under the Minister of National Enlightenment was deliberately left vacant. Instead, expert Jews were absorbed as full members of the Ministry's *Uchenyi komitet* (Expert Committee). The Jewish members of the Expert Committee included

Dr. Nikolai Bakst (in the 1880s), Baron David Gintsburg (until 1910), and Dr. Naum Pereferkovich (from 1910).[39]

Expert Jews under the governor-generals in the provinces of the Pale of Settlement were Jewish officials of the Ministry of Internal Affairs, appointed by the governor-generals and approved by the Minister from qualified candidates holding gymnasium diplomas and university degrees. Their work included official missions requiring "special knowledge of the rules and procedures of Jewish religious law."[40] The MVD allowed expert Jews to hold more than one office within the religious administration for the Jews, including the office of government rabbi. The MVD consistently rejected baptized Jews applying for the position, on the grounds that the cadres of the religious administration for the Jews, including expert Jews, should belong to the Jewish faith.[41]

The post of expert Jew at the Ministry of Internal Affairs was a Jewish official position established in 1877, due to the growing demand for expertise in Jewish matters in the central offices of the MVD that could not be satisfied by the occasional assistance of the Rabbinical Commission and the government rabbi of St. Petersburg. This expert Jew also served the governors of Kurland and Lifland, who were not assigned Jewish officials upon the dismantling of the Baltic governor-generalship in 1876. Therefore, the position was often occupied by government rabbis of Riga, who provided their services to the governors and the MVD without leaving the capital city of Lifland. These expert Jews included Aaron Pumpianskii (1877–1894), Solomon Pukher (1894–1898), and Isidor Mikhelson (1900–1907). In 1907, the MVD relocated this office to St. Petersburg in order to put an expert Jew in charge of preparation of the forthcoming session of the Rabbinical Commission and the Rabbinical Congress.[42] The last expert Jew at the MVD was the chief rabbi of the Jewish agricultural colonies of Kherson province, Moisei Kreps (1907–1917).[43]

This typology delineates the two principal echelons of the Jewish bureaucracy. The first echelon included expert Jews who were elected officials of the Jewish communities, serving as assistants to the government rabbis in matters of ritual and religious law. Their Hebrew title, *more-horaa*, officially designated by Russian law, specifically referred to their traditional Jewish learning and expert skills. The second echelon included expert Jews who were government officials appointed by the governor-generals and Russian ministries serving as bureaucrats in the provincial and central chancelleries of the MVD and MNP. Their expertise covered matters of Jewish religion and traditional way of life along with official Russian policies of integration of the Jews into Russian society. Besides the conventional classification as *uchenye evrei*, the law categorized these expert Jews as *evrei dlia ispolneniia osobykh poruchenii* (Jews for special missions), which explicitly indicated their bureaucratic function, similar to the Russian category of officials for special missions.[44]

The first echelon of expert Jews was made up of a few thousand mostly traditional Russian Jews, with a number of traditional rabbis among them. This amorphous bureaucratic category had little social or ideological integrity, and no particular group identity. By contrast, the second echelon of expert Jews, made up of only a few dozen Jewish bureaucrats, was demarcated by clear-cut social and ideological boundaries. As a rule, these expert Jews had common social and educational experience as graduates of the imperial rabbinical seminaries.[45] Their integration within contemporary Russian officialdom and their bureaucratic careers within the ministerial system further shaped their distinctive ethos and social status within Russian Jewry.

The Official Limits of Jewish Bureaucracy: Rules and Regulations for Expert Jews

The acute dearth of adequate bureaucratic cadres and the MVD's determination to divest the Jewish bureaucracy of any administrative authority, just as it abolished autonomous power of the kahals, significantly hampered the implementation of the consistorial model on Russian soil. As a result, the MVD had to reshape and redefine the institutions and functions of the consistorial system in order to adapt them to the actual needs and limitations of the religious administration for Russian Jews. However, its key office—expert Jews—can be directly traced to the French institutional prototype.

In France, the departmental consistories regularly dispatched their special officials, *commissaires-surveillants*, to inspect far-flung Jewish communities in their districts. The *commissaires-surveillants* reported directly to the consistorial boards, and were banned from direct official communication with the central government and local authorities. According to an instruction of 1821, the *commissaires-surveillants* were to inform the consistories about the social conduct, sources of income, and morality of the Jews, including any abuses of the law. Their official mandate also included the audit of communal finances and promotion of loyalty to the government and of productive labor and useful occupations among the Jews.[46]

In Russia, the bureaucratic mandate of the expert Jews absorbed the full scope of inspectorial duties of the *commissaires-surveillants*. In 1850, the MVD provided the governor-generals with a *Sekretnoe nastavlenie o sluzhbe uchenykh evreev* (Secret Regulation of the Service of Expert Jews), a comprehensive guideline for the selection and application of Jewish bureaucrats. Fourteen paragraphs of the Secret Regulation set the official status of the expert Jews, requirements for the candidates, responsibilities and routine commissions of Jewish bureaucrats, as well as official means and procedures for their realization.

The Secret Regulation lay down the fundamental principles of the practical application of expert Jews by the governor-generals.[47] It emphasized the full administrative dependence of expert Jews on their immediate superiors, and their direct subordination to the Minister of Internal Affairs, to whom the governor-generals should report all expert Jew assignments. The assignments should be given in a proper official manner, by executive order of the governor-generals. The governor-generals should proceed with due caution and secrecy in order to keep their use of expert Jews concealed from the "fanatical" Jewish masses. The same caution should be applied to the use of Jewish bureaucrats who should not be "vested with authority of any kind, and should not be given fiscal tasks."[48]

Candidates for the position of expert Jew were required to have proficiency in matters of Jewish tradition and rituals. The governor-generals should look for qualified "spiritual" rabbis, and absolutely avoid appointing rabbis from the "Hasidic and other sects" and government rabbis as expert Jews.[49]

The bureaucratic scope of expert Jews was broadly defined as the "religious affairs of the Jews, excluding censorship of Jewish religious books and other literature."[50] As directed by the Secret Regulation, the governor-generals should use the moral influence of the expert Jews in order "to correct the contemporary Jewish misrepresentations of the original teachings of the Old Testament" and to alleviate the incongruity between Jewish religious law and imperial legislation. Thus, expert

Jews would aid the administration in overcoming Jewish "fanaticism," i.e., isolation, the major obstacle to rapprochement between the Jews and other subjects of the empire. The Secret Regulation identified this fanaticism as a both religious and social impediment to the integration of the Jews. Religious fanaticism included the general anti-Christian thrust of Judaism and its messianic aspect, which prevented Jews from turning to a "solid settled way of life" while still in exile. The social fanaticism of the Jews included subversive patterns of social behavior based on their atavistic medieval legacy, such as false testimony in general courts, concealment from police investigation, evasion from proper civil registration, and early marriages.

The everyday use of expert Jews was at the discretion of their superiors and subject to the due bureaucratic procedure outlined by the Secret Regulation.[51] The governor-generals were encouraged to use the help of Jewish bureaucrats whenever they saw fit, and, especially, when taking action based on "private" (i.e., unofficial) information about fanaticism and subversive activity among the Jews. However, when the same facts were reported through official channels, including petitions and police intelligence, the governor-generals should not use expert Jews but conduct official investigations by other means at their disposal. The prospective missions of expert Jews, delineated by the Secret Regulation, included unofficial and unpublicized investigation of occurrences of Jewish fanaticism in the provinces; study of local forms and roots of fanaticism in the provinces; inspection of synagogues, religious communities, and institutions in the provinces; moral influence of the Jews aimed at inculcation of loyalty to the government and to its policies of social amelioration and integration.

Finally, the Secret Regulation defined the official means available to Jewish bureaucrats and described their work procedure.[52] Moral influence, the most important part of the expert Jews' official mission, should be exerted through "articulation of their guidance and advice" among Jews. They should base their arguments in the plain meaning of the Old Testament in order to expose the misinterpretations of the talmudists who were generating religious fanaticism. They should maintain awareness of the everyday proceedings of the Jewish communities, including rabbis and lay personnel. The Secret Regulation required expert Jews "to penetrate into the hearts" of traditional Jewry. The service of expert

Jews should be protected by strict measures of confidentiality and even complete secrecy. Expert Jews were forbidden from maintaining any paperwork related to their official missions except their reports to the governor-generals. When on their missions, they should proceed with extreme caution in order to preserve the essence of their assignments from being discovered by the Jews.

Expert Jews were sworn into office by taking an oath of service according to the procedure established by the MVD. Similar to the "Statute" and "Secret Regulation" of 1850, the oath did not give expert Jews any official authority or accompanying liability. Moreover, the oath lacked any reference to Jewish matters, except that Jewish bureaucrats swore by "the Lord, God of Israel."[53] The rest of the oath included the staple vows obligatory for all official servants of the Russian emperor, including pledges of loyal service, obedience to orders, contribution to the benefit and prevention of loss to the country, and protection of entrusted secrets.[54]

Therefore, from the MVD's rules and regulations, the perfect type of Jewish bureaucrat emerged. It was an expert Jew who was fully loyal to the government on the basis of his own ethos, in agreement with government goals, bound by the official oath of service. He possessed traditional Jewish learning and expertise in religious matters. He was held in high esteem among Russian officialdom, keeping a safe distance from the Hasidic and other illegitimate sects. He enjoyed the reasonable trust of the Jews, being uninvolved with the repressive roles of the government rabbis and censors. These characteristics entitled expert Jews to the privileged status of the Jewish bureaucratic elite, which was both their official commission and their social reward.

In sharp contrast with the French consistorial system, the status of the Russian Jewish bureaucratic elite did not enable expert Jews to represent Russian Jews officially in government agencies, or represent the government officially among the Jews. The Russian institution of expert Jews functioned as a bureaucratic means for the advancement of the official policy of rapprochement between Russian Jews and the rest of the imperial subjects. Expert Jews helped the government blaze the best path to its ultimate goal, while trying to persuade the Jews to follow it.

The MVD provided provincial administrators with Jewish officials for special missions, expert Jews, who were a mere bureaucratic extension of the administrative authority of Russian officialdom. Expert Jews depended

Я, нижепоименованный, обѣщаю и клянусь Господомъ Богомъ | въ еврейскомъ текстѣ Адонай|, Богомъ Израилевымъ, съ чистымъ сердцемъ и не по иному, скрытому во мнѣ смыслу, а по смыслу и вѣдѣнію приводящихъ меня къ присягѣ, въ томъ, что хочу и долженъ ЕГО ИМПЕРАТОРСКОМУ ВЕЛИЧЕСТВУ, своему истинному и природному ВСЕМИЛОСТИВѢЙШЕМУ ВЕЛИКОМУ ГОСУДАРЮ ИМПЕРАТОРУ Н И К О Л А Ю А Л Е К С А Н Д Р О В И Ч У, САМОДЕРЖЦУ ВСЕРОССІЙСКОМУ, и ЕГО ИМПЕРАТОРСКАГО ВЕЛИЧЕСТВА Всероссійскаго Престола НАСЛѢДНИКУ, ЕГО ИМПЕРАТОРСКОМУ ВЫСОЧЕСТВУ ГОСУДАРЮ ЦЕСАРЕВИЧУ ВЕЛИКОМУ КНЯЗЮ А Л Е К С Ѣ Ю Н И К О Л А Е В И Ч У вѣрно, и нелицемѣрно служить, и во всемъ повиноваться, не щадя живота своего до послѣдней капли крови, и всѣ къ высокому ЕГО ИМПЕРАТОРСКАГО ВЕЛИЧЕСТВА Самодержавству, силѣ и власти принадлежащія права и преимущества, узаконенныя и впредь узаконяемыя, по крайнему разумѣнію, силѣ и возможности предостерегатъ и оборонять, и притомъ по крайней мѣрѣ стараться способствовать все, что къ ЕГО ИМПЕРАТОРСКАГО ВЕЛИЧЕСТВА вѣрной службѣ и пользѣ государственной во всякихъ случаяхъ касаться можетъ; объ ущербѣ же ЕГО ВЕЛИЧЕСТВА интереса, вредѣ и убыткѣ, какъ скоро о томъ увѣдаю, не токмо благовременно объявлять, но и всякими мѣрами отвращать и не допущать тщатися, и всякую ввѣренную тайность крѣпко хранить буду, и повѣренный и положенный на мнѣ чинъ какъ по сей | генеральной|, такъ и по особливой, опредѣленной и отъ времени до времени ЕГО ИМПЕРАТОРСКАГО ВЕЛИЧЕСТВА именемъ отъ предустав-

Expert Jew's official oath of service taken and signed by Moisei Kreps on May 18, 1907 (RGIA, f. 821, o. 8., d. 469, l. 127) on the everyday necessities and bureaucratic routines of the provincial chancelleries, and on the individual approach of the governor-generals to matters of Jewish policy, which sometimes diverged from the mainstream policies of the MVD. As a result, in addition to laws, statutes, and regulations, the service of expert Jews was significantly affected by the intertwined factors of time, location, and personality of their superiors.

Size, Staff, and Structure of the Jewish Bureaucratic Elite

Despite the many diverse features that shaped the lives and careers of expert Jews scattered over the vast territory of the Pale of Settlement, Jewish bureaucracy was nonetheless one solid political institute and a cohesive social group. As the following chapters show, contrary to conventional perceptions, Jewish bureaucracy was by no means an eclectic group of marginal idealists, opportunists, and self-appointed informers cum intercessors.[55] Expert Jews were an important dedicated segment within general Russian officialdom, and, at the same time, a skilled elite at the core of the religious administration for Russian Jews.

From 1850 to 1917, the office of expert Jew was an indispensable feature at every provincial chancellery in the Pale of Settlement, and at the central offices of the MVD in St. Petersburg. Expert Jews were appointed by the administrations of seventeen Russian provinces (every governor and governor-general in the Pale of Settlement), two city administrations (the city governors of Odessa and Nikolaev), and the central offices of the MVD (at the DDDII in St. Petersburg). Within seven decades, a total of forty-eight expert Jews were appointed to these twenty bureaucratic offices.[56]

Based on rough calculations, the full bureaucratic staff of the religious administration for Russian Jews, comprising the government rabbinate, Rabbinical Commissions, censors, and supervisors of government-sponsored Jewish schools, included some fourteen hundred Jewish officials.[57] Expert Jews, 1.5 percent of this figure, constituted an elite segment of Russian Jewish bureaucracy. On the whole, the proportion of the bureaucracy within the 5.2 million-strong general Jewish population of the empire in 1897 amounted to one Jewish official per 3,714 Jews. This proportion is comparable to the similar ratio of Russian officials to the general population of the country, including Jews.[58] These ratios show the sweeping bureaucratization of Russian and Jewish society, implemented by the government with the help of Russian and Jewish bureaucrats during the 1880s through the 1910s. While the total size of Jewish officialdom remained the same, the total number of Russian bureaucrats grew significantly.[59] Therefore, the Jewish bureaucracy that, in 1851 constituted 2 percent of the total number of all imperial officials, in 1897 constituted only 0.4 percent of that number. This proportion shows the trend of unification and standardization of administration for Russian Jews. However, Jewish bureaucracy remained an integral and indispensable institute of government policies toward the Jews, and of imperial domestic policy as a whole.

For many decades, expert Jews were steadily featured in the institutional structure of provincial administration under the MVD. As demonstrated by Table 1, for seven years, from 1850 to 1857, expert Jews were appointed by administrations of all major centers in the Pale of Settlement. (For detailed information see Appendix.) In the following decades, the offices of expert Jews, once dissolved due to major changes in administration of the provinces, were consistently reestablished with newly formed provincial chancelleries. In 1857, upon the dissolution of the Vitebsk, Mogilev, and Smolensk governor-generalship, the office of expert Jew was promptly reestablished under the governor of Minsk province, who administered the territories of the former governor-generalship. Moreover, in critical circumstances emerging due to large-scale political campaigns launched by the government or due to growing political and social instability, Russian administrators of several regions appointed additional expert Jews. Such appointments were made in the 1860s by the governors of several Ukrainian and Lithuanian provinces in connection with the implementation of the universal court system in the western region of the empire. In the 1900s, due to the rising tide of revolutionary activity among the population of the southern region of Russia, including the Jews, a new expert Jew position was created under the governor of Ekaterinoslav province.

Bureaucratic procedures constituted the core activity of policymaking and implementation in late imperial Russia. Political and administrative measures were developed behind the closed doors of the bureaucratic chancelleries of the imperial ministries and other agencies in the capital

Table 1. Establishment and Dissolution of Offices of Expert Jews under Provincial and Central Administrations of the MVD, 1850–1917

Date	Administrative unit	Establishment and dissolution of offices of expert Jews within the administration
1850	governorships of Lifland and Kurland	position of expert Jew established
1852	governor-generalship of Novorossiia and Bessarabiia	position of expert Jew established
1853	governor-generalship of Vitebsk, Mogilev, and Smolensk	position of expert Jew established
1856	governor-generalship of Vilna, Kovno, and Grodno; governorships of Mogilev and Poltava; DDDII at the MVD	position of expert Jew established
1857	governor-generalship of Kiev, Podolia, and Volhyn; governorship of Chernigov	position of expert Jew established
1857	governor-generalship of Vitebsk, Mogilev, and Smolensk	position of expert Jew dissolved along with the administration of the governor-generalship
1857	governorship of Minsk	position of expert Jew established
1867–1868	governorships of Volhyn, Podolia, and Kovno	additional positions of expert Jews established
1874	governor-generalship of Novorossiia and Bessarabiia	position of expert Jew dissolved along with the administration of the governor-generalship
1900s	governorships of Vilna and Grodno	additional positions of expert Jews established
1900s	governorship of Ekaterinoslav; city governorships of Nikolaev and Odessa	position of expert Jew established

city of St. Petersburg and in the Russian provinces. Domestic policy in social, economic, and cultural spheres was by and large conceived of and implemented by purely bureaucratic means, including the establishment, reestablishment, and improvement of bureaucratic institutes, agencies, and procedures, aimed at registration, control, and regulation of society. This approach was an institutional representation of the fundamental gap between the authorities and society, a prominent feature of Russian history. In the eyes of the Russian authorities—that is, the tsar and his bureaucratic servants—the ministries, as the principal institutions of executive and police power, were leading uncivilized Russian society toward historical progress. They were above class interests and served an absolute social good. In these conditions, bureaucrats, the cadre base of the Russian monarchy, had paramount importance as the mobilized progressive vanguard of society.[60]

In the eyes of the government, expert Jews, the loyal Jewish bureaucratic elite, represented the vanguard of Russian Jews. In that capacity, expert Jews were assigned the most important bureaucratic missions among those given to Jewish bureaucracy. Expert Jews' functions and appointments, presented in Table 2, encompassed the full spectrum of official policies toward Russian Jews in the spheres of education, religion, official expertise in Jewish matters, and policymaking.

One definitive feature of the Jewish bureaucratic elite—expert Jews—was their specialized training. As shown in Table 3, nearly half the expert Jews graduated from the rabbinical seminaries of Vilna and Zhitomir—specialized schools that trained bureaucratic servitors of the state, including government rabbis and teachers. Therefore, expert Jews were professional bureaucrats who were prepared for service by specialized education tailored to the needs of the government. Moreover, as presented in Table 4, the geographical distribution of the graduates of rabbinical seminaries appointed as expert Jews reveals the government's intention to use these professional bureaucrats in the regions that they presumably knew well. The figures show that most of the graduates of the Vilna Rabbinical Seminary served in Lithuanian provinces, while graduates of the Zhitomir Seminary served exclusively in Ukrainian provinces.

The total number of expert Jews appointed by the Russian provincial administration, presented in Table 3, reveals the key geographical points of the application of government policies toward the Jews. The greatest

Table 2. Joint Bureaucratic Appointments of Expert Jews within the Religious Administration for Russian Jews, and within the General Administration within the MVD, 1850–1917

Appointment	Number of Jewish bureaucrats assigned to this appointment while holding the office of expert Jew
Government rabbi	14
Member or secretary of the Rabbinical Commission	7
Censor of Jewish literature	4
Instructor or supervisor of a rabbinical seminary or other government-sponsored Jewish school	9
Editor of official periodical	1
Member of provincial or governmental advisory commission on the Jewish question	2
Member of municipal, provincial, or state legislature	2
Other appointments	2

Note: Based on data about 34 expert Jews. For detailed information, see Table 4 in Appendix.

concentration of Jewish bureaucrats was directly related to the concentrated efforts of the government in the implementation of its policies in such regions as the northwestern and western provinces of the Pale of Settlement.

The official status of expert Jews as the Jewish bureaucratic elite entitled them to a privileged social status. Their compensation was on par with that of their Russian colleagues in positions of comparable rank. The total budget for compensation of expert Jews, itemized in Table 5, amounted to some 10,000 silver rubles annually. This figure was a relatively high proportion—6 percent—of the total annual compensation budget of the DDDII staff, and shows the importance of this Jewish bureaucratic sector within the government administration.

The monetary compensation of expert Jews was complemented by substantial social privileges. As shown in Table 6, many expert Jews

Table 3. Geographical Distribution of Expert Jews, including Those Graduated from Rabbinical Seminaries, by Region, 1850–1917

Region	Total number of Jewish bureaucrats appointed as expert Jews	Number of Jewish bureaucrats-graduates of rabbinical seminaries appointed as expert Jews
Northwest[a]	24	10
West[b]	18	7
Southwest[c]	5	0
Central[d]	7	3[e]
Total	54	20

Notes:

a. Including provinces of Vilna, Kovno, Grodno, Vitebsk, Smolensk, Mogilev, Minsk, Lifland, and Kurland

b. Including provinces of Kiev, Volhyn, Podolia, Chernigov, and Poltava

c. Including provinces of Novorossiia, Bessarabiia, and Ekaterinoslav, and city of Odessa

d. DDDII at the MVD in St. Petersburg

e. This number represents those expert Jews jointly appointed by governors of the North-Western region and by the DDDII in St. Petersburg

Table 4. Geographical Distribution of Expert Jews / Graduates of the Rabbinical Seminaries, by Region, 1850–1917

Region / Seminary	Vilna Rabbinical Seminary	Zhitomir Rabbinical Seminary
Northwest	10	0
West	4	3
Southwest	0	0
Central	3	0

Note: Based on data about 17 expert Jews. For detailed information, see Table 2 in Appendix.

acquired the privileged status of honorary citizens, and a few of them rose quite high in the official hierarchy of civil service, achieving ranks of the sixth class—*kollezhskii sovetnik* (collegiate councilor)—out of the fourteen classes of the official Table of Ranks. These privileges contributed to the successful social integration of expert Jews into the Russian

Table 5. Compensation of Expert Jews, 1850–1917

Amount of annual compensation (silver rubles) of expert Jews	Number of expert Jews in the group
250–450	9
600–800	15
900	11
1,500–3,000	2

Note: Based on data about 36 expert Jews. For detailed information, see Table 5 in Appendix.

Table 6. Social Status of Expert Jews, 1850–1917

Rank, title, and social status of expert Jews	Number of expert Jews in the group
Attorneys	1
Honorary citizens	10
Officials in the ranks of XII-VI classes	5

Note: Based on data about 16 expert Jews. For detailed information, see Table 3 in Appendix.

Table 7. Service Terms of Expert Jews, 1850–1917

Service term (years) of expert Jews	Number of expert Jews in the group
1–10	16
13–21	6
22–35	7
43–52	3

Note: Based on data about 32 expert Jews. For detailed information, see Table 6 in Appendix.

bureaucratic class, and made a bureaucratic career—implying high official and social standing—an attractive opportunity in the eyes of Russian Jews. As presented in Table 7, this opportunity was much appreciated and valued by expert Jews, who remained in their positions for decades.

This statistical survey of the Jewish bureaucratic elite will serve as the background for the following detailed examination of the institutional history of expert Jews.

Institutional History of Expert Jews

The office of expert Jew existed within the central and provincial administration of the MVD from 1850 to 1917. During these seven decades, official perceptions of the MVD and provincial governors regarding the Jewish bureaucrats changed considerably. The bureaucratic functions of expert Jews evolved accordingly over time. Several times, the government reassessed the official role of Jewish bureaucrats and considered eliminating the office of expert Jew altogether. However, the prolonged existence of expert Jews demonstrated both the secure integration of Jewish bureaucrats into the power structures of the MVD and the institutional stability and continuity of official Jewish policy.

The institutional evolution of the office of expert Jew had four distinct phases. The first phase, the 1840s, was the prologue to actual institution building in the field of official Jewish policy. In those years, based on the successful experience of the French consistorial system and the deliberations of the MVD-summoned committees on the establishment of the provincial rabbinate, such as the Odessa Committee in 1840, a blueprint emerged for the Russian hierarchical system of Jewish religious bureaucracy. During the second phase, in the 1850s, the realization of this plan was set in motion. The Rabbinical Commission was convened in St. Petersburg. The governor-generals deployed their newly appointed Jewish officials, expert Jews, in the provinces of the Pale of Settlement, for the most part with great enthusiasm and relative success. In the third phase, from the 1860s to the 1880s, official Jewish policy reached its institutional maturity. In those years, the positions of expert Jew went for the most part to specially trained religious bureaucrats, graduates of the Russian rabbinical seminaries. Those same bureaucrats constituted the majority of participants in the Rabbinical Commission of 1861. As a result, expert Jews had a central role in the bureaucratic procedures of Jewish policymaking and implementation. Also, in this phase, due to the general atmosphere of emerging political reaction in the empire and rising conservative tendencies within the MVD, Jewish bureaucracy was increasingly dominated by structural stagnation and political conservatism. During the fourth phase, the 1890s–1910s, these tendencies prevailed. The MVD and the governors increasingly commissioned expert Jews to perform a variety of police functions aimed at the prevention of subversive political activity, the chief concern of the MVD until the fall of the empire in 1917.

In the 1840s, at the beginning stages of Jewish bureaucracy, the MVD planned to allot a broad scope of functions—similar to the official mandate of the French departmental consistories—to the provincial rabbis, mid-level Jewish bureaucrats. On August 1, 1840, a circular directive from Minister Lev Perovskii outlined their prospective responsibilities, including inspection of the district government rabbinate, official certification of political loyalty of the district rabbis and other elected officials of the Jewish communities, and supervision of the provincial Jewish religious boards and of their proceedings on examination and settlement of complaints and disputes related to Jewish religious matters.[61] In November 1840, the draft "Statute on Jewish Clergy" of the Odessa Committee proposed broadening the scope of the provincial rabbis with the mission of acculturation and social regeneration of the Jews, thus bringing this office closer to the fundamental institutional role of its French prototype. The draft recommended that the provincial rabbis be given authority over Jewish ritual, including public worship, and the public education of the Jews. The provincial rabbis should also provide general guidance to the Jews, "directing them toward civil improvement."[62]

Due to the dearth of adequate Jewish personnel, the institution of the provincial rabbinate was postponed until its cadre base emerged from the pool of prospective graduates of the newly founded rabbinical seminaries of Vilna and Zhitomir. In 1844, instead of the provincial rabbinate, a provisional office of "Jewish inspectors from among the expert Jews," or, simply, "expert Jews," was instituted to aid the governor-generals in administration of the Jews' religious affairs. Due to the provisional nature of their position, expert Jews were never fully integrated into the originally conceived hierarchy of the religious administration for the Jews. Instead, expert Jews became an integral part of the Russian bureaucratic structure of the MVD, as officials for special missions under the provincial governors. Jewish bureaucrats had no administrative authority and acted on the orders of their superiors. Their bureaucratic objective included only general tasks such as "weakening Jewish fanaticism through exposure and eradication of the religious fallacies of the Jews," and other elements of Jewish social isolation that did not comply with state law and order.[63] In 1846, the governor-generals of the Pale of Settlement approved the new bureaucratic design proposed by the MVD, and in 1850 the position of expert Jew was given permanent status.[64] Thus, the first page in the history of expert Jews had been turned.

When the first modern Russian rabbis graduated from the rabbinical seminaries of Vilna and Zhitomir, the MVD reconsidered the establishment of the provincial rabbinate. In 1855, an MVD circular directive requested that governors nominate their candidates for the positions of provincial rabbi. In response, the governors presented nine candidates, and one additional candidate was nominated by the DDDII.[65] Four nominees were incumbent expert Jews under the governor-generals, including Avraam Neiman, Solomon Pukher, Arnold Mandel'shtam, and Markus Gurovich. Two nominees held other positions within the Jewish bureaucracy, including Iakov Tugendgold, censor of Jewish literature, and Samuil Fin, expert Jew under the superintendent of Vilna's educational district. One nominee was a traditional rabbi—Iankel' Barit, the *rosh yeshiva* and prominent leader of the Jewish community in Vilna. Three other nominees represented the modern Jewish economic elite and included the Odessa merchants Simkha Pinsker, Faddei Berezkin, and Isaak Gurovich.[66]

Only two of the nine nominees, Solomon Pukher and Arnold Mandel'shtam, were graduates of the Russian rabbinical seminaries; both graduated from the Vilna Rabbinical Seminary in 1853. The governors obviously believed that these specially trained and promising young rabbis were still inexperienced youth in their early twenties and thus it was premature to engage them in serious matters of government. Vladimir Nazimov, the governor-general of Vilna, Kovno, and Grodno, and Prince Mikhail Vorontsov, governor-general of Novorossiia and Bessarabiia, in their responses to the MVD circular directive insisted that the lack of life and service experience—essential for the successful overcoming of Jewish fanaticism—disqualified both young graduates of the rabbinical seminaries from the office of the provincial rabbinate.[67] Therefore, in the 1850s, the positions of expert Jew were by and large filled by seasoned personnel in their thirties and forties with university degrees and substantial life experience, like Moisei Berlin, Markus Gurovich, and Avraam Neiman. Likewise, in the following decades, the position of expert Jew was normally the apex of the successful bureaucratic careers of Jewish bureaucrats, usually in their forties and fifties, with fifteen to twenty years of service experience.

Finally, in 1861, the plan to establish a hierarchical religious administration for the Jews, including the institution of the provincial rabbinate, was submitted for examination by the Rabbinical Commission. The commission supported the idea in principle, but recommended postponing it, mostly due to the lack of adequate cadres.[68]

The substitute for the provincial rabbinate—the office of expert Jew—had its own cadre problems. Unlike the provincial rabbinate, which existed only on paper, the office of expert Jew was established, staffed, and operating, contributing to the everyday bureaucratic routines of official Jewish policymaking and implementation. Therefore, its cadre problems involved practical issues related to the adaptation of the governors and the Jews to the newly established Jewish bureaucracy.

In 1857, the Jews of Chernigov petitioned the MVD to replace Leiba Shikin, expert Jew under the Chernigov governor.[69] The petition maintained that by appointing Shikin, the governor "had selected a person with neither the sufficient skills, nor the trust of the Jewish community" indispensable for an expert Jew.[70] Apparently, the Jews of Chernigov would never have endorsed Shikin, a mere teacher at the government-sponsored Jewish elementary school, if it had been subject to their approval. In 1888, an internal memorandum of the MVD maintained that lack of trust and prestige in the Jewish community would significantly impede the work of expert Jews, expected to exert their moral influence. However, in 1857, based on the law stipulating the absolute authority of the governors in the appointment of expert Jews, the MVD simply ignored the petition of the Chernigov Jews.[71]

The provincial administrators also had their own opinions about the qualifications and skills of their expert Jews. In 1846, the acting governor-general of Novorossiia and Bessarabiia, Pavel Fedorov, recommended recruiting Jewish bureaucrats from among "virtuous Jews who have accepted Christian teaching."[72] The governor-general of Kiev, Volhyn, and Podolia, Prince Illarion Illarionovich Vasil'chikov, put this recommendation into action. In 1858, he sought MVD approval for his appointment of a baptized Jew, collegiate assessor Vladimir Fedorov, to the office of expert Jew. Prince Vasil'chikov argued that, since modern educated Jews did not have the trust of the traditional Jewish masses and could not influence them, and since traditional Jews were trusted by the masses but not by the government, expert Jews should then be recruited among Jews who had converted to Christianity and completely broken their ties with the Jewish community but still possessed broad knowledge of the Jewish religion, languages, traditions, and lifestyle.[73] The MVD approved the appointment, but it did not set a precedent. The appointment of converted Jew Iakov Brafman to the office of expert Jew at the MVD in 1870 was just another isolated example. As a rule, the MVD reserved such opportunism for very special cases, and encouraged the governors to follow the spirit and letter of the "Secret Regulation," which clearly stipulated that the office of expert Jew was limited to candidates not only well versed in but also belonging to Judaism in order "to eradicate any groundless fears among the Jews regarding the persecution of their religion."[74]

In 1856, the large territorial conglomerates under the governor-generals of Poltava, Chernigov, and Kharkov, and of Vitebsk, Mogilev, and Smolensk, were dismantled. The chancelleries of the former governor-generals and their staff, including expert Jews, were discharged. As a result, several provinces densely populated by Jews were excluded from the administrative realm of the governor-generals and their expert Jews. The MVD promptly revised the previous regulation limiting the appointment of expert Jews as officials under governor-generals, and extended the office of expert Jews to ordinary governors. Thus, expert Jews were appointed under the governors of Chernigov, Poltava, Vitebsk, and Poltava provinces. Introducing this measure to the Jewish Committee, the Minister of Internal Affairs pointed out that expert Jews under the governor-generals were appointed to aid the government in "the dissemination of productive labor among the Jews, overcoming Jewish fanaticism, and the [social] integration of the Jews," so that, with the elimination of the governor-generals and their Jewish officials, "the noble goal of the institution of expert Jew would remain unaccomplished."[75]

Reorganization of the provincial administration was not the only factor affecting the growth of the Jewish bureaucracy. In the 1840s–1850s,

Jewish bureaucratic offices were established throughout the Russian ministerial system. The positions of expert Jew were instituted under the superintendents of the educational districts of the Ministry of National Enlightenment "for supervision of Jewish schools and necessary explanation of special Jewish subjects."[76] By the 1860s, the Jewish bureaucracy had come of age.

The MVD started the new decade with another reassessment of the position of expert Jew, its bureaucratic scope, official status, and overall political role in the implementation of official Jewish policy.

In 1858, the responsibilities of expert Jew Vladimir Fedorov, according to his superior, Prince Vasil'chikov, included the interpretation of Jewish religious law to assist in the decision-making process in the everyday administration of the Jews, reviewing and translating documents and publications in Jewish languages, and secret inquiry into various issues of Jewish traditions, history, and everyday life. The governor-general emphasized that the need for such involvement of the expert Jew in the bureaucratic proceedings of the provincial administration "emerged on a daily basis."[77] However, the essential agenda of expert Jews—the promotion of productive labor and social integration among Jews and suppression of Jewish fanaticism—repeatedly outlined by the statutes and regulations of the MVD was remarkably absent from Prince Vasil'chikov's list. Instead, the tasks devised by the governor-general amounted to a purely bureaucratic mission—accumulation of comprehensive and accurate information on the Jewish population, necessary for the development of administrative decisions and legislation.

In the 1860s, Vasil'chikov's approach was adopted by the leadership of the MVD. In 1863, Minister of Internal Affairs Petr Aleksandrovich Valuev argued that "rapprochement between the Jews and the general mass of the population, and the implementation of the planned transformation of the Jewish [social and religious] organization could only proceed gradually and slowly."[78] Therefore, structural changes and institutional innovations in the life of Russian Jews required the same gradual pace. Initial government measures, such as the establishment of expert Jews under the governor-generals, were preliminary and provisional, and were meant to collect "accurate data needed for systematic deliberation upon the establishment of a [permanent] religious administration for the Jews."[79] As soon as the data were collected and processed by bureaucratic organs like the Rabbinical Commission, the MVD, according to Valuev, decided to introduce "the traditional Jewish approach repudiating the principle of hierarchical religious authority" into the foundation of a permanent framework of religious administration for the Jews.[80] As a result, the MVD proposed replacing the echelons of bureaucratic control embodied by the hierarchy of the rabbinate with direct government supervision of the "religious and administrative affairs of the Jews, including rituals of substantial civil significance," such as marital acts and official oaths. According to Valuev, Jews would be granted full freedom in purely religious matters, such as resolution of their religious disputes. Thus, "indirect interference in matters of conscience executed by the government-appointed rabbinate" would be eliminated.[81]

Thus, the MVD seriously questioned its own hierarchical principle of institution building in the field of Jewish policy. The official status of expert Jew was jeopardized as well. On the one hand, expert Jews had never been an official part of the rabbinical hierarchy. They were not direct subordinates of its central organ, the Rabbinical Commission, and were not in direct control of its lower echelon, the district rabbis. Therefore, the MVD proposal did not threaten the existence of the provincial Jewish bureaucrats. On the other hand, the MVD specifically pointed out the preliminary and provisional function of expert Jews, but it did not make clear whether or not the bureaucratic mandate of expert Jews had expired. In this ambiguous situation, the immediate superiors of expert Jews, the governors, attempted to take the fate of Jewish officials into their own hands.

The position of expert Jew under the governor of Minsk province was vacant for twelve years, from 1864 to 1875, because the governor deemed it "unnecessary."[82] During these years, three Russian officials succeeded one another as Minsk governors.[83] Apparently, none of them spent enough time in office to grasp all the details of the provincial administration. Without the incumbent expert Jew inherited from his predecessor, each subsequent governor was totally unaware of this opportunity and its actual "necessity." Finally, in 1876, governor Valerii Ivanovich Charykov (in office 1875–1879) appointed Samuil Katsenelenbogen, a math teacher at the Jewish school in Minsk, as expert Jew, and assigned him cases related to Jewish military service.[84]

In 1870, the governor of Poltava province Mikhail Alekseevich Martynov (in office 1866–1878) sought MVD approval for the dismissal of his expert Jew, Aaron Tseitlin. According to the governor, for four years, from 1866 to 1870, "there was no single case demanding the service of an expert Jew" in his province.[85] However, in seven years, from 1859 to 1866, under the previous governor Aleksandr Pavlovich Volkov (in office 1853–1866), expert Jew Tseitlin had accomplished dozens of missions ordered by the governor and earning his high praise.[86] According to Tseitlin, the new governor was influenced by corrupt officials in his chancellery who had unsuccessfully tried to extract a bribe from the expert Jew in exchange for securing his official position.[87] As a result, in 1872 Tseitlin was transferred from Poltava to Kiev to assume the office of third expert Jew under the governor-general of Kiev, Volhyn, and Podolia.[88] The government rabbi of Poltava, Lev Zaidiner, replaced Tseitlin as expert Jew under the governor of Poltava province, and, according to the governor, was provided with a modest bureaucratic workload, including "twenty assignments a year (mostly, settlements of disputes between Jews)."[89]

In 1875, the governor of Bessarabiia Nikolai Ignat'evich Shebeko (in office 1871–1879) sought MVD approval for his decision to eliminate the office of expert Jew, which he considered a useless and irrelevant office within his chancellery.[90] The governor's opinion provoked strong criticism from a member of the Council of the Minister of Internal Affairs, Fedor Karlovich Girs, a veteran Russian bureaucrat in the field of religious administration of *inorodtsy*, including the Jews.[91] In his memorandum to Count Emmanuil Sivers director of the DDDII, Girs judged Shebeko's decision to be uninformed and counterproductive: "I was in charge of the chancellery of the governor-general [of Novorossiia and Bessarabiia] for nine years, so I can testify that expert Jews proved to be very useful not only for the development of measures related to the Jews; they were immensely useful as a liaison between the Jews and the Christian population in cases of mutual misunderstanding and open conflict. The influence of expert Jews was particularly successful when they did not break with the faith of their ancestors and maintained close ties with the traditional milieu. Thank God, during those nine years, [their intervention resolved] in this manner all complaints and conflicts arising between the two sides, which otherwise could have easily escalated, as the last fact clearly demonstrated, into bloody carnage. There is no Polish question in Novorossiia, however, there is another plague—the Jewish question, which is equally relevant and of great significance for bordering Bessarabiia."[92]

Girs was referring to the first Jewish pogroms in Russia, which shocked Odessa, the major urban center of Novorossiia, in 1859 and 1871. Apparently, the Novorossiia governor-generals handled these incidents differently.[93] As a result, in 1859 under Governor-general Aleksandr Grigor'evich Stroganov (in office 1855–1862) the violence was promptly extinguished; in 1871, under Governor-general Pavel Evstaf'evich Kotsebu (in office 1862–1874) the pogrom rapidly turned into a major calamity with many victims. In Girs's opinion, these cases demonstrated that "the ability to make use of the institution [of expert Jews] provided by law belongs entirely to the governor's office. He [Governor Shebeko] would be bitterly wrong if he tries to approach the Jews directly through his chancellery and [Russian] officials."[94] Girs concluded that, since the office of expert Jew was established by law, and there was no reason to anticipate any changes, the private opinion of Governor Shebeko should be dismissed as insignificant.[95]

However, the MVD ignored the judgment of this prominent official in its general approach to the position of expert Jew in the 1870s and 1880s. When the territorial conglomerate under the former governor-general of Novorossiia and Bessarabiia was dismantled in 1874, the position of expert Jew was eliminated and never reestablished. Moreover, the MVD rejected requests for the institution of expert Jew under the governors of the newly formed Kherson and Ekaterinoslav provinces because of the scarcity of Jews, who constituted less than 23 percent of the total population. The city governor of Odessa was the only administrator in the former Novorossiia entitled to the office of expert Jew in 1875. In 1877, two expert Jew positions in the Baltic provinces were replaced by one expert Jew, who worked simultaneously for the MVD and the governors of Lifland and Kurland.[96] In sharp contrast with the 1850s and 1860s, the MVD in the 1870s and 1880s considerably reduced the size of the Jewish bureaucracy and yet again reassessed the institute of expert Jew and its political role.

In 1873, the official for special missions under the Minister of Internal Affairs, Viktor Iakovlevich Fuks, voiced official disappointment with the contribution of expert Jews to government Jewish policy. In his report, "On the Attitude of the Government toward Manifestations of the

Religious Life of the Jews," presented to the Committee on the Settlement of Jewish Life, Fuks came to conclusions diametrically opposed to the observations of Fedor Girs. Fuks argued that expert Jews had proven to be completely ineffective, since "for almost a quarter of the century their work demonstrated an inability to expose the real plagues [i.e., hidden motivation] of Jewish [traditional] ways."[97]

Apparently, Fuks, like many of his colleagues at the MVD, was under the strong influence of the *Kniga Kagala* (Book of the Kahal) (Vilna, 1869) by Iakov Brafman, who was believed to be the genuine "expert in Jewish matters."[98] It was Iakov Brafman who had exposed "the real plague of Jewish ways"—the kahal, the secret autonomous Jewish international republic based on the teachings of the Talmud. According to Brafman, this political entity was the real impediment to rapprochement, so official Jewish policy had completely missed the target by engaging in a desperate fight against the mythical religious fanaticism of the Jews.[99] In Brafman's view, the goals of acculturated and traditional Jews paradoxically coincided. In 1888, based on Brafman's conclusions, the DDDII memorandum "On Jewish Charitable Organizations in the Empire" declared that the educational programs of the Society for the Spread of Enlightenment among the Russian Jews (*Obshchestvo dlia rasprostraneniia prosveshcheniia mezhdu evreiami v Rossii* [OPE]) were a "promotion of Jewish education in the exclusive national Jewish spirit."[100]

In this context, expert Jews who were unable to expose the deep roots of Jewish social isolation, "successfully" unearthed by Brafman, naturally became the targets of official criticism, at best, as ineffective bureaucrats, at worst as violators of their oath of service. Therefore, Fuks proposed that this office should no longer be entrusted to Jews, including their traditional, acculturated, and even completely assimilated factions. Fuks argued that "if they are Jews only in name and in reality they belong to the cosmopolitan group, they cannot qualify as experts in religious and national matters; if they are so-called reformers, then they represent the absolute minority among the Jews and their expertise would be one-sided; and if they are Orthodox, i.e., true followers of the Talmud, then they should be believed even less than the cosmopolitans. All these people can tell the sincere truth only in the rare cases when their particular national interests do not conflict with the interests of the government and the native population of the country."[101]

The provincial commissions on the Jewish question, convened in 1881 by the MVD under the provincial governors, developed Fuks's conclusions further. Members of these commissions considered the office of expert Jew as a major institute of Jewish social isolation. Thus, paradoxically, expert Jews ultimately thwarted the progress of Jewish social integration that the government was promoting through the institution of Jewish bureaucracy. The members of the Volhyn provincial commission believed that the government should stop its special tutelage of the Jews and their religious life, and proposed dismantling the institutional structure of the Jewish religious administration including the office of expert Jew.[102] Similarly, the members of the Bessarabiia, Mogilev, Podolia, Kherson, and Chernigov provincial commissions considered the special official Jewish institutions, including the Jewish bureaucracy and means of its financial support, *korobochnyi sbor*, the special Jewish tax, detrimental to rapprochement between the Jews and the native population, and proposed eliminating them.[103] In sum, these attitudes significantly altered the general thrust of official policy toward the Jews and *inorodtsy* as a whole. Because the integration of non-Russian and non-Christian minorities within imperial society had proven to be a failure, the neutralization of *inorodtsy* leading toward bureaucratic centralization and unification of their administration became the priority of the government, including the MVD.[104]

In 1886, the bureaucratic apparatus of the MVD included thirteen expert Jews under the governor-generals and the governors. The annual budget of the Jewish bureaucrats, consisting mostly of their compensation, amounted to 9,000 silver rubles financed from the funds of the *korobochnyi sbor*. For four decades, these officials successfully completed hundreds of missions assigned to them by the provincial authorities and the central offices of the MVD. However, according to the conclusions of the DDDII, their principal goal remained unreached, and thus their overall bureaucratic performance and political role were cast into doubt. Or, as the DDDII official memorandum put it, "Since the social isolation of the Jews continues, the provisional institution of expert Jews, in the provincial centers, aimed at overcoming Jewish religious fanaticism through their influence, has failed to satisfy the expectations of the government."[105]

At the end of the 1880s, the DDDII seriously considered replacing expert Jews with Russian Christian officials, presumed to be a more efficient means for the accomplishment of the "insignificant agenda" of Jewish bureaucrats, including inspection of Jewish religious and communal institutions. Moreover, the government sought "more influential and powerful" means of support for its measures against Jewish fanaticism among the "emerging Russian Jewish press, and the considerable contingent of Jews educated in Russian gymnasia and universities and serving in the Russian Army."[106] The DDDII concluded that the position of expert Jew "could be easily eliminated without causing any discomfort either to the government or to the Jewish population."[107] In sum, the DDDII considered the provisional bureaucratic mandate of expert Jews as expired, and Russian Jews ready for direct administration by Russian bureaucrats. The absence of expert Jews among official Jewish experts of the Highest Commission on the Reexamination of Laws on the Jews (the Palen Commission) convened by the MVD in 1883 signified a crisis of Jewish bureaucracy.[108]

However, the office of expert Jew endured in the 1890s through the 1910s, and its political role was adjusted by the MVD. The bureaucratic functions of expert Jews were significantly altered. Generic tasks, including supervision of Jewish religious and communal institutions, exposure, and eradication of Jewish fanaticism disappeared from their agenda. Their presence in the Rabbinical Commission and in other expert bodies under the MVD was less if not completely removed. The new pressing social and political problems of the late Russian empire gave Jewish bureaucrats a second chance. The rapid growth of radical political opposition to the regime, the emergence of mass political movements and parties including Jewish political organizations, produced a strong political reaction from the MVD. It turned to conservative policies implemented by its bureaucratic agencies using administrative, repressive, and police methods.[109] In these circumstances, the MVD reclaimed the service of expert Jews. Under increasing pressure from multiplying political issues, the MVD redirected the efforts of the Jewish bureaucracy from its former target— the vestiges and prejudices of the premodern Jewish past that prevented rapprochement between the Jews and the rest of the imperial subjects. Radical politics and anti-government activities, uniting Jews and non-Jews in the joint struggle for a socialist future, became the new bureaucratic focus of expert Jews.

Already in 1882, the governor-general of Kiev, Volhyn, and Podolia and the former Chief of the Corps of Gendarmes, general *aide-de-camp*

Aleksandr Romanovich Drentel'n, anticipated a new role for expert Jews. While supporting the dismantling of the religious administration for the Jews in principle, Drentel'n maintained that the special function of supervision of the Jews, "preventing them from pursuing any subversive goals," should be preserved as a crucial aspect of the imperial administration.[110] In 1898, the governor-general of Vilna, Kovno, and Grodno, general *aide-de-camp* Vitalii Nikolaevich Trotskii, did not even mention the possibility of elimination of expert Jews. Conversely, Trotskii petitioned the MVD for a substantial increase in the salaries of the three expert Jews working in his chancellery. The governor-general supported his petition, pointing out that with the escalation of political instability in the empire, the bureaucratic scope of expert Jews had changed and their workload increased significantly. He wrote that "since the introduction of the Court Reform [in 1864] and, especially in recent years with the emergence of the labor movement and the illegal import and wide circulation of prohibited subversive publications in various languages including Jewish languages, the pressing need for expert translation and other assistance in the investigation of anti-government crimes is constantly rising. Not to mention the rising demand for expert Jews by local chiefs of gendarmes and courts."[111] The MVD granted the governor-general's request and set the annual compensation of his expert Jews, Mikhail Vol'per, Abram Tsuntser, and Grigorii Shkliaver, at 900 silver rubles, the highest limit stipulated by the law.[112] Thus, the MVD recognized the new significance of Jewish bureaucracy and used it extensively in the coming decades.

In 1906, the city governor of Nikolaev, rear-admiral Vasilii Maksimovich Zatsarennyi, solicited the DDDII and the Minister of Internal Affairs for the appointment of an expert Jew to his chancellery. Zatsarennyi planned to assign the expert Jew the "translation of subversive publications and secret correspondence in Jewish languages confiscated as evidence by the police."[113] The city governor pointed out that the close proximity of Nikolaev to the "largest centers of revolutionary propaganda" in southern Russia, including Odessa, Kiev, Ekaterinoslav, and Kharkov, and the high concentration of industrial workers attracted "large masses of revolutionaries who settled in Nikolaev and transformed it into a major center of anti-government propaganda." According to Zatsarennyi, Jews, one-third of the city population, were among the most active propagandists and largely dominated the anti-government political scene. They occupied leadership positions in the general Russian revolutionary parties, including the social democrats and social revolutionaries, and "formed their own Jewish parties," including Zionists, the Bund, and Poale Zion. Therefore, the city governor argued, in order to aid the police and gendarmerie, the office of expert Jew should be established in Nikolaev and be filled by a bureaucrat "who is loyal and proficient in the Hebrew [*sic!*] language, so he could be assigned with official translation without fear of any distortion and with the full confidence that the translated, sometimes very serious, documents would be completely safe from disclosure."[114]

In addition to translation for the police, the city governor of Nikolaev planned to use his expert Jew in matters related to Jewish tradition, religious institutions, rituals, and law. Zatsarennyi reported that his chancellery was flooded with cases of Jewish "family disputes and divorce proceedings; petitions requesting correction of metrical books; disputes among officials of Jewish religious organizations, and between these organizations and other institutions and individuals; spending of the funds of the *korobochnyi sbor* and budget issues of the Jewish communities and organizations, and many other issues insufficiently addressed by the imperial legislation regarding the Jews."[115] According to the city governor, these pressing issues clearly demanded the involvement of an expert Jew with special linguistic and theological skills. The appointment of an expert Jew under the city governor of Nikolaev is undocumented; however, the general MVD approach to Jewish bureaucracy in the 1890s through the 1910s would have made it inevitable.

In that period, the last doubts of the MVD about the political utility and bureaucratic functionality of expert Jews were cast aside. On the eve and in the aftermath of the first Russian Revolution of 1905, the MVD approved the appointments of expert Jews to the provincial chancelleries on a routine basis. The MVD also increased the compensation of Jewish bureaucrats and supplemented its major source, the funds of the *korobochnyi sbor*, with funds provided by the MVD Department of Police.

In 1911, the governor of Minsk province, Iakov Egorovich Erdeli (in office 1906–1912) solicited the MVD for an increase in compensation for expert Jew Osip Gurvich recently reinstituted in his chancellery.[116] The MVD approved the increase and appointed Gurvich as official interpreter of the investigative division of the Minsk city police department, thus providing him with supplementary income.[117] This appointment was also a considerable upgrade in his official status, and the expert Jew was thus granted the full benefits of civil service, including a government pension upon retirement, a substantial reward for the seventy-two-year-old Gurvich. In 1904, the city governor of Odessa, Dmitrii Borisovich Neidgart, supported by the MVD Department of Police, solicited the same benefits for his expert Jew, Iakov Dynin.[118] The cases of Gurvich and Dynin exemplified the late nineteenth-century imperial policy of centralization and unification of the administration for the *inorodtsy*, including the Jews, accomplished through the amalgamation of Jewish bureaucracy within general Russian officialdom.

Recent scholarship demonstrates that in the 1890s through the 1910s the social and legal integration of a significant portion of the Jewish population into the social fabric of the Russian estates, classes, and categories became a tangible fact.[119] However, legal dualism—the fundamental incongruity between the general laws and the special laws for the Jews, and between these laws and Jewish religious law, the *halacha*—was never fully resolved. This situation created a considerable demand among Russian administrators and courts for the interpretation and reconciliation of the legal systems. Such demand was largely met by Jewish bureaucrats, including the Rabbinical Commission, and, especially, expert Jews.

In 1906, the city governor of Nikolaev, Rear Admiral Zatsarennyi, emphasized the central role of expert Jews in examining cases "insufficiently addressed by the imperial legislation regarding the Jews."[120] In 1912, the city governor of Odessa, Ivan Vasil'evich Sosnovskii, solicited MVD approval for the candidate to replace the retired expert Jew Iakov Dynin. Similar to his colleague from Nikolaev, Sosnovskii reported that his office was receiving dozens of cases demanding substantial help of an expert Jew with "broad knowledge of the imperial laws on the Jews, in addition to expertise in the laws and rituals of the Jewish religion, as well as awareness of the actual needs of Jews and about their social organization."[121] According to the city governor, his candidate, Gavriil Lifshits, a graduate of the University of Novorossiia, was perfectly qualified for the office as "a Jew by background and a lawyer by education," with considerable bureaucratic experience as secretary of the Odessa city magistrate.[122]

The interpretation and reconciliation of halachic norms and categories with imperial legislation and confessional policies, and expert assistance in monitoring of contemporary Jewish political activity, were major priorities on the agenda of the expert Jew of the MVD, Moisei

Kreps, until the last days of the Russian empire.[123] After the Revolution of 1917 in February, the Provisional Government, which replaced the monarchy, incorporated the MVD and preserved its structure, including the DDDII and expert Jew Kreps. In October 1917, the government planned to reorganize the MVD and transfer the functions of the DDDII to the forthcoming Ministry of Faiths. On October 20, 1917, Kreps applied to the Minister of Internal Affairs, social democrat Aleksei Maksimovich Nikitin, for an appointment to the new ministry to continue providing "consulting services on Jewish matters, similar to my previous ten-year-long official service at the DDDII."[124] However, in a week's time, Minister Nikitin was arrested by the Bolsheviks along with the other members of the Provisional Government. A new Ministry of Faiths was never established, and the oldest agency of the Russian government, the MVD, was eliminated by the new regime. The office of expert Jews followed its path into history.

3

"Without Haste and Without Rest"

Enlightened Bureaucrats

In Sholem Aleichem's novel *Funem yarid* (From the Fair, 1916), the protagonist Sholom moves from a provincial town to the big city of Kiev in search of a new life and better opportunities—"some business, occupation, profession or position."[1] Even this novice has learned that to achieve his goal he needs the patronage (*protektsiia*) of the government rabbi for, as conventional wisdom would have it, this is the way the world works. The office of the government rabbi turns out to be a dull Russian bureaucratic chancellery with a cheap popular print of the portrait of the tsar hanging on the wall and an old desk that has seen better times. The rabbi's assistant, an old man with the faded face of a corpse, is present along with ragged and miserable visitors waiting for an appointment. The room has only one Jewish detail, a torn map of Palestine hanging on the wall. However, the appearance of the rabbi surpasses even Sholom's expectations. While all the small-town rabbis were short and pathetic, the rabbi of Kiev cuts a magnificent figure: he is fit (*bogatyr'*) and handsome. His only "flaws" are his red hair and his tendency to be slow. More important, as Sholom discovers, the government rabbi is completely powerless: "It turned out that the rabbi could do nothing, absolutely nothing."[2] The only "patronage" the rabbi can provide to Sholom is a letter of recommendation to his friend German Markovich Barats, an attorney and expert Jew under the auspices of the governor-general.

Armed with his letter, the protagonist imagines the expert Jew as both a scholar and a high-ranking Russian official, "a professor decorated with medals like a general."[3] One can't judge a book by its cover: the expert Jew receives visitors in his private study, crammed with bookcases filled with religious and secular books. However, Sholom is quickly disappointed by this man with thin side whiskers. He is nearsighted and extremely nervous. "Was this really an expert Jew under the governor-general? If he did not have a beard shaved in the middle of his chin, you would swear that he was a melamed, a Talmud teacher."[4] Upon reading the rabbi's letter, Barats "grabbed his head and started pacing the room begging to be left alone because he did not know anything, could not do anything, and would not do anything. He was exasperated by the rabbi, who sent young people to him every day. What could Barats do for them? What did he know? Who was he? Who does he think he is? He is not Brodskii! One felt pity looking at this expert Jew!"[5] After calming down, the expert Jew decides that the only thing he can do for the young man is to recommend him to his best friend and colleague, the famous lawyer Lev Abramovich Kupernik. Barats assures Sholom that the patronage of Kupernik "would knock down walls; he is capable of moving the most influential people."[6]

Sholem Aleichem's vivid caricatures of Jewish officials at work capture many contemporary realities, such as the gap between the image of the high official status of government rabbis and expert Jews and their lack of power in real life.[7] Sholem Aleichem also reveals the everyday official routines of government rabbis, who were constantly besieged by impoverished petitioners, and of expert Jews, who spent their office hours inside their insulated studies, surrounded by shelves of religious and secular books. However, both Jewish bureaucrats are at a loss when faced with a real-life situation beyond their limited scope.

Leo Tolstoy's novel *Anna Karenina* portrays the Russian bureaucrat Aleksei Aleksandrovich Karenin, a high-ranking official at the MVD who would be the contemporary and, perhaps, the superior of expert Jew Barats. Karenin's appearance is immaculate as he dons "a white tie and tailcoat decorated with two medals [orders]," which perfectly matches his high official status. Every minute of his time is scheduled for important government matters; "without haste and without rest—is his motto."[8] The main feature of Karenin's distinctive bureaucratic attitude, "which, in combination with his ambition, reticence, integrity and self-confidence, shaped his career, included his irreverence to bureaucratic paperwork . . . and, if possible, involvement in actual issues."[9] Thus, in the fictional "Committee on the *Inorodtsy*" where Karenin represents his ministry, he not only promotes departmental interests, but seeks to resolve real-life problems within the context of his office. Karenin cannot tolerate the idea that "the rival ministry, inimical to the ministry of Aleksei Aleksandrovich," has failed to understand, let alone reform the situation of the *inorodtsy*. Ultimately, Karenin himself makes an inspection trip to the "distant provinces" to examine the situation, and pointedly refuses to take his official travel allowance. However, as the novel's plot demonstrates, this outstanding bureaucrat is at a loss when confronted with real-life situations. As Tolstoy put it, "All his life Aleksei Aleksandrovich lived and worked in the official sphere, which only dealt with reflections of real life. And every time, when he encountered real life itself, he distanced himself from it."[10]

The fictional portraits of the wretched Jewish bureaucrat Barats and the model Russian bureaucrat Karenin share one characteristic—the inability to respond adequately to the challenges of real life. The obvious difference in the level of administrative power at their disposal is not the point here. Their alienation from real life stems directly from their bureaucratic occupation. Both Barats and Karenin are quintessential bureaucrats not only by career but also by their education, social status, general outlook, and lifestyle. Jewish bureaucrats—expert Jews—and their Russian colleagues shared many social and cultural characteristics and political beliefs, which constituted their service ethos. The service ethos of expert Jews was an offshoot of the ethos of the vanguard of Russian officialdom, the enlightened bureaucrats.

Contemporary scholarship provides a new perspective on Russian officialdom by treating the government administration as an independent historical agent distinguished by a unique social and ideological identity, rather than a faceless bureaucratic apparatus simply reacting to social developments.[11] This scholarship demonstrates that in the 1840s and 1850s, the major institutional and social developments within Russian officialdom significantly affected the outlook and ethics of Russian bureaucrats. As a result, a group with a new service ethos—the enlightened bureaucrats—emerged. This cohort conceived of and successfully implemented the Great Reforms—an unprecedented transformation of the Russian state and society in the 1860s.

The key factor that influenced the emergence of the enlightened bureaucrats and development of their group identity and ethos was their education, which they received at the elite imperial boarding schools, Tsarskosel'skii Lyceum and the School of Jurisprudence. The previous generations of Russian bureaucrats were not subject to any special training requirements, and had a very low educational profile. As a rule, they learned bureaucratic skills and traditions at the chancelleries from their more experienced colleagues. The special atmosphere of the new schools, the Lyceum and the School of Jurisprudence, created an insular space where students were cut off from the influence of institutional, social, and family ties. In this environment, future bureaucrats sought guidance in their education and formulated their own ideas cultivated by teachers and readings. The influence of the Lyceum and the School of Jurisprudence on the future careers of enlightened bureaucrats was not limited, however, to their curriculum. The general emotional ambience, shared life experience, and values contributed to the maturation of the young men as much as their classes and books. This unique institutional spirit was ultimately realized in the esprit de corps and special ethos of the graduates of these schools. The future enlightened bureaucrats cherished and preserved this spirit throughout their lives and careers. When they began their service in government administration, the graduates of the elite schools considered themselves to be a chosen group dedicated to the lofty mission of positive social change. Their shared mission created a sense of group cohesion and identity.

These idealistic young bureaucrats, many of whom were in their early twenties, immediately encountered the drudgery of the mundane bureaucratic routines of the Russian ministerial system, especially the mountains of dreary bureaucratic paperwork. They had no other choice, since the law stipulated mandatory service for graduates of the Lyceum and the School of Jurisprudence: six years for government-funded students and four years for the others. Inspection trips to the provinces were the only service assignments which sparked enthusiasm among the young officials and provided them an opportunity to demonstrate their skills and abilities. While on these assignments, the young bureaucrats felt their importance as they exposed administrative injustices and flaws and tried to overcome them. Thus, the future enlightened bureaucrats acquired substantial firsthand knowledge of the provincial administration and developed a vision for its improvement.[12]

In the 1840s, the Russian ministerial system began to recognize and integrate the new generation of educated and motivated bureaucrats. From 1836 to 1840, the Minister of State Domains, Count Pavel Kiselev, appointed many educated young men and regularly dispatched them as officials for special missions to the provinces to study the local conditions. Kiselev's practice was emulated by the offices of the MVD starting in 1841, when Lev Perovskii became Minister of Internal Affairs. Working under Kiselev and Perovskii, young bureaucrats with demonstrated ability to collect, analyze, and present information in comprehensive reports had a good chance of being noticed by their superiors. Demonstrated expertise in a particular area of administration became a significant criterion for promotion. However, besides education and theoretical skills, firsthand knowledge of local conditions was required, since the official statistics provided by the provincial administration were inadequate and unreliable. The young enlightened bureaucrats did not regard the collection of information in the provinces as a mere mechanical task. For them, it was an important part of their mission, aimed at the improvement of the administration and general welfare of imperial subjects. This mission motivated their statistical, ethnographic, economic, and social research and contributed to the dynamic nature of their work. Moreover, in the process of exploring the data, the young bureaucrats started to perceive the inevitability of reforms.

Eventually, during the 1840s and the 1850s when the first graduates of the Lyceum and the School of Jurisprudence acquired influence and authority from among the ranks of Russian bureaucracy, they recreated the institutional environment of their alma mater, encouraging learning, talent, diligence, and integrity throughout the chancelleries of the Russian ministerial system. In this environment, the new generations of young educated bureaucrats were assigned meaningful and large-scale tasks befitting the talents, education, and mission of novice officials, from the very beginning of their bureaucratic careers. Ministers Perovskii and Kiselev cultivated the policymaking skills of the young enlightened bureaucrats, engaging them in the preparation of key political decisions and laws. Thus, the self-confidence of the enlightened bureaucrats grew along with their belief that the situation in Russia could be improved using their talents, skills, and knowledge applied within the bureaucratic structures of the government.[13]

As a result, the enlightened bureaucrats came of age in the mid-1850s as a competent, dynamic, and politically cohesive elite group within Russian bureaucracy. The powerful formula of their service ethos was made up of the following: a positive attitude with the assurance of the possibility and necessity of progress and change; inseparability of private life and service, enabling the enlightened bureaucrats to consider their official work as their personal calling, and to enhance their service with their personal enthusiasm; diligence and determination, which helped them cope with ubiquitous bureaucratic routines by using the motto—"hard work and sense of duty"; ethical mission, calling for the amelioration and civilization of the administrative and social order; intellectual exclusivity, based on the serious education and special training required for a successful career; and faithful service to the monarch.

From the 1840s to 1870s, the service ethos and esprit de corps of the elite group of enlightened bureaucrats put them at the vanguard of the Great Reforms. During the 1880s and 1890s the reforms lost momentum while the bureaucratization of the government administration and its cadres, triggered by the reforms, intensified. Ultimately, the enlightened bureaucrats, especially at the MVD, gave way to a new generation of bureaucrats who based their policies on a doctrine of ministerial power and total police control, which dominated the domestic policy of late imperial Russia.[14]

Service Ethos and Mission of Expert Jews

The service ethos of the Russian Jewish bureaucratic elite—expert Jews—was shaped by their educational experience at the rabbinical seminaries of Vilna and Zhitomir.[15] These schools played a key role in the history of Jewish bureaucracy. Like the Lyceum and the School of Jurisprudence, the rabbinical seminaries were elite educational institutions where students, isolated from the traditional institutional and social milieu and from their families, matured as individuals and emerged as a distinctive group, united by shared experiences and values and the common goal of improvement of the traditional social order. Both Russian elite schools and the rabbinical seminaries were supported by government policies aimed at the professionalization and bureaucratization of civil service in the Russian empire. However, Russian and Jewish elite schools cultivating bureaucratic cadres differed in several respects.

The Russian elite schools educated the young generation of the Russian nobility, the traditional elite of Russian society. By contrast, the majority of students at the rabbinical seminaries were Jewish youth from the lower strata of traditional Jewish society.[16] These students began to consider themselves the new Jewish elite only when they graduated from the rabbinical seminaries. Russian elite schools as well as the rabbinical seminaries nurtured a sense of high civic mission and prepared their students for a career aimed at the realization of that mission. In the Russian schools, the most significant influence on the students was the unique atmosphere. The special emotional ambience encouraged a sense of brotherhood among the students, based on their mutual support and common ideals, which transcended social and material obstacles. The Lyceum and the School of Jurisprudence enjoyed the special patronage of the Russian emperor and members of his family, which promoted an elitist consciousness among the students. The rabbinical seminaries provided a similar atmosphere of nurturing unity, and a sense of belonging to a common cause.[17] The emperor Alexander II demonstrated his personal support of these institutions when he paid a visit to the rabbinical seminary of Vilna in 1858.[18] Many mundane details of everyday life in the rabbinical seminaries significantly affected the future Jewish bureaucratic elite and contributed to the development of its service ethos. The uniforms provided to the students by the government signified their personal modernization and break from Jewish tradition, as well as their integration into the uniformed ranks of Russian bureaucracy. For many students of impoverished backgrounds who were accustomed to wearing only second-hand clothing, these brand-new uniforms gave them a sense of dignity and worth. They also signified the government's patronage and care for Russian Jews. As a result, many graduates of the rabbinical seminaries felt a sense of sincere gratitude to the Russian government throughout their lives and careers. By the same token, the outfits of the seminary teachers, which were the official uniform of the Ministry of National Enlightenment, complete with shiny buttons (a special detail that stuck in the memories of the students), signified the high social status of their mentors, which the students could also achieve in the future by pursuing a bureaucratic career.[19]

The rabbinical seminaries served as a testing ground for practical rapprochement between Jews and Russians, where Jewish students encountered the values and lifestyle of Russian society in general and Russian bureaucracy in particular. On the one hand, some aspects of this new life such as the culture of pre-reform Nikolaevan officialdom were foreign if not downright unappealing to the students. Particularly difficult were the hierarchical subordination, military discipline, total control, and authoritarianism accompanied by ubiquitous corruption, procrastination, and deception. On the other hand, the mentors and lecturers, especially Russian Christian instructors who taught the secular subjects in the curriculum, employed the most advanced pedagogical techniques developed by Konstantin Ushinskii and Vladimir Stoiunin, pioneering Russian thinkers in the field of pedagogical theory.[20] According to Mikhail Morgulis, a graduate of the rabbinical seminary in Zhitomir, the Russian teachers were able to make a crucial impact on the spiritual development of the students and instill in them a true love for Russia and Russian literature. The textbooks on Judaic subjects, which for the most part were made up of contemporary works by Russian maskilim written in Russian, promoted the principles of enlightenment—rationalism, humanism, tolerance, and morality—in addition to Russian patriotism. Moreover, these textbooks cultivated a dedication to the Jewish people among the rabbinical students and aided them in adapting Jewish values to the surrounding political reality of imperial Russia.[21]

As a result, the Russian Jewish bureaucratic elite, brought up and educated in the rabbinical seminaries, acquired a solid ideological and ethical foundation, with the following components: a firm belief in the good intentions and positive program of the government aimed at the social transformation and integration of the Jews; the civic mission of bureaucratic service to the government and its policy of reforms; a positive outlook based on the principles of the European enlightenment and the Haskalah; Russian Jewish patriotism comprising love of the fatherland and its culture along with a dedication to the Jewish people and strong belief in the ultimate success of rapprochement; the value system and lifestyle of the Russian bureaucracy; and "maskilic solidarity"[22]—a distinctive esprit de corps and group consciousness of the Russian Jewish bureaucratic elite. This Jewish variety of the Russian enlightened bureaucrats' ethos strongly affected the service of expert Jews, their official careers and everyday lives.

Upon graduation, some students of the rabbinical school chose to serve as government rabbis, an office that lacked legitimacy in the eyes of traditional Jewish society. This was in large measure due to their inadequate training in Jewish law at the state rabbinical seminaries. A recent study argues that while the rabbinical seminaries failed to staff the Russian government rabbinate with fresh cadres of educated rabbis, they nevertheless succeeded in bringing up a whole new generation of Russian Jews committed to the transformation of traditional Jewish life. The government rabbinate, with its core institutional weakness, disorganization, and low repute among Jews, provided an unwelcoming environment for the integration of the young educated rabbis. The official mandate and work conditions of the government rabbis impeded rather than encouraged the realization of the elitist service ethos of the graduates of the rabbinical seminaries. Limited authority and excessive responsibilities effectively prevented them from properly executing their official duties. Several important factors further damaged the official role and bureaucratic capacity of the government rabbinate: their institutional and financial dependence on the Jewish communities, which elected and funded these officials; short three-year terms of service, which prevented any institutional and political continuity; lack of decisive and adequate support from the government, which divested the rabbinate of any means of enforcement; and lack of demand for the enlightened service ethos of the educated rabbis in the traditional Jewish environment and in the milieu of petty bureaucracy of the district administration. Moreover, the most important component of the Jewish bureaucratic service ethos, a strong commitment to the mission of civilizing and enlightening traditional Russian Jews, ultimately contributed to the alienation of the young Jewish bureaucrats and made them outsiders in traditional Jewish society in general and in the government rabbinate in particular.[23] Even when elected to positions of government rabbi, graduates of the rabbinical seminaries found little support for their service ethos. Instead, they were significantly challenged by this ethos, which created difficult dilemmas in their everyday rabbinical routines. According to Iulii Gessen, the young educated rabbis "acting in the spirit of the government policies, encountered significant resentment in their congregations, on which they depended financially; however, failure to implement government policies also led to troubles."[24] As a result, these government rabbis lived "with the constant struggle between their conscience and sense of duty versus concerns about sustaining themselves and their families."[25]

In contrast to the government rabbinate, the position of expert Jew, integrated within Russian bureaucracy, provided the graduates of the rabbinical seminaries with a unique opportunity for practical application of their education and realization of their mission. In the institutional environment of the Russian ministerial system, especially at the MVD, the service ethos of the young Jewish bureaucrats was perfectly relevant. Moreover, in this milieu their ethos was considered an essential qualification for bureaucratic office, and was substantially compensated and rewarded by career growth.

Therefore, the service ethos of the graduates of the rabbinical seminaries determined their aspiration toward a bureaucratic career within Russian officialdom, while a career in the government rabbinate, within the traditional Jewish milieu, scared educated Jewish youth away. Many graduates of the rabbinical seminaries who were appointed to the office of expert Jew (including government-funded students who had no choice but to accept mandatory appointment) served responsibly and eagerly. They believed in the positive effect of their work and in the universal justice of the bureaucratic system, and demonstrated outstanding initiative and enthusiasm.

Aaron Tseitlin, expert Jew under the governor of Poltava province, described the relationship between his education, service ethos, and bureaucratic career thus: "After completing studies at the rabbinical seminary in Vilna as the top student of the class, with award certificates in every grade, in 1859 I was appointed by the authorities to the office of expert Jew in Poltava.... Since I was a government-funded student, nobody asked me if I agreed to accept this appointment.... Since I was brought up by the government for a special mission and spent the best years of my life in government service, and due to my religion I was unable to look for any other occupation or job. Thus, if I am dismissed from the office of expert Jew, which I currently occupy, I would lose all means of support and, worse, I would lose my faith in justice, which inspires me to this minute."[26]

Tseitlin maintained his belief in justice despite the unseemly actions of his Russian colleagues at the provincial chancellery, who demanded a bribe, disguised as a charitable donation, in order to keep his position. Tseitlin wrote that when the governor decided to dismiss him from office, "the officials of the provincial chancellery suggested that he make a donation of 25 rubles to the orphanage."[27] Tseitlin reacted in the most impractical manner. He honestly admitted: "I could not afford such a sum (since every month a major part of my salary goes to support my family: 10 rubles to my mother, 5 rubles to my brother).... One of the officials at the provincial chancellery pointed out my impracticality, since being warned [about the dismissal], I was unable to keep my position by making a timely contribution."[28]

Even in these desperate circumstances, expert Jew Tseitlin was unwilling to consider the career of government rabbi as a viable alternative. Tseitlin argued: "I do not have enough money to travel to different places to offer myself for rabbinical office and depend on the random results of elections.... Having occupied a rabbinical office twice in Kremenchug, I am convinced that due to the present condition of Russian Jews, even the most loyal rabbi, inspired by a sense of lawfulness, is frequently forced to breach the laws and, consequently, the oath of service. This regrettable situation is caused by the dependence of the rabbi on the Jewish community, and by the fact that many imperial laws concerning the Jews have not yet been adapted to Jewish religious laws and traditions."[29]

For four years, 1866–1870, when according to the governor of Poltava province Mikhail Martynov, "there was no single case demanding the service of the expert Jew" in his province,[30] even without any work assignments from the governor, expert Jew Tseitlin, committed to his ethos and mission, tried to be useful to the government and cherished the hope of continuing his career at the central offices of the MVD. Tseitlin pointed out that "four years, free from official service, were used for a special theoretical and practical study of the Jewish question. Long-term research yielded many conclusions, including the following: the increase of the Jewish population is inversely proportional to the level and continuity of religious tolerance in a given country. My a priori assumption is supported by the numbers, but, since I live in the provinces, I lack several sources [for the completion of this work]; thus, I seek an appointment at the central offices of the MVD, at least temporary, so I could be useful to the government and the fatherland."[31]

Tseitlin's commitment was noticed, utilized, and rewarded by the MVD. In 1870, he was dismissed from the position of expert Jew under the governor of Poltava province,[32] but as early as 1872 he was appointed expert Jew under the governor-general of Kiev and Podolia provinces, and his annual compensation was increased from 600 to 900 silver rubles.[33] In 1887, the governor-general nominated the expert Jew for an official award for "long-term flawless service," and it was thus that the Minister of Internal Affairs personally expressed his appreciation of Tseitlin's service, awarding him a bonus in the amount of 900 silver rubles, and allowing him a vacation for medical treatment abroad.[34] In 1897, Tseitlin was promoted to the office of censor of Jewish literature in Kiev.[35]

During his long and successful bureaucratic career, Tseitlin's service was influenced by Russian Jewish patriotism—a combination of love of the fatherland and dedication to the Jewish people—another important feature of the service ethos of Jewish bureaucrats. According to the expert Jew, his service "promoted the simple yet important idea for the fatherland that every subject of the Russian tsar, despite his origins and religious faith, is nothing but a Russian."[36] Tseitlin declared, "This simple truth will ultimately triumph. When this truth is absorbed by the civil consciousness of my compatriots of different faiths, then there will be as many Russians as there are people in my great fatherland."[37] The contemporary developments of Russian and Jewish politics challenged Tseitlin's hopes for the triumph of integration, but the expert Jew never lost his basic sympathy for the Jews and never abandoned his concerns about the historical destiny of his people. In 1903, Tseitlin, on assignment for the MVD's Main Directorate of Press Affairs (*Glavnoe upravlenie po delam pechati*), presented his report on Zionism, written in a "very sympathetic tone" to the MVD.[38]

In sum, the service ethos of Jewish bureaucrats was not a straightforward emulation of the service ethos of Russian enlightened bureaucrats. The values, beliefs, and mission of Jewish bureaucrats, while similar to those of Russian enlightened bureaucrats, developed independently through their special education, life experience, and service. As a result,

Jewish bureaucracy emerged as an elite group distinguished by its ethos among both modernized and traditional Russian Jews. The common goals and similar ideals of Jewish and Russian bureaucrats contributed to the successful integration of the Jewish bureaucratic elite, mainly in the official capacity of expert Jews, within Russian bureaucracy, a sizeable and politically significant segment of Russian society.

Social Profiles of Expert Jews

Unlike the amorphous cohort of government rabbis, expert Jews constituted a socially homogeneous elite group of professional Jewish bureaucrats united by their service ethos. The integrity of this group was well protected by the MVD's policy of keeping the office of expert Jew distinct from other groups including the lay Jewish intelligentsia who sought the social privileges and rewards of civil service and the traditional Jewish religious elite who strove for political gain provided by official status. The law granted exclusive authority to provincial administrators, namely the governor-generals and governors, to nominate candidates for the office of expert Jew from among those who sought the appointment. The final choice and approval of the official appointment was left to the Minister of Internal Affairs.

Thus, in 1871, titular councilor Iona Gurliand, who received his bachelor of jurisprudence and master of Oriental languages degrees at St. Petersburg University and became an associate at the Imperial Public Library in St. Petersburg, was denied an appointment to the office of expert Jew under the governor-general of Kiev, Volhyn, and Podolia provinces.[39] Instead, the appointment of German Barats, the incumbent expert Jew, was confirmed by the governor-general and approved by the MVD. It was an obvious choice, since Barats, who lacked the academic credentials demonstrated by the other candidate, had, however, a solid bureaucratic background as a member of the Rabbinical Commission, expert Jew, and censor of Jewish literature.[40]

In 1891, the appointment to the office of expert Jew under the governor-general of Vilna, Kovno, and Grodno provinces was denied to Meer Vygodskii, a young lawyer who graduated from St. Petersburg University in 1886,[41] and to baptized Jew Pavel Dreizin, nominated by the

Orthodox archbishop of Lithuania and Vilna. Vygodskii was rejected by the governor-general, while Dreizin was denied the office by the Minister of Internal Affairs. The minister, Ivan Nikolaevich Durnovo, pointed out that the law explicitly disqualified baptized Jews from the appointment.[42] Finally, the MVD appointed Mikhail Vol'per, a teacher of Russian language at the model elementary Jewish school in Vilna.[43]

In 1899, physician Aaron Shavlov was denied an appointment to the office of expert Jew under the governors of Lifland and Kurland provinces and under the DDDII. Instead, the MVD appointed Isidor Mikhel'son, who also held a medical degree from Moscow University and, as government rabbi of Riga, had considerable bureaucratic experience.[44]

In 1908, Rabbi Leib Tsirelson, the traditional religious authority and official government rabbi of the town of Priluki in Poltava province, was denied an appointment to the office of expert Jew under the DDDII. According to Aleksei Nikolaevich Kharuzin, director of the DDDII, the candidate was disqualified due to his "insufficient level of education."[45] Instead, the MVD appointed Moisei Kreps, who, in addition to extensive experience as government rabbi in many localities of southern Russia, held a doctorate in philosophy from the University of Berlin.[46]

During the entire history of expert Jews, the MVD carefully screened candidates for the office to maintain political conformism, social cohesiveness, and the elite status of Jewish bureaucracy.[47] The analysis of the life and service of three generations of expert Jews[48] presented on the following pages demonstrates how the evolving cadre base and ethos of Jewish bureaucracy adapted to the shifting priorities and methods of official Jewish policy.

Lay Maskilim: Moisei Berlin

The first generation of expert Jews was made up of diverse amateur bureaucrats, for the most part of maskilic background, who served from the 1850s to the early 1870s.[49] Their primary bureaucratic function was to collect basic information about the religion, history, and traditional lifestyle of Russian Jews, and about their current social and economic conditions in order to provide knowledge for making and implementing official Jewish policy. These bureaucratic pioneers came from diverse social backgrounds, and found their way into government service through various channels and under different circumstances. They did not have any special bureaucratic training. Many of them did not have any secular education at all or were educated abroad.

They were an eclectic group that spanned the broad social and ideological spectrum of mid-nineteenth-century Russian Jewry, including German-trained rabbi and doctor of philosophy Avraam Neiman, Lubavicher hasid and traditional rabbi Avraam Madievskii, and baptized Jew and Russian titular councilor Vladimir Fedorov. Their service was inconsistent, due to the newness of their office, which still lacked a firm basis in Russian bureaucracy. Consequently, the length of their official careers greatly fluctuated, from the three years of Avraam Madievskii to the twenty-two-year term of Markus Gurovich. The first generation of expert Jews had neither a collective service ethos nor a common mission. Their service was motivated by individual goals and aspirations largely based on their maskilic ideals. Thus, according to Moisei Berlin, he used a "scientific and literary" approach in his work,[50] based on the ideas and methods of the German *Wissenschaft des Judentums* (Science of Judaism), which emphasized positive belief in the historical progress of the Jewish people and Judaism. Another expert Jew of the first generation, Markus Gurovich, demonstrated a more down-to-earth attitude. Based on his strong belief in the social and cultural integration of Russian Jews, Gurovich invested substantial effort into the promotion of secular Jewish education among traditional Jews. The initial institutional volatility of Jewish bureaucracy, the eclecticism of its cadres and the diversity of its motivations, maintained the low level of bureaucratization of the first generation of expert Jews and contributed to the dynamic nature of their service, which frequently circumvented official procedures and regulations.

The biography of Moisei Berlin is representative of expert Jews of the first generation. Moisei Iosifovich Berlin (1821–1888) was born in the town of Shklov in Mogilev province, an important center of traditional Jewish learning and a hotbed of the Russian Haskalah.[51] Berlin's father was a wealthy merchant who provided his son with a solid traditional Jewish education along with the basics of secular education, including several European languages. In 1840, when his father died and the family's fortune deteriorated, Berlin went to Europe in order to complete his secular education and acquire a profession. As Berlin put it, while

Moisei Berlin (Evreiskaiia entsiklopediia: svod znanii o evreistve i ego kul'ture v proshlom i nastoiashchem [St. Petersburg, 1908–1913], vol. 4, 271)

supported by the family's wealth, he peacefully enjoyed the "honey and nectar of the Torah and the sages."[52] However, when his financial security was gone, Berlin had to "seek shelter under the canopy of secular science and enlightenment."[53] He studied in Germany for five years, attending lectures at the universities of Koenigsberg and Bonn. In 1845, Berlin defended a doctoral dissertation on logic, which was published in Koenigsberg under the title *Ars Logica*.[54]

After returning to Russia in 1849, Berlin found employment as a teacher of Hebrew and German languages at the government-sponsored Jewish school in Mogilev. During the five years of his teaching career, Berlin achieved considerable results in introducing secular education to Russian Jews. According to the superintendent of the Vilna school district who inspected the Mogilev school in 1852, Berlin significantly improved the quality of instruction and expanded attendance, which grew to 100 pupils.[55]

In 1853 Berlin was appointed expert Jew under the governor-general of Vitebsk, Mogilev, and Smolensk provinces. Berlin served in this office, which, in his words, "gave him access to the sphere of useful work for the common good of my people, as well as for the lofty goals of the beneficial government,"[56] until 1855. From 1856 to 1866, Berlin held the nominal appointment of expert Jew under the governor-general of Kiev, Volhyn, and Podolia provinces, but in fact he served as expert Jew under the DDDII at the central offices of the MVD in St. Petersburg. Berlin combined his service with active literary and research work. In 1859, he published his Russian translation of a Jewish historical chronicle describing the mass execution of Jews during the Cossack uprising in Ukraine in the 1640s.[57] In 1861, Berlin published an ethnographical survey of Russian Jews.[58] These publications brought him prestigious membership in the Society for Russian History and Antiquities and in the Imperial Russian Geographic Society.

Moisei Berlin died in St. Petersburg in 1888. His only child, daughter Fanni (1850–1896), received a degree in jurisprudence from the University of Bern in Switzerland, and his son-in-law, prominent economist and statistician Illarion Ignat'evich Kaufman (1848–1915), served as acting expert Jew under the DDDII in the 1870s.[59]

Berlin's choice of bureaucratic career was largely accidental. His education was eclectic and suited to many occupations including science,

Moisei Berlin's official service record, September 6, 1856 (RGIA, f. 821, o. 8, d. 456, ll. 111ob.-112)

commerce, and even the rabbinate. His first official appointment as a teacher at the government-sponsored Jewish school coincided with the large-scale government reforms, which created an auspicious institutional environment and provided material support to rank-and-file Russian maskilim. However, Berlin's attitude perfectly matched the contemporary bureaucratic agenda of the government, which singled him out among expert Jews of the first generation. The MVD singled out the exceptional service of expert Jew Berlin who "provided the administration with secret evidence of illegal activity of the Jews."[60] Like many Russian enlightened bureaucrats, Berlin spent a significant amount of time in the beginning of his career on inspection trips in the provinces, and collected critical data, which enabled efficient policymaking.[61] As a result, Berlin was noticed by his superiors and promoted. The education and career of Berlin's children (including his son-in-law) followed the path of integration and acculturation paved by this expert Jew and his service.

Graduates of the Rabbinical Seminaries: German Barats

The second generation of expert Jews, in service from the late 1850s to the 1890s, was dominated by graduates of the rabbinical seminaries.[62] Their principal bureaucratic role was to make and implement official policies aimed at rapprochement between Jews and Russians in areas of administration, legislation, and education. This generation of expert Jews was made up of specially trained bureaucratic professionals. They constituted a homogeneous elite group united by shared educational and life experiences, common mission, and service ethos. Many of them knew each other personally. The MVD's selective approach to the cadres of expert Jews promoted the elite status of these Jewish bureaucrats, making the position inaccessible to non-bureaucratic outsiders. The careers of expert Jews of the second generation were steady and spanned lengthy terms. More than half of these expert Jews served twenty to fifty years. The MVD considered them an essential and ongoing cadre base of official Jewish policy. Therefore, even when dismissed from office at some point in their careers, the Jewish bureaucrats were later reappointed to other offices, as demonstrated by the careers of Aaron Tseitlin, German Barats, and Osip Gurvich.[63] Some of these expert Jews acquired non-bureaucratic professions while in office, such as in jurisprudence and finance,[64] which provided them with useful skills demanded by the increasing bureaucratic expansion of the state into new spheres of social life in post-reform Russia. The ethos and mission of expert Jews of the second generation were manifest in their service and extracurricular pursuits, which included historiography, pedagogy, public service, and politics.[65] The institutional maturity of the Jewish bureaucracy and stability of its cadres in combination with the well-developed official routines of policymaking and implementation contributed to the increased level of bureaucratization of expert Jews of the second generation. Their work moved from the Jewish world to the chancelleries of the central and provincial administration under the MVD. Their modus operandi also shifted to bureaucratic procedures, with extensive paperwork, participation in legal proceedings, and administrative commissions.

The biography of German Barats is representative of expert Jews of the second generation.[66] German Markovich Barats (1835–1922) was born in the town of Dubno in Volhyn province. His social background is

German Barats (German Barats, Sobranie trudov po voprosu o evreiskom elemente v pamiatnikakh drevnerusskoi pis'mennosti [Paris: Imprimerie d'Art Voltaire, 1924–1927])

unclear but apparently he came from a poor Jewish family, since in 1853 when Barats was admitted into the third grade of the rabbinical seminary in Zhitomir, he received a full government stipend. Among his classmates in the seminary were several future expert Jews, including Lev Binshtok, Faitel' Bliumenfel'd, and Lev Zaidiner.

In 1859, Barats graduated from the seminary with an official rabbinical certificate. The same year, at the request of the authorities, Barats and Bliumenfel'd ran for election to the office of government rabbi of Odessa. The elections ended up a fiasco for both graduates of the rabbinical seminary, neither of them receiving even one vote. In the opinion of the authorities who were monitoring their protégés, the main reasons for this failure were the youth and inexperience of the freshly minted educated rabbis.[67] From 1860 to 1861, Barats lived in Odessa and worked as a secretary on the editorial staff of *Tsion*, the Russian-language Jewish periodical and successor to *Rassvet*. In 1861, with the support of the governor-general of Novorossiia and Bessarabiia, Barats was elected to the Rabbinical Commission, where he represented the Jews of these provinces. Barats was noticed by officials of the DDDII during a session of the Rabbinical Commission in St. Petersburg, and in 1862 the MVD used him as an auxiliary official complementing the work of the acting expert Jew under the DDDII, Moisei Berlin. The same year, the governor-general of Kiev, Volhyn, and Podolia provinces, Nikolai Nikolaevich Annenkov (former governor-general of Novorossiia and Bessarabiia, who had actively engaged his expert Jew, Markus Gurovich, in the mid-1850s), learned of the outstanding service of Barats and solicited the MVD for Barats's appointment to the office of expert Jew in Kiev. Thus, upon the MVD's approval, Barats went to Kiev and served as expert Jew under the governor-general of Kiev, Volhyn, and Podolia provinces from 1862 to 1881.

According to a contemporary account by Mikhail Morgulis, in his capacity as an expert Jew, Barats "travelled all over the southwestern region [of Russia] popularizing the enrollment of Jewish children into government-sponsored Jewish schools; as a result, in hasidic localities such as Kamenets-Podol'sk, Jews frequently threw stones at him."[68] In addition to trips to the provinces, expert Jew Barats was on a regular basis involved, either by the Jewish vote or by official appointment, in the work of many expert and administrative commissions in various areas of official Jewish policy. After 1861, Barats won election to the Rabbinical Commission twice, in 1879 and 1893. However, in 1879 Barats willingly surrendered his mandate to Baron Goratsii Gintsburg. Barats, on a par with another expert Jew Avraam Neiman, was the veteran member of the Commission, having participated in more than one of its sessions.[69] In 1881, after the Kiev pogrom, the governor-general of Kiev, Volhyn, and Podolia provinces appointed his expert Jew Barats to the Kiev provincial commission on the Jewish question.[70]

From 1871 to 1901, by the order of the MVD, expert Jew Barats held a parallel appointment as censor of Jewish literature under the Kiev branch of the MVD's Main Directorate of Press Affairs (*Glavnoe upra-vlenie po delam pechati* [GUDP]). His lenient and even encouraging approach to censorship enabled the publication of such authors as Mendele Moikher-Sforim and Sholem Aleichem. His approach was well known among Jewish literati and publishers, so the number of texts sent for approval to the Kiev branch of the GUDP grew in proportion to Barats's reputation as a liberal censor.

Based on his own calling and with the permission of the governor-general, expert Jew Barats combined his bureaucratic service with a successful legal career. In 1870, he received a bachelor's degree in jurisprudence (*kandidat prava*) from Kiev University, which entitled him to independent legal practice. From 1872, with permission from the governor-general, Barats worked as a lawyer specializing in civil law and appealing the courts on behalf of private clients. In 1881, his professionalism and profound expertise in general civil law and in the special laws on Russian Jews were acknowledged by the Kiev District Court Chamber, which granted him a full attorney's certificate without his having served the mandatory term of assistant attorney.

In 1881, Barats resigned from the office of expert Jew and devoted himself entirely to legal practice. Still, in the 1880s and 1890s, Russian and Jewish officials and public figures used his expertise and experience in Jewish matters on a regular basis. In the early 1880s, Barats advised Pavel Pavlovich Demidov San-Donato, former councilor of the Podolia provincial chancellery and former head of the Kiev city council, who worked on the proposal of the legal emancipation of Russian Jews.[71] In the late 1880s, Barats visited Warsaw to consult Ivan Stanislavovich Bliokh, a wealthy entrepreneur, banker, and railroad developer, who was undertaking a major comparative social, statistical, economical, and political study of current conditions of European and Russian Jews.[72] Barats complemented Bliokh's research with materials on the history of the Jews in Europe and on contemporary antisemitism.

Barats's own research, an important component of his extracurricular activities from the 1860s, focused on the history of the Jews in Kievan Rus. He published several studies on the history of the Jewish community in Kiev in the ninth, tenth, and eleventh centuries, and on Hebrew elements in Old Slavonic language and literature. In 1900, the historical society of Nestor the Chronicler, a prestigious academic association under the auspices of Kiev University, recognized the scholarship of the expert Jew by awarding him associate membership.[73]

In 1902 the governor-general of Kiev, Volhyn, and Podolia provinces Mikhail Ivanovich Dragomirov, who needed an assistant "competent in the Jewish religion and other matters,"[74] turned to Barats for information on hasidim and their *tzadikim*. Soon Barats was officially reappointed to the office of expert Jew. As an expert Jew, Barats was also instrumental for Jewish public causes. Thus, in 1903, the branch of the OPE opened in Kiev thanks to his support, and, moreover, Barats headed the society's commission for the dissemination of Jewish public libraries. Barats served as expert Jew until 1915, when his office was eliminated along with the post of governor-general. He died in Soviet Kiev in 1922.

Barats's son Leon (b. 1871) was educated at the best Kiev gymnasium and the law school of Kiev University. Leon Barats did not follow in his father's footsteps in bureaucracy, but instead made a fast and successful career in commerce and banking, working for various enterprises of the Brodskii family, a dynasty of wealthy Jewish entrepreneurs in Kiev. Leon also demonstrated an interest in Jewish public initiatives. During the First World War he volunteered for the Kiev society for aid to the Jewish population (the KOPE). In 1923, Leon Barats emigrated from the USSR, first to Germany and then to France, where he taught, conducted research, and was active in Russian immigrant institutions and associations, the Union of Russian Jews in Germany and the French-Russian Institute for Social and Legal Studies in Paris.

In sum, German Barats's choice of bureaucratic career was predetermined by his special education received in the rabbinical seminary, by his ethos and mission, common to the graduates of the rabbinical seminaries, and by his status as a government-funded student, which bound the future expert Jew to mandatory service. Barats's career was jumpstarted by bureaucratic appointments at the highest level—membership in the Rabbinical Commission and an appointment as expert Jew under the governor-general of a key region of the Pale of Settlement. His career was propelled by a favorable environment, the dynamic spirit of the Great Reforms, and the positive attitude toward the social integration of Russian Jews. Barats, like many other expert Jews of the second generation, was at the vanguard of implementation of official Jewish policy. Thus, he was appointed a censor at the GUDP, a key political agency under the MVD during the era of the Great Reforms.

Barats's service ethos enhanced his bureaucratic approach to official missions, with sympathy for the Jews and a strong commitment to their social and cultural improvement. Barats supported and even cultivated contemporary Jewish literature and Jewish social and cultural initiatives. Essentially a Russian bureaucrat, he was integrated within Russian society socially, culturally, and intellectually. This integration was manifest in his extracurricular pursuits such as jurisprudence and historiography. His commitment to universal justice and rule of law epitomized a fundamental belief in the ethos of Russian enlightened bureaucrats. His historiography featured a nationalist perspective of contemporary Russian scholarship, seeking to establish the historicity of the Russian nation by exploration of its most distant past. Using this approach, Barats's own scholarship aimed to demonstrate the ancient and organic presence of the Jews in Russian history.

Barats's steady career as expert Jew spanned the most critical decades in the modern history of Russian Jews and the entire epoch of the evolution of official Jewish policy. Examination of the biography and service of this expert Jew reveals that for many decades, both the making and implementation of state policies concerning Jews consistently relied on dedicated bureaucratic cadres of expert Jews such as Barats.

The education and career of Barats's children continued in the path of integration and acculturation. They preserved a great devotion to Jewry, which was a basic element of their father's ethos.

Professional Career Bureaucrats: Moisei Kreps

The third generation of expert Jews, serving from the late 1870s until 1917, was made up of professional bureaucrats, for the most part motivated by pure career goals and a conservative ethos, conforming to the general conservative policies of the late imperial MVD.[75] Their bureaucratic mandate was shaped by the conservative thrust of the MVD, aimed at the preservation of the autocratic regime. Their work included many auxiliary police and administrative tasks, which supported the reactionary domestic policy of the late Russian empire. This generation of expert Jews was affected by two parallel processes—the gradual extinction of the previous generation of Jewish bureaucrats along with their service ethos, and the emergence of new Jewish bureaucrats pursuing successful and rewarding careers, whose service ethos was based on political and bureaucratic conformism. Unlike that of the previous generation of expert Jews, this new ethos was a direct projection of the dominant conservatism of the contemporary MVD. Moreover, due to the closing of the rabbinical seminaries, the majority of expert Jews of the third generation was educated at Russian and European universities. Due to the sweeping bureaucratization of late imperial Russian society, including Russian Jews, the service and extracurricular pursuits of expert Jews of this generation were intertwined in the institutional fabric of Russian and Jewish bureaucratic routines and social life, including such institutes as the rabbinate, Jewish scholarly organizations, the Russian provincial administration, and the Russian parliament, the State Duma.[76] The bureaucratization of the service of expert Jews of the second generation reached new heights, but the expert Jews of the third generation were mostly confined to the chancelleries and engaged in petty bureaucratic tasks.

The biography of Moisei Kreps is representative of expert Jews of the third generation. Moisei Lazarevich Kreps (1866–1942) was born in the city of Kerch in Tavrida province. In the late 1840s, his father moved to Kerch from Kherson and his mother from Kutaisi. Both of Kreps's parents came from a wealthy and traditional Jewish background. From the age of six, Kreps went to *cheder*, Talmud Torah, and yeshiva, since his father, according to Kreps, wanted him to become "a spiritual [traditional] rabbi."[77] After the death of his mother, Kreps lived with his married older sisters who insisted that he pursue a career as a government rabbi and, in addition, that he acquire some secular profession. As Kreps put it, "The contemporary condition of the Jews, deprived of civil rights, and the peculiar conditions of rabbinical life and service, and the short three-year term of elected rabbinical office" forced aspiring rabbinical candidates to learn, in addition to religious education, some useful occupation to earn a living in the event of hard times.[78] Since the rabbinical seminaries were already closed at the time, Kreps studied the Talmud and *Shulchan Aruch* at home with a private tutor, a melamed. Simultaneously, he attended the Kerch Aleksandrovskaia gymnasium and worked, for two hours a day,

Moisei Kreps (private blog with miscellaneous historical photographs, at irlovin-dreams. diary.ru, accessed on December 20, 2015)

in the chemistry laboratory in a factory owned by his relative.[79] In 1888, Kreps received a certificate of secondary education from the gymnasium but, in his words, he "did not want to become a rabbi without receiving a higher education."[80] Therefore, Kreps went to Germany where he studied at the Jewish Theological Seminary of Berlin and took courses in "philosophy, logic, natural, and social sciences," specializing in chemistry at Berlin University.[81] While pursuing his studies in Berlin, Kreps was chairman of the local Russian Jewish student scholarly society, where he presented a study entitled "The Essence of Kabbalah and Its Relationship to Hasidism." He planned to develop this study into a doctoral thesis in philosophy. However, taking into account the goals of his education and future career, Kreps defended a dissertation in chemistry, and, in 1893, received a doctoral degree from Berlin University.[82] In 1895, Kreps confirmed his professional credentials in Russia. After passing the qualification exams at the Institute of Experimental Medicine and at the Military Medical Academy in St. Petersburg, Kreps obtained the right to have a private laboratory practice and the certificate of an assistant pharmacist, which entitled him to unrestricted residence outside the Pale of Settlement. After completing his education, Kreps finally decided to "devote himself to rabbinical work."[83]

In 1897, Kreps was elected to the joint office of government rabbi of Kherson and chief rabbi of the Jewish agricultural colonies of Kherson province, replacing the previous rabbi, Faitel' Bliumenfel'd, a graduate of the Zhitomir Rabbinical Seminary who died in 1896. Kreps took on one of the most challenging rabbinical offices in the empire. As chief rabbi, he supervised the entire Jewish population of Kherson province, more than 50,000 people. He also supervised sixteen district government rabbis, who worked in twenty-three colonies.[84] The responsibilities and daily routine of chief rabbi were also extraordinary. In this way, Kreps supported the economic development of the colonies. In 1901, he initiated the establishment of a collective agricultural farm in the colony of Romanovka. This farm incorporated the ten poorest Jewish families, who shared the land, labor, and equipment. The chief rabbi raised 150 rubles in charitable contributions and donated this money to the farm in order to purchase a reaping machine and other agricultural equipment.[85] In 1904, Kreps delivered a series of public fundraising lectures in Odessa and other cities of southern Russia "on the question of the aptitude of Jews for agricultural labor, on the basis of the hundred-year experience of the Russian government."[86] Kreps donated the money raised by these lectures to the Jewish agricultural colonies, which were suffering from a bad harvest.[87] Essentially a modern and educated rabbi, Kreps tried to base his work on Jewish public opinion. He sought to publicize his work, reporting it in the Jewish press. However, Kreps signed his reports and opinions with pseudonyms, such as M. Krymskii, *Russkii Evrei* (Russian Jew), and *Ia Grazhdanin* (I the Citizen), to disguise his official status.[88] According to Kreps, in his capacity of chief rabbi, he delivered weekly sermons and speeches "on Biblical topics, ethical themes, and the pressing issues of public life linked to the contemporary matters of politics and government" for Jews in various localities of Kherson province.[89]

As chief rabbi, Kreps tried to coordinate the work of the government-sponsored and the unofficial traditional rabbinates, both on the local and imperial level. His initiatives in this area were fully supported by the DDDII. Kreps organized and chaired the "first regional rabbinical conference on various religious and daily life issues," which convened in the colony of Nagartav in Kherson province in 1899, and the "first all-Russian congress of government and spiritual [traditional] rabbis" in Nikolaev in 1901.[90] Kreps presented his reports on these conventions, including "the decisions and their substantiation by the rabbis," to the DDDII, which made use of these materials when developing the agenda for the Rabbinical Congress in St. Petersburg in 1910.[91] Kreps's organizational and bureaucratic talents as well as his practical accomplishments were noted by MVD officials and consequently, in 1907, he was appointed to the office of expert Jew under the DDDII at the MVD central offices in St. Petersburg. However, Kreps continued to work as chief rabbi of the Jewish colonies of Kherson province until 1917. Moreover, from 1902 to 1905, he was elected chief government rabbi of Odessa, the largest Jewish community in the Russian empire.[92]

During his ten-year tenure as expert Jew under the DDDII, Kreps was mostly assigned routine bureaucratic tasks, such as expert surveys of "various religious, private, public, political and other topics and issues of contemporary Jewish life" and monitoring and creating digests of the Jewish press in Russian, Hebrew, and Yiddish.[93] From 1908 to 1910, Kreps prepared the full compendium of resolutions and verdicts of the

Rabbinical Commission for use in the practical administration of the Jews. He also conducted substantial preliminary work for the last session of the Rabbinical Commission in 1909. Kreps summarized dozens of cases and did extensive legal research for examination by the Rabbinical Commission and by the Rabbinical Congress, which took place after the Commission's last session in 1910. Furthermore, Kreps worked as an official interpreter for the Rabbinical Congress.[94] In the 1900s and 1910s, based on the extensive official materials at his disposal, Kreps prepared entries "on alimony, marriages, divorces, rite of *chalitsa*, the Rabbinical Commission, rabbinical congresses, expert Jews and censorship of Jewish literature in Russia" for the fundamental Jewish encyclopedia in the Russian language.[95]

In 1917, after the February revolution, the Provisional Government granted full citizenship to the Russian Jews and declared freedom of conscience and religion for all Russian citizens. However, the new Russian government for the most part preserved the imperial MVD, including the DDDII and its expert Jew Moisei Kreps. In the fall of 1917, the government planned to transform the DDDII into a new Ministry of Faiths, and to appoint Kreps as its official. The Bolshevik Revolution of 1917 ultimately buried this initiative.

Kreps died in February 1942 in Leningrad, when the city was besieged by the German army.[96]

The bureaucratic career of Moisei Kreps was determined by his own early and deliberate choice. Kreps considered this career his priority, despite his solid training in chemistry, which he regarded as a backup alternative. Kreps did not consider a position in the government rabbinate as a mere means of material support. On the contrary, he saw it as a launching pad for an ambitious career in Jewish bureaucracy. This career path, blazed and developed by expert Jews of the previous generations, had become a feasible and desirable option for expert Jews of the third generation.

Despite the closing of the rabbinical seminaries and the liberal approach of the government to the cadres of the government rabbinate, the MVD still paid significant attention to the professionalism of the Jewish bureaucratic cadres. Kreps, who went through extensive traditional and modern rabbinical training, obviously realized its importance for a successful career. Consequently, his first appointment was a crucial position in the government rabbinate, and his performance in this office propelled his career to the top of the imperial Jewish bureaucracy.

However, Kreps's special education did not include the unique service ethos of the previous generation of expert Jews. The service ethos of the enlightened Russian bureaucrats, which inspired the ethos and mission of the Jewish bureaucrats of the second generation, had ultimately vanished from Russian officialdom. The spirit of reforms that permeated the MVD's policies from the 1850s to the 1880s was gradually replaced by a spirit of conservatism embodied by the repressive policies and sweeping bureaucratization of the government and society in late imperial Russia. Therefore, during his tenure as an expert Jew, Kreps was for the most part assigned routine, paperwork-centered, bureaucratic tasks. Furthermore, his extracurricular activities also reflected the ubiquitous bureaucratization. The topics of his entries for the Russian Jewish encyclopedia mostly represented areas of his bureaucratic scope, rather than his own research interests. The end of Kreps's career was the culmination of the bureaucratization of expert Jews. After the fall of the empire, Kreps naturally moved from the imperial MVD to the MVD under the Provisional Government, and expected to have an organic bureaucratic reincarnation within the new Ministry of Faiths. Kreps obviously considered his position an inherent and indispensable bureaucratic function, independent from the collapsed *ancien régime*. Thus, the expert Jew confidently anticipated a smooth transition of his office to yet another agency for perpetual "consulting work on Jewish matters, as exemplified by [Kreps's] more than decade long career at the DDDII."[97]

Official and Social Status of Expert Jews

The elite bureaucratic corps of expert Jews was a product of social engineering by the Russian government, which created the Jewish bureaucracy as an institutional and cadre base of official Jewish policy. The invention of the Jewish bureaucracy was an emulation of the archetypal imperial confessional policy, based on the co-optation and cooperation of traditional non-Russian and non-Christian elites.[98] The emergence of a Jewish bureaucratic elite also paralleled the modernization of the Russian administration, civil service, and bureaucratic cadres. The

MVD, the key institution responsible for the social and bureaucratic modernization of the whole empire, also shaped the Jewish bureaucratic elite and effectively integrated it into Russian officialdom.

What made expert Jews a unique group, a new secular Jewish elite? What, in other words, allowed them to rise above other Jews, and what brought them closer to Russians? First of all, expert Jews had official status: they were essentially Russian bureaucrats. This status was based on the common features of Russian and Jewish bureaucrats, including special training, official rank, material (salary), and non-material (social privileges and honors) benefits of bureaucratic service. Expert Jews enjoyed a relatively high official status, which provided a solid basis for their material well-being and elevated social status. Second, expert Jews had social status: they were a distinctive segment of the Russian bourgeois intelligentsia. This status was based on the commonalities between Jewish bureaucrats and the Russian bourgeoisie, including their family life, education, and the careers of their children, as well as extracurricular pursuits such as scholarship, journalism and belles-lettres, philanthropy, and business.

An analysis of the official and social status of expert Jews will demonstrate that their privileged position within officialdom and their bourgeois lifestyle, not only their service and mission, elevated expert Jews above traditional Jewish society and brought them closer to Russian bureaucracy.

Official Status

The history of Russian officialdom in the nineteenth century was marked by the growing professionalization and social prestige of the civil service. A successful bureaucratic career became dependent on special training received at educational institutions controlled by the government.[99] The economic and social success of professional bureaucrats also became more dependent on the government, which had at its disposal powerful mechanisms of control, including ranks, compensation, and honors, established by the all-encompassing system of the Table of Ranks.[100]

Expert Jews, with rare exceptions,[101] were not formally included in the Table of Ranks, since they were not entitled to the full benefits of civil service. Nevertheless, the careers of expert Jews were framed by the conceptual context of the Table. Thus, a long and unblemished service career had the same import for Russian as well as for Jewish bureaucrats, since it was linked to the concomitant acquisition of civil rights through honorary citizenship and nobility, privileged social status attainable by outstanding service.[102]

The bureaucratic careers of expert Jews were comparable to the typical career of a Russian provincial bureaucrat. As a rule, the career of an average Russian bureaucrat in the provinces started at the ranking position of the XIV class and culminated at the ranking position of the VIII class. The rank of the VIII class granted its holder the status of nobility, a most desirable goal and the culmination of the life-long service of bureaucrats of non-noble origin.[103] For Russian bureaucrats of the first category, those with higher education, the average interval between the rank of XIV and VIII classes was twenty-six years, and for bureaucrats of the second category, those with only secondary education, this interval was thirty years. The length of service was calculated from the appointment to the first ranking position and included all subsequent appointments.

According to the law, expert Jews could receive honorary citizenship (of comparable significance to Jewish bureaucrats as nobility for their Russian colleagues) after fifteen years of continuous unblemished service in the office of expert Jew, excluding service terms in any other office. The statistics of the service terms of Jewish bureaucrats in the office of expert Jew and other Jewish bureaucratic offices, such as the government rabbinate and teaching positions in government-sponsored Jewish schools,[104] demonstrate that the average Jewish bureaucrat started his career at the age of twenty-four, was appointed to the office of expert Jew at thirty-eight, and served in this office for sixteen years. Therefore, the majority of Jewish bureaucrats who served more than fifteen years in the office of expert Jew in addition to their previous appointments were obviously seeking honorary citizenship. The full length of service of the average Jewish bureaucrat, including his term in the office of expert Jew, was thirty years, similar to Russian bureaucrats of the second category, seeking nobility. The status of nobility was off-limits for Jewish bureaucrats, but for them honorary citizenship was a social stimulus of equal significance. Thus, expert Jews who achieved honorary citizenship through their service typologically matched Russian bureaucrats in ranks of the V–VIII classes, which made them members of the nobility.

Service in the central offices of the Russian ministerial system in St. Petersburg granted the maximal career and social success to Russian bureaucrats. Service in the provinces meant less prestige, less compensation, slower career growth, and lower social status. So the choice between the imperial capital and the provinces, for a service career, was a key factor for Russian bureaucrats.[105] Jewish bureaucrats did not have this choice, since all permanent Jewish bureaucratic offices, including expert Jews and government rabbinate, were in provincial and district administrations. However, the office of expert Jew was at the very top of the Jewish bureaucracy and was perceived as the culmination of a successful career. Only two people were appointed to the office of expert Jew at the very beginning of their careers. The majority of Jewish bureaucrats came a long way before reaching this office; eight of them started their careers as government rabbis, nine as teachers at government-sponsored Jewish schools.[106] The only Jewish bureaucratic position in St. Petersburg, expert Jew under the DDDII, was staffed on an irregular basis by a temporary[107] or joint appointment (combining the office of expert Jew under the DDDII with that of expert Jew under the governors of Kurland and Lifland provinces),[108] or by the occasional services of St. Petersburg government rabbis.[109] Only in 1907 did the MVD make a permanent appointment,[110] giving this office the status of a top destination for career Jewish bureaucrats.

Throughout the nineteenth century, special training and general education increasingly contributed to the career success of Russian bureaucrats. However, the capacity of the Russian educational system hardly met the growing needs of the bureaucracy. From 1857 to 1860, the annual pool of graduates of all Russian universities and other institutions of higher education resulted in 400 potential candidates for the 3,000 bureaucratic vacancies that opened annually in the same period.[111] The rabbinical seminaries, which produced the same number of graduates, about 400 certified rabbis and teachers in twenty-five years,[112] were also unable to satisfy the needs of the government rabbinate, in need of thousands of new recruits. In 1859–1860, there were 240 openings in the government rabbinate in just three out of fifteen provinces of the Pale of Settlement.[113]

However, for the institute of expert Jew, which throughout its history consisted of thirteen to twenty offices in all the provinces of the Pale, the situation was different. The position of expert Jew was mainly occupied by specially trained bureaucrats, that is, graduates of the rabbinical seminaries. Moreover, the overall educational profile of Jewish bureaucrats far exceeded the qualifications of their Russian colleagues. Forty-six percent of expert Jews had higher education (thirteen people, including three graduates of the rabbinical seminaries), and the remaining fifty-four percent of expert Jews had secondary education (fifteen people, including fourteen graduates of the rabbinical seminaries).[114]

The Russian cadres of the MVD and other imperial ministries demonstrated far less impressive credentials. From 1841 to 1859, among all Russian bureaucrats with ranks of V–VIII classes, only six percent had higher education, and twenty-six percent had secondary education.[115] By the end of the century these figures had grown modestly. From 1,096 Russian bureaucrats appointed by the MVD from 1894 to 1896, seventeen percent had higher education and ten percent had secondary education.[116] Thus, the educational level of expert Jews made them an outstanding phenomenon within Russian officialdom, and the high educational profile of Jewish bureaucrats also represented the ultimate realization of government policies aimed at the modernization and professionalization of the civil service and its bureaucratic cadres.

According to the law, the compensation of expert Jews ranged from 300 to 900 silver rubles annually. This range remained unchanged through all seven decades of the history of expert Jews. The exact amount of compensation of each expert Jew was decided by his immediate superior, the governor, on an individual basis, and was subject to the approval of the Minister of Internal Affairs. As a rule, governors adhered to the lower and upper limits stipulated by the law; however, in the middle, compensation of expert Jews varied.[117] Thus, three expert Jews received 250 rubles, four received between 300 and 450, fourteen received 600, fifteen received 900, one received 1,500, and one received 3,000. The rare cases when the amount of compensation was set below the limits stipulated by the law reflected part-time and auxiliary appointments, as in the case of the government rabbi of Poltava, Lev Zaidiner. In 1872, he was appointed acting expert Jew under the governor of Poltava province with an annual salary of 260 rubles, which supplemented a 500-ruble salary in his principal position as government rabbi.[118] The cases when the amount of compensation was set above the prescribed limits include the example of expert Jew Moisei Kreps. His salary was increased from 1,800 to 3,000 rubles to compensate for his resignation from the office of government rabbi of Kherson in order to devote himself fully to the service of expert Jew, which meant the loss of his rabbinical salary of 1,200 rubles.[119] In the 1900s and 1910s, the MVD adjusted the salaries of some expert Jews to the current economic conditions and growing inflation. Thus, the salary of expert Jew Osip Gurvich was increased from 900 to 1,500 rubles,[120] and the salary of expert Jew Moisei Kreps was increased from 900 to 1,800 rubles.[121]

The material compensation of Jewish bureaucrats challenged the choice made by Daniel Chwolson, who converted to Christianity "out of true conviction that it is better to be a professor in St. Petersburg than a melamed in Eishishok." The professional bureaucratic career of expert Jews also constituted a solid alternative for social mobility and integration as opposed to conversion to Christianity and an academic career pursued by St. Petersburg professor Chwolson. The service compensation alone, without other benefits and auxiliary income provided by such an official status, put expert Jews on a level of financial success inaccessible to melamdim and even to employees of the profitable Jewish excise tax-farming enterprises (*aktsizniki*). According to Abram Paperna, in the 1850s in the western provinces of the Pale of Settlement, Jews considered annual income from petty trade or from a *parnosa*—traditional communal occupations such as melamed or *dayyan* (member of the Jewish religious court)—in the amount of 150–200 rubles to be "enviable," and the 400–500 rubles of annual compensation of the *aktsizniki* "far exceeded the limits of happiness."[122] However, while the tax-farming business required from the Jews "just basic knowledge of the Russian language and arithmetic,"[123] a bureaucratic career required a substantial education and service ethos.

The material compensation of Jewish bureaucrats was also on a par with that of their Russian colleagues.[124] Russian bureaucrats of equal rank and in comparable positions under different Russian ministries were compensated differently. The largest compensation figures were for the Ministry of Finances (*Ministerstvo finansov* [MF]); the second ministry in terms of compensation was the MVD, followed by the Ministry of Justice (*Ministerstvo iustitsii* [MIU]), and the Ministry of National Enlightenment (*Ministerstvo narodnogo prosveshcheniia* [MNP]). In the 1840s and 1850s, the compensation of expert Jews was on a par with the following Russian bureaucrats: head of the governor's chancellery (MVD), who received 600 rubles; chairman of the provincial court chamber (MIU), from 700 to 1,000 rubles; and senior teacher in a provincial gymnasium (MNP), 393 rubles. However, unlike the salaries of expert Jews, salaries of Russian bureaucrats were regularly adjusted to the current economic conditions and growing inflation, and rose with increasing departmental budgets. In thirty years, from the mid-1850s to the mid-1880s, the salaries of Russian bureaucrats serving in the central agencies of the Russian ministerial system had a growth of 50 percent. Therefore, in the 1890s and 1900s, the compensation of expert Jews was on a par with the following Russian bureaucrats: deputy head of the governor's chancellery (MVD), who received 800 rubles; district police officer (*uchastkovyi pristav*) (MVD), 1,000 rubles; assistant district police officer (MVD), 600 rubles; teacher in a provincial gymnasium with university degree and five years' teaching experience (MNP), 900 rubles; and university professor (MNP), 3,000 rubles. As a result, while in the 1850s at the onset of Jewish bureaucracy, the compensation of expert Jews was on a par with compensation of Russian bureaucrats in the rank of the VIII class, a critical career point linked to a significant upgrade in social status, in the 1900s, the late years of Jewish bureaucracy, the compensation of expert Jews became comparable to salaries of Russian bureaucrats in the rank of the IX class.

Russian bureaucrats whose service required frequent travel were entitled to an official travel allowance (*raz"ezdnye*). For mid-level provincial bureaucrats, such as a district police officer and his assistant, this allowance was 300 rubles annually. Expert Jews, whose service also involved considerable travel, especially during the first period of their service history, with rare exceptions[125] did not receive a travel allowance.

What kind of lifestyle could expert Jews and their Russian colleagues afford based on their official salaries? As demonstrated by the sources, these salaries barely allowed both Russian and Jewish bureaucrats to maintain a high social status comparable to their official position. In the 1860s through the 1890s, the expenditures of the average Russian provincial bureaucrat in ranks of the XII–XIV classes, single, and living in rented quarters, amounted to 240 rubles a year.[126] Based on this figure, expert Jew Aaron Tseitlin, a single renter, could not afford 25 rubles to pay a bribe in order to keep his position.[127] With his annual compensation of 600 rubles, Tseitlin earned 50 rubles a month. Thus, his monthly expenditures, including 20 rubles for average living expenses, 15 rubles to aid his mother and brother, and 25 rubles for the bribe, would leave a 10-ruble deficit in his budget. In such circumstances, Russian bureaucrats had to supplement their official salaries with income from auxiliary sources such as private translation, editorial, and tutoring jobs, which provided about half of their total income.[128] As a rule, Jewish bureaucrats followed this example. In the 1900s, expert Jew Osip Gurvich, who had to feed a large family of eight, his wife, and seven children, earned in addition to his record salary of 1,500 rubles an additional 1,611 rubles annually by teaching the basics of the Jewish religion in two Minsk gymnasia.[129]

Medals, orders, and other signs of honor were as important a means of upward mobility and high social status for Russian bureaucrats as ranks and material remuneration. There was a hierarchy of these rewards, similar to the hierarchy of ranks. Medals were awarded for continuous unblemished service, gems were given for particular accomplishments, and orders were conferred for outstanding service achievements. Moreover, these awards were symbols of the high social status of the recipients and provided them with substantial benefits. Thus, until 1861, any Russian order granted nobility to its recipient.[130] The widow of a bureaucrat with an order was entitled to a government pension. Holders of the most prestigious orders gained access to the imperial court and were expected to attend its ceremonies, which shortened the physical and symbolic distance between the Russian emperor and his loyal servants, and let them into the confined circle where imperial politics was made. Medals, orders, and gems were coveted by bureaucrats of all ranks, since these awards signified recognition of service by the monarch and his personal favor toward the recipient, regardless of rank or office.[131]

Three expert Jews[132] were honored with medals—Osip Gurvich was given three,[133] Markus Gurovich four,[134] and Ruvim Shnitkind one.[135] Osip Gurvich's medals and other awards included a bronze medal "For active participation in the suppression of the Polish revolt of 1863–1864," awarded to him in 1864; a silver medal "For diligence" on the ribbon of the order of St. Stanislav, awarded to Gurvich in 1870 for "translation into

Russian of Jewish liturgical books and excellent execution of assigned missions"; a silver medal of the Red Cross society awarded in 1908 "as a tribute to [Gurvich's] contribution to the society's mission during the Russian-Japanese War"; and a diamond ring for presenting the emperor with the Russian translation of a Jewish prayer book.[136] Markus Gurovich was the only expert Jew honored with imperial orders. The orders of St. Anna and of St. Stanislav were conferred on him "for his diligence and hard work demonstrated by his service."[137]

In sum, the official status of expert Jews was comparable to the status of mid-level Russian provincial bureaucrats. The career objectives, education, compensation, and honorary awards of Jewish bureaucrats were on a par with similar attributes of their Russian colleagues, provincial bureaucrats of the second category, that is, those with secondary education, in the ranks of the V–VIII classes, and seeking the high social status of nobility as the ultimate reward for their service. Still, compared to their Russian counterparts, expert Jews were second-class bureaucrats, since the terms of their service did not entitle them to the full benefits of civil service, limited their upward social mobility to the status of honorary citizenship, and confined their career growth to the provincial administration.

Social Status

The new generation of educated Russian officials—enlightened bureaucrats—who came to work at the Russian ministries in the 1840s and 1850s not only represented the bureaucratic "vanguard of the reforms" but also the social transformation and enlightenment of Russian society. The enlightened bureaucrats were the trailblazers of social success through education and bureaucratic careers, and ultimately made that path attractive and prestigious. In the mid-1850s, some Russian government officials expressed their concern that "all enlightened Russians" preferred civil service to any other type of career. State Council members Dmitrii Nikolaevich Bludov and Iakov Ivanovich Rostovtsev warned, "If we remain on this track, which drags along enlightenment only through bureaucratic privileges, then Russia will not move forward in trade, industry and agriculture."[138] However, this warning did not change the situation when the civil service became an essential source of social prestige and the bureaucratic elite became the social elite.[139]

Like the service ethos of Russian enlightened bureaucrats, which influenced that of Jewish bureaucrats, shaping their careers and reinforcing their official status, the culture and lifestyle of Russian bureaucrats affected the social characteristics of Jewish bureaucrats. As a result, despite the Jewish background and the inherent traditional Jewish values of most expert Jews, Jewish bureaucrats gradually acquired the social—essentially bourgeois—characteristics of Russian bureaucracy and ultimately became one of its integral parts.

The family status of expert Jews was an important indicator of the social transformation and integration of Jewish bureaucrats.[140] In the family sphere, expert Jews for the most part maintained traditional Jewish values and practices. They did not marry outside their faith. The family lives of half the expert Jews had traditional Jewish features, including early marriage between the ages of sixteen to twenty,[141] large families with three to seven children,[142] frequent divorces, and new marriages, sometimes due to the infertility of a spouse.[143] However, the families of the other half of the expert Jews were smaller, with one to two children.[144] As a rule, children from these modernized families were given secondary and higher education at the best Russian and European schools,[145] and their careers testified to their integration in both Russian educated society[146] and in the Russian bureaucratic elite.[147] Thus, in the smaller families of Jewish bureaucrats, the secular education and professional careers of their children attested to the general modernization of the traditional Jewish family and the gradual acculturation of Jewish bureaucrats.

All expert Jews, excluding rare and marginal exceptions,[148] belonged to the Jewish faith. Information about the individual religiosity of expert Jews, for the most part scarce, indirect, and subjective,[149] suggests, however, that most expert Jews were rather indifferent toward religion. Expert Jews, both as individuals and as a group, never articulated any explicit position toward Judaism. They were neither atheists, nor pietists, nor reformers. In short, they were Russian bureaucrats of Jewish faith.

Although religion occupied a peripheral place in the private lives of expert Jews, it played a central role in their service. The majority of expert Jews had a solid religious education, acquired both at traditional and modern Jewish schools in Russia and Europe.[150] During their careers, many expert Jews served as government rabbis.[151] However, the performance of expert Jews in rabbinical office was affected not only by their individual attitudes toward religion, but also by their high official status as Russian bureaucrats, their mission of positive transformation of traditional Jewish society, and their service ethos based on devotion to Jewry.

According to Genrikh Sliozberg, Lev Zaidiner, expert Jew under the governor of Poltava province and government rabbi of Poltava in the 1860s and 1870s, "did not play any role in the life of the local Jewish community."[152] Zaidiner, a graduate of the rabbinical seminary of Zhitomir, was "an insignificant person, without any Jewish erudition, shy and characterless before his superiors; he did not demonstrate any courage or initiative with the Jews either. He did not have any authority . . . he never delivered any sermons. He lacked piety altogether."[153] In sharp contrast to Zaidiner, his predecessor in the rabbinical office of Poltava and graduate of the rabbinical seminary of Vilna, Iona Gurliand, according to Sliozberg, "used his [rabbinical] authority as a real bureaucrat, personifying the watchful eye of the government."[154] In particular, Gurliand prohibited dancing at the synagogue during *Simchat Torah* celebrations, and even ordered a pious Jew celebrating in a particularly cheerful manner removed from the synagogue. Thus, Gurliand tried to fulfill "the responsibility of government rabbi, who, according to the law, should enforce order during public worship."[155] At the same time, some expert Jews who served as government rabbis, such as Aaron Pumpianskii, government rabbi in Riga and expert Jew under the governors of Lifland and Kurland, considered their rabbinical authority not only an instrument of government control, but also a means of social amelioration of the Jews.[156]

Pumpianskii and several other expert Jews in the posts of government rabbi proved to be actual leaders of their communities. These expert Jews and rabbis were able to promote Jewish interests without circumventing the limits imposed by their official status.[157] The role of Jewish bureaucrats as the new Jewish social elite was fully manifest in their work as government rabbis. For the most part, Jewish bureaucrats held rabbinical positions in the largest urban centers of the Russian empire, St. Petersburg, Moscow, Odessa, and Riga, which were situated beyond the Pale of Settlement. The Jewish population of these cities had a high level of modern education and high degree of integration in Russian society.

Therefore, the Jewish bureaucrats serving as rabbis in these communities assumed the status of a social and political, rather than religious, elite within the essentially bourgeois social environment of acculturated Russian Jews.[158] The authority of these rabbis was based not on their traditional religious erudition and piety, but on their organizational abilities and political resources, held in esteem by their modern communities.

The extracurricular activities and non-bureaucratic occupations of expert Jews provide additional insight into their social status.[159] Literary pursuits such as journalism, literary translations and criticism, and belles-lettres were a major extracurricular activity of expert Jews. Many expert Jews taught Jewish subjects at Russian and Jewish schools and gymnasia. Three expert Jews, Iona Gurliand and Markus Gurovich in Odessa and V. L. Kagan in Vilna, were founders and directors of private Jewish schools.[160] Five expert Jews, including Iona Gershtein in Vilna, Avraam Neiman in St. Petersburg, and Aaron Pumpianskii in Riga, worked for Jewish public and charitable causes as overseers and executives of non-official Jewish organizations, ranging from a gymnasium fund for the support of needy students, to a Talmud Torah, to the OPE.[161] Two expert Jews ran their own businesses or were involved in larger enterprises— Sheftel Kliachko owned profitable real estate in Vilna,[162] and Grigorii Schkliaver sat on the board of the Vilna main inspection office of a Russian insurance company.[163] The scholarship of expert Jews Moisei Berlin and German Barats brought them official recognition from the Russian academy, and they were given membership in prestigious scholarly societies—the Society for Russian History and Antiquities, the Imperial Russian Geographic Society, and the Historical Society of Nestor the Chronicler.[164] Finally, expert Jews pursued liberal professions such as jurisprudence practiced by attorney-at-law German Barats,[165] and medicine practiced by Dr. Isaak Kaminer.[166]

On the one hand, extracurricular activities and non-bureaucratic occupations provided expert Jews with a living, since they were barely sustained by their official compensation. On the other hand, these activities and occupations significantly contributed to the social integration of Jewish bureaucrats in Russian society, to their embourgeoisement, and their transformation into the rudimentary Russian middle class.

In sum, the biographical materials on expert Jews reveal two parallel processes that shaped their social status and bureaucratic careers. Their professional activity and service ethos were affected by the process of bureaucratization of the Russian state and society, while their social and family lives and public activities were affected by social integration into Russian society and embourgeoisement. The cumulative effect of these processes was to drive expert Jews away from traditional Jewish values and lifestyle and bring them closer to the social environment of Russian bureaucracy. Ultimately, Jewish bureaucrats became less Jewish and increasingly resembled their fellow Russian bureaucrats, whose service ethos, political beliefs, and culture they emulated.

4

Jews, Law, and Order

Service of Expert Jews

The "Statute" and the "Secret Regulation" of 1850 put expert Jews under the exclusive control of the provincial governors and limited their bureaucratic scope to the exposure of Jewish religious "fanaticism" and its eradication through moral influence on traditional Jews. In practice, the central and provincial branches of the MVD increasingly commissioned expert Jews with diverse assignments, including the collection of statistical data on the Jewish population, monitoring of the implementation of legislation and administrative regulations, and even administrative intervention in the religious and social lives of the Jews. Thus, the office of expert Jew became the key institute of imperial Jewish policy.

The service history of expert Jews parallels their institutional history described in chapter 2. There were three distinct periods in the evolution of the official mission and objectives of the bureaucratic work of Jewish officials. These periods are defined by the common functions and specific tasks assigned to expert Jews by their superiors (governors and governor-generals) within the broader political agenda of the MVD. The shifting bureaucratic priorities and routines of expert Jews therefore reflect major turns and shifts of official Jewish policy as a whole, most notably its increasing bureaucratization.

In the 1850s, during the first period of the service history of expert Jews, their primary mission was the accumulation of essential and accurate information on the Jewish population of the empire. Expert Jews shared this mission with the district government rabbinate, the lower echelon of religious administration for the Jews.[1] The district rabbinate collected vital statistics on the Jews, the critical hard data on which the MVD's decisions and administration of the Jewish population were based. Expert Jews provided the authorities with information on various aspects of the history, ethnography, culture, religion, and the economy of traditional Eastern European Jewish society. This information constituted the fundamental knowledge base for the MVD's policymaking and everyday administration of imperial Jewish subjects. In addition to information on Jewish life, the MVD commissioned expert Jews with assessing changes in traditional Jewish society brought by the government reforms of the 1830s and 1840s. According to Osip Lerner, "The top administration needed to know whether and how its [reformative] designs, so significant de jure, caught on de facto; which fruits did two decades of government efforts, aimed at bringing order to the Jewish lifestyle and inculcating basic civic values in the Jews, yield?"[2]

In the 1850s, the service of expert Jews consisted mostly of assignments related to the institutions and operations of the newly established religious administration for the Jews.[3] The governors on a regular basis dispatched expert Jews to inspect the local Jewish officials and institutions, including district government rabbis, religious boards of prayer assemblies, synagogues, communal asylums and hospitals; and to expose illegal remnants of kahal autonomy, including unofficial "spiritual" rabbis, Hasidic leaders (*tzadikim*), unauthorized religious courts (*batei din*), and private prayer assemblies (*minyanim*). When on their missions, expert Jews inspected official population registers kept by Jewish officials and institutions: *metricheskie knigi* (metric books) for the registration of births, deaths, marriages, and divorces, and *shnurovye knigi* (lit., string books, in which pages are bound together with string and sealed by official seal to ensure the integrity of the records) for the registration of members of Jewish prayer assemblies, or "synagogue parishioners." Expert Jews also audited the communal financial transactions that local Jewish communities were required to submit to the government.

Official assignments related to government initiatives aimed at the dissemination of secular education and productive labor among Jews constituted a significant proportion of the service of expert Jews. The Jewish bureaucrats regularly inspected both government-sponsored and private secular Jewish schools. The provincial administration even attempted, unsuccessfully, to place traditional private Jewish teachers (melamdim) under the control of expert Jews. Expert Jews sat on many administrative committees for the implementation of official educational policy, including the promotion of private boarding schools for Jewish girls, and the establishment of the official qualification examination for melamdim by boards of the provincial gymnasium directors and expert Jews. Expert Jews contributed to the promotion of productive labor among the Jewish population. The MVD and the provincial governors commissioned expert Jews with developing projects and regulations to introduce Jews to agriculture, including vocational classes at government and community-sponsored Jewish schools, such as Talmud Torah, promotion of gardening, and regulation of the social status of the *evrei-zemledel'tsy* (Jewish farmers).

Expert Jews provided their official expertise on Judaism and Jewish culture, especially when state policies targeted particular Jewish customs or whole areas of traditional Jewish life as antisocial manifestations of Jewish "fanaticism." This expertise covered such areas as the validity of the civil and court oaths of the Jews, the social impact of the Hasidic religious schism, and the subversive aspects of Jewish liturgy, such as the ritual of *Kol Nidre*.

In the 1850s, the service of expert Jews included a few odd assignments based on the individual approach and immediate concerns of the governors, violating the limits set by the "Statute" and "Secret Regulation" of 1850.[4] However, some of these assignments, including participation in police investigations, arbitration in disputes between Jews, and censorship of Jewish publications, eventually became common tasks of expert Jews.

Thus, in the 1850s, during the first period of the service history of expert Jews, their official niche within government bureaucracy was established. Russian bureaucrats used expert Jews as a chief means of control of the newly established state administration for the Jews, including its religious, communal, and educational institutions. In addition, expert Jews aided the MVD, providing critical information for policies aimed at overcoming Jewish social isolation (or "fanaticism," in bureaucratic parlance) through the adaptation of traditional Jewish social structure and religious law to the social and legal frameworks of imperial society.

In the 1860s, during the second period of the service history of expert Jews, the adoption of the Great Reforms—especially the Court Reform of 1864—became the priority for Jewish bureaucrats. The Great Reforms were first implemented by the government in the *vnutrennie gubernii* (inner provinces) of central Russia. In the remote parts of the empire, including the western and southwestern provinces populated by Jews, the government implemented reforms gradually and on a selective basis. Therefore, in the 1860s, the administrative, social, and legal order in the provinces of the Pale of Settlement had both pre-reform and post-reform features. Expert Jews contributed to the implementation of the new order through their routine bureaucratic assistance to the authorities as well as through involvement in direct actions and administrative measures. This new aspect of the expert Jews' service reflected the increased trust of the Russian administrators in their official Jewish aides. The central and provincial administration of the MVD started to consider the Jewish officials—expert Jews—an integral part of Russian officialdom. As a result, the bureaucratic scope of expert Jews often went beyond the limits set by the MVD regulations and became closely intertwined with the functions of Russian bureaucrats.

During the second period of the service history of expert Jews, assignments related to the institutional control of the state administration for the Jews still made up a substantial proportion of the workload.[5] However, the nature of these assignments changed. In the 1850s, they were mostly bureaucratic inspections of Jewish religious and communal institutions and their official records, while in the 1860s they included some administrative functions, including the official appointment of expert Jews to the normally elected office of government district rabbis. During this period, the MVD and the provincial administrators increasingly appointed expert Jews to their advisory policymaking institutions for the development of administrative measures and legislation. These institutions included the Rabbinical Commission of 1861 under the MVD, where expert Jews were the majority, and the Special Commission on Jewish Burial Societies (*chevra kadisha*) of 1868 under the governor-general of Vilna, Kovno, and Grodno, which included three expert Jews.[6]

The government also sanctioned the direct involvement of expert Jews in the implementation of the government-sponsored Jewish school system. On assignment and with support from the Ministry of State

Domains, the Patronage Committee for Foreign Settlers in Southern Russia, and the governor-general of Novorossiia and Bessarabiia, the expert Jew under the governor-general engaged in substantial fieldwork aimed at the establishment of government-sponsored elementary Jewish schools in Kherson province. Expert Jews' activities ranged from mobilization of communal support to renting, renovating, and equipping classrooms with basic furniture.

Before the introduction in the provinces of the Pale of Settlement of the universal public justice system and its institutions created by the Court Reform of 1864, the expert Jew on assignment from the governor of Poltava province arbitrated in disputes between Jews when at least one of the sides was appealing to the provincial administration. In most cases, including divorce proceedings and small material claims, the expert Jew managed to "reach a settlement between the sides."[7] When reformed courts and procedures were finally established across the provinces of the Pale of Settlement, expert Jews were commissioned to reconcile the general Russian legal system and court proceedings with the norms of *halacha*, Jewish religious law, and its institutions, such as *batei din*, rabbinical courts. In particular, the Jewish bureaucrats adapted the general forms and procedures of the court oaths of witnesses, jurors, and attorneys for the Jews.

At the end of the second period of the service history of expert Jews, their service niche expanded considerably due to the unification of the bureaucratic functions of Jewish officials with the general bureaucratic administration under the MVD. During the era of the Great Reforms, the bureaucratic role of expert Jews grew beyond that of a mere instrument of control—to active practical implementation of government Jewish policies.

During the third period, from the 1870s to the 1910s, the service of expert Jews was affected by the growing political conservatism and mounting administrative and police functions of the MVD. In the 1870s, the service missions of expert Jews still involved social reforms and the institutional transformation of Jewish life. However, as the political discord between the Russian government and society, including Jews, intensified, the expert Jews' work became focused on purely bureaucratic tasks supporting conservative political order and policing of the Jewish population.

From the 1870s through the 1910s, assignments linked to the official policy of social integration of the Jews, including overcoming "fanaticism," promotion of modern education, and productive occupations, completely disappeared from the service agenda of expert Jews.[8] The proportion of assignments related to supervision of Jewish religious and communal institutions considerably shrank in the official workload of the Jewish bureaucrats. Moreover, these assignments reflected the consolidation and mounting bureaucratization of the state administration of Jewish religious affairs. In 1908, the DDDII commissioned its expert Jew to prepare a full compendium of the resolutions and verdicts of the Rabbinical Commission for use in the practical administration of the Jews. The expert Jew under the DDDII conducted substantial preliminary work for the last session of the Rabbinical Commission in 1909, including summaries and extensive legal research of the cases on the agenda, and for the Rabbinical Congress that followed the Commission's session in 1910. At the congress, which was initiated and sponsored by the DDDII and the MVD, the religious leaders of Russian Jews along with representatives of the secular Jewish elites discussed the unification of religious administration, including such measures as elimination of the "double" ("spiritual" and government) rabbinate and bureaucratization of the rabbinical office.[9]

By the 1880s, expert Jews' assignments related to social and administrative reform faded away along with era of the Great Reforms. However, the Jewish bureaucrats were still commissioned with adapting imperial legislation to the Jews, including reconciliation of the Jewish tradition and *halacha* with post-reform Russian court procedures and compliance of Jews with universal military service introduced by the Military Reform of 1874. Instead, chancellery paperwork grew to constitute the major component of the service of expert Jews. These assignments reflected the contemporary realities of Jewish life, such as the mass emigration of Jews from the Russian empire, manifest in the "rapidly mounting demand" for travel documents and passports dutifully met by the expert Jew on the assignment of the governor.[10]

In the 1900s and 1910s, expert Jews' assignments were mainly related to the administrative and police measures of the MVD aimed at suppression of radical political opposition and containment of the revolutionary movement in the empire. These assignments included involvement of expert Jews in a range of procedures, from monitoring the Jewish press for the Department of Police to auxiliary functions such as translation and forensic expertise in the investigation of political crimes.

In the third period of the service history of expert Jews, their firm integration within the structures of the MVD saved the institute of Jewish officials from becoming an atavistic remnant of the Jewish reforms from the 1840s to the 1860s. Expert Jews had become an indispensable part of Russian officialdom. The evolution of the political role and functions of Jewish bureaucracy paralleled the institutional development of the MVD and the Russian ministerial system as a whole.

In the early stages of Jewish bureaucracy, the MVD, the largest and most powerful agency of the Russian government, was the driving force of the unprecedented political, social, and economic reforms affecting all strata of imperial society, including Jews. The enormous breadth of the Great Reforms resulted in the vast institutional expansion of the MVD and its bureaucratic functions, with the purpose of consolidating the entire spectrum of social life of imperial subjects under government administration, including the religious administration for Jews. Thus, in post-reform Russia, all issues of domestic policy were concentrated within the departments of one government agency, the MVD. Despite its inflated authority, this oversized institution was overloaded and ultimately paralyzed by the avalanche of pending bureaucratic cases, which considerably impeded any structural or functional improvement. As a result, the MVD's policies largely relied on essentially bureaucratic methods, including the growing involvement of its numerous officials.[11] This bureaucratization of official domestic policy in the late Russian empire was fully manifested in the service history of expert Jews. From 1850 to 1917, Jewish bureaucrats, initially intended to be the vanguard of government reforms aimed at the social transformation of the Russian Jews, evolved into chancellery pettifoggers, buried in bureaucratic cases.

Typology of Expert Jews' Missions

The "Statute" and "Secret Regulation" of 1850 outlined the basic categories of service missions for expert Jews. However, these categories, such as "investigation," "inspection," "exposure," and "influence," were ambiguously and loosely defined, thus leaving interpretation and practical initiative up to the superiors of the Jewish bureaucrats.[12] As a result, from 1850 to 1917 the provincial governors and central departments of the MVD charged the expert Jews with the following basic commissions: (1) inspection trips, (2) investigations and legal proceedings, (3) legal, religious, ethnographic, and historical expertise, (4) policymaking and implementation of administrative measures, and (5) official translation and chancellery work.

The priority and proportion of these missions in the service of expert Jews varied considerably from period to period of their service history. In the 1850s during the first period, inspection trips to monitor implementation of official Jewish policy and improve institutions, including rabbinical, educational, religious, and communal organizations, dominated the work of expert Jews. In the 1860s during the second period, direct involvement in policymaking and administrative implementation of official Jewish policy prevailed. Expert Jews actively contributed to many administrative agencies dealing with various aspects of Jewish policy; they served as the legal authority—surrogate justices of the peace—in disputes between Jews, and even used their moral influence, a technique usually prescribed by official regulations but rarely implemented in real life. In the 1870s to the 1910s during the last period, the work of expert Jews moved from Jewish social and religious life to the insulated world of bureaucratic chancelleries and departments. In these years, the service agenda of expert Jews involved for the most part pure bureaucratic tasks, including monitoring of Jewish public opinion through translation and digesting the Jewish press; formal chancellery paperwork on the registration and issuing of official documents such as passports; investigation of political crime in the capacity of official interpreters and experts of the police and courts; and technical expertise in various matters related to the history, religion, and lifestyle of the Jews necessary for bureaucratic proceedings of the provincial governors, DDDII, and other departments of the MVD.

The changing priorities apparent in the missions of the expert Jews were due to their increasing bureaucratization, which paralleled the general development within Russian officialdom.[13] However, the sprawl of bureaucratization in late imperial Russia reached far beyond officialdom. The government sought to extend its bureaucratic control over all unofficial and even private aspects of social life, thus establishing a universal bureaucratic order. Increasing and all-encompassing bureaucratization was also a fundamental feature of official Jewish policy, as demonstrated by the following survey of typical missions of expert Jews.

Inspection Trips

In the 1850s and early 1860s, inspection trips were the main official work of expert Jews. Jewish officials reported their findings, including information about Jewish religious, communal, educational, and charitable institutions, their personnel and record-keeping practices, to the governors. Expert Jews often supplemented their official reports with memoranda on those aspects of Jewish religious rituals, traditional lifestyle, and economy targeted by the special policies of the provincial administration and central departments of the MVD. Starting in the early 1850s, the governors usually included data accumulated by the expert Jews' inspections in their annual reports submitted to the emperor through the MVD.[14] As a rule, the governors used the information collected by expert Jews during their inspections as a basis for planning and implementing administrative measures.[15] In general, the governor-generals and governors highly valued the utility of the inspection trips of expert Jews and expressed appreciation for this service through official rewards.

In 1853, the governor-general of Vitebsk, Mogilev, and Smolensk provinces, Prince Andrei Mikhailovich Golitsyn (in office 1845–1853), dispatched his expert Jew, Moisei Berlin, to inspect Jewish religious institutions in the city of Mogilev. On the verbal order of the governor-general, Berlin was also told to "delve into Jewish rites and customs, and report about practices which had no basis in pure Mosaic law, but were initiated by perverse interpretations of rabbis promoting ignorance and moral degradation."[16]

In four months, while on his inspection trip, the expert Jew accomplished his mission and presented three reports to the governor-general. The first included information on thirty-one Jewish religious, communal, and charitable organizations. This report was based on the *perechnevaia vedomost'* (tabulated data sheet), a special statistical format developed by Berlin for inspection missions. It had twenty categories, including "location, term of operation, number of parishioners, dominant mode of rituals, income, expenses, assets and properties, names of wardens, cantors and Torah readers."[17] The two other reports of the expert Jew addressed the verbal commission of the governor-general and exposed the illegal activity and "fanaticism" of the Jews of Mogilev. One report, in addition to a description of "disorder and deviation from the organizational principles established by the law, the endemic feature of the Jewish religious organization in Mogilev," included information on the Jewish burial society, *chevra kadisha*, the constant concern of the imperial administration due to its alleged violations of the government fiscal monopoly. Another report exposed the practice of "early marriages between the Jews, lacking any basis in Mosaic law, and the harmful consequences of these marriages."[18]

Governor-general Pavel Nikolaevich Ignat'ev (in office 1853–1855), who replaced Prince Andrei Golitsyn, approved the official use of the statistical format developed by the expert Jew "for all future inspections of the districts."[19] However, Ignat'ev did not take any administrative action on the information that the expert Jew provided. Instead, he forwarded Berlin's reports to the DDDII for further consideration. As a result, the issue of early marriages between Jews was placed on the agenda of the Rabbinical Commission during its session in 1861.[20] Jewish burial societies became a subject of discussion initiated by the MVD in the 1860s, and were the exclusive matter on the agenda of the Special Commission on Jewish Burial Societies under the governor-general of Vilna, Kovno, and Grodno provinces in 1868.[21]

In 1854, Governor-general Ignat'ev dispatched expert Jew Berlin to sixteen Jewish communities in the Orsha and Senno districts of Mogilev province. In addition to the regular inspection of Jewish religious and communal organizations, the expert Jew was told to inspect Jewish schools, both government-sponsored and private. On the verbal order of the governor-general, Berlin was also to "explore the way of life of the Jewish farmers, determine any disorders and their causes."[22]

For three months the expert Jew traveled extensively through the two districts and finally presented six reports to the governor-general summarizing his findings and conclusions. In his main report, Berlin listed unofficial Jewish communal organizations and violations of the law in the work of official organizations, including inadequate record keeping and improper conducting of rituals. The report was supplemented by statistical data sheets with information on sixty-three Jewish religious and communal organizations. The expert Jew's additional five reports covered important aspects of Jewish social and religious life. The first of these reports surveyed the government-sponsored Jewish schools of the city of Orsha and the town of Liubavichi in the Orsha district. Berlin pointed out the inadequate qualification of the teachers and general poor condition of these schools. He declared the patronage of the *pochetnyi popechitel'* (honorary superintendent), Hasidic rebbe Menachem Mendel Shneerson, over this Liubavichi government-sponsored Jewish school as well as its exemplary status to be "fictional." In fact, according to Berlin, the condition of the school was unsatisfactory.[23] The second report described the condition of traditional private Jewish schools, *chadarim*, and their teachers, melamdim, and proposed measures aimed at improving and regulating these educational institutions.[24] The third report described inadequate record-keeping practices of Jewish religious and communal organizations. The law stipulated the registration of members of Jewish prayer assemblies, or "synagogue parishioners" in *shnurovye knigi*.[25] According to the expert Jew, the majority of the communities did not keep *shnurovye knigi*, and, moreover, local Jewish officials intentionally "evaded following the procedure stipulated by law."[26] The fourth confidential report exposed the problem of the double rabbinate, defined by the expert Jew as "the illegitimate yet influential office of spiritual rabbis, existing throughout the inspected communities without the approval or even knowledge of the authorities, while the official rabbis approved by the authorities were essentially fictional and formal figures of the humblest backgrounds and without any influence in the community."[27] Berlin supplemented this report with a list of clandestine spiritual rabbis and official government rabbis in every inspected Jewish community, including all available private information for each rabbi on the list.[28] The fifth report examined the issue of Jewish farmers. According to the expert Jew, he "sincerely described the conditions of this estate," pointing out the deficiencies of the Jewish farmers as well as the administrative flaws of the local authorities who regulated them. As part of his assignment, Berlin developed instructions for the Jewish farmers, outlining their basic "duties and responsibilities, rights and privileges" and also translating it into Yiddish.[29]

On the basis of the information provided by the expert Jew, Governor-general Ignat'ev ordered immediate administrative actions. He initiated circular directives by the governor of Mogilev province aimed at tightening the regulation of Jewish religious and communal institutions and melamdim. Moreover, Ignat'ev dispatched several of his officials for special missions to the districts to "bring order to the Jewish religious organizations according to the letter of the civil laws."[30] The governor-general paid special attention to the materials on Jewish farmers presented by the expert Jew. Ignat'ev solicited official approval of the MVD for the implementation of the measures proposed by Berlin in the Vitebsk, Mogilev, and Smolensk provinces, or at least for partial realization of these measures, such as the establishment of the *pochetnye popechiteli* (honorary patrons) of Jewish farmers, appointed from the local nobility.[31]

In 1854, the governor-general of Novorossiia and Bessarabiia, Nikolai Nikolaevich Annenkov (in office 1854–1855), sent his expert Jew Markus Gurovich on an inspection trip to the Jewish communities of Kherson, Ekaterinoslav, and Tavrida provinces and the city of Taganrog. As in Berlin's case, the principal objective of the mission, by order of the governor-general, was to inspect Jewish religious and charitable organizations and assess their compliance with the law and "conformity to their official mandate."[32]

For four months, the expert Jew inspected Jewish communities in eleven cities and towns and in seven Jewish agricultural colonies.[33] Gurovich presented the results of his mission to the governor-general in two reports: one on the cities, another on the colonies. According to Osip Lerner, the reports of the expert Jew revealed the "wide gap between law and life, between words and deeds."[34] Gurovich's descriptions of Jewish religious life and its institutions in every city he visited featured the same "uniformly depressing phenomena":[35] illegal religious and charitable institutions;[36] inadequate record keeping and procedural violations in lawful institutions, including unauthorized spending of the funds of the *korobochnyi sbor*, lack of religious boards, parish registers (*shnurovye knigi*) and proper accounting prescribed by the law;[37] ritual disorder and predominance of chaotic traditional, and even Hasidic, rites in public worship in synagogues;[38] widespread existence of unofficial spiritual rabbis; and general incompetence, greed, and abuse of power by official government rabbis.[39]

In addition to these facts, pointed out by Moisei Berlin as well, Markus Gurovich paid special attention to the improvement of the

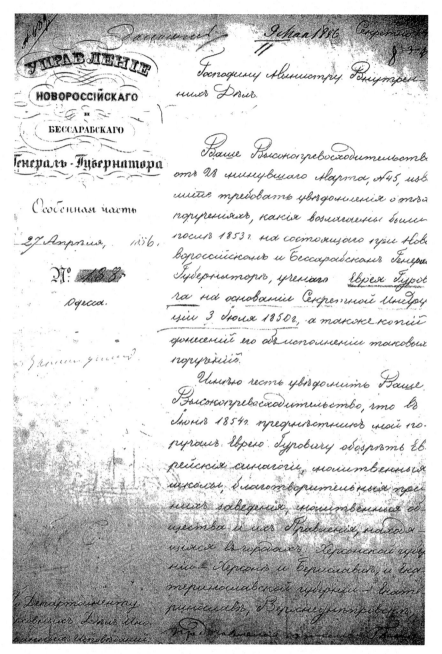

Novorossiia and Bessarabiia Governor-general's report about inspection trip of expert Jew Markus Gurovich, April 27, 1856 (RGIA, f. 821, o. 8, d. 397, l. 8)

existing practices of collection and distribution of the funds from the kosher meat excise tax (*korobochnyi sbor*), the main financial basis of the religious administration for the Russian Jews.[40] Gurovich proposed putting the distribution of these funds under the control of expert Jews. Thus, the draft budgets of Jewish communities and organizations, subject to approval of the provincial administration, would be examined by the expert Jews under the governor-generals, since "these expert Jews, being in charge of inspection of the synagogues and [Jewish] charitable institutions, knew the needs of the Jewish communities better than anyone else."[41]

Besides data on Jewish religious and community organizations, Gurovich's report on Jewish agricultural colonies provided information on the economy and lifestyle of Jewish farmers. According to the expert Jew, the general condition of the colonies was poor and in economic decline. Gurovich laid the blame for this on Jewish colonists themselves, who preserved their "unproductive" occupations and traditional lifestyle.[42] This situation was particularly evident in the older populous colonies such as Efingar' and Bobrovyi Kut, funded by the government and periodically replenished (in 1808, 1822, and 1840) by an influx of fresh migrants perpetuating traditional lifestyles.[43] Conversely, according to the expert Jew, the newly established private colonies, such as one founded in 1846 by Khaskel Morgonovskii, demonstrated rapid economic growth "unheard of in the government-sponsored colonies."[44] Gurovich concluded that the poor condition of the government-sponsored colonies was mostly due to their inadequate administration by the authorities. The expert Jew argued that as soon as this administration was improved, "through agricultural labor and increasing enthusiasm of the Jews, the elements of civic awareness would emerge among them."[45]

The expert Jew proposed several measures aimed at the amelioration of the substandard social and economic conditions of the government-sponsored colonies. For the most part, these measures would establish administrative obstacles against the preservation and spread of the traditional Jewish lifestyle. They included a ban on non-agricultural occupations for the colonists, restriction on their free migration, and establishment of a maximum age limit for new colonists preventing the influx of older Jews, guardians of the traditional lifestyle.[46]

The expert Jew also recommended appointing acculturated and educated rabbis capable of instilling diligence in the colonists.[47] Gurovich boldly moved from words to deeds in his practical work. In 1856, the chairman of the Patronage Committee for Foreign Settlers in Southern Russia pointed out the significant role of the expert Jew, which was apparent during his inspection trip. According to the chairman, expert Jew Gurovich "presented the advantages of the agricultural occupation to the Jewish settlers, instilled in them absolute respect for the authorities, educated them about their responsibilities to society, family and children; in short, he left no subject untouched and provided appropriate and helpful advice. . . . If the Jewish colonies were visited more frequently by people like Mr. Gurovich, who had an appropriate outlook and clear understanding of the government's purposes, then Jewish farmers would better understand their own goals and would aim to achieve them, since admonitions by officials of a different religion would never have the same beneficial impact among the Jews, as the words of those who practiced the same religion and belonged to the family of the Jewish people."[48] This documented example of "moral exhortation" of the Jews demonstrated that this method, essential to the mandate of expert Jews according to official regulations, was actually, though rarely, implemented in the practical work of Jewish bureaucrats and was greatly appreciated by their superiors.

In 1854 due to the outbreak of the Crimean War, which directly affected the provinces inspected by the expert Jew, "the official reaction to Gurovich's reports was postponed until more favorable circumstances arose."[49] However, in 1856 the new governor-general of Novorossiia and Bessarabiia, Aleksandr Grigor'evich Stroganov (in office 1855–1862), ordered administrative actions based on the expert Jew's findings. These included a ban on unofficial spiritual rabbis, dismissal of the incompetent government rabbis misusing their official authority, and abolishment of illegal synagogues and prayer houses discovered by the expert Jew. Stroganov ordered the governors of Kherson and Ekaterinoslav provinces to study the feasibility of the expert Jew's proposal on the distribution of funds of the *korobochnyi sbor* and, when possible, to implement the measures recommended by Gurovich. The governor-general sent another proposal of the expert Jew, recommending the establishment of a central hospital and central school for the Jewish agricultural colonies, for examination by the Patronage Committee for Foreign Settlers in Southern Russia. Yet another of the expert Jew's proposals, recommending the publication and distribution of the regulations on official record-keeping and accounting for Jewish religious and communal institutions, was supported by the governor-general and submitted for approval to the MVD.[50]

Official missions similar to the inspections of Moisei Berlin and Markus Gurovich were assigned to expert Jew Aaron Tseitlin by the governor of Poltava province, Aleksandr Pavlovich Volkov (in office 1853–1866). In 1860, the governor ordered the expert Jew to inspect the private Jewish schools, synagogues, and prayer houses in Poltava province. Tseitlin was told to verify the legitimacy of the Jewish religious and communal institutions, which had to have valid formal authorization, and to examine the record-keeping practices of community officials, including registration of lifecycle events and parishioners as well as accounting. The governor recommended that the expert Jew conduct such inspections on a regular basis, without special order, while traveling through the province on other missions.

In open violation of the "Secret Regulation" of 1850, which absolutely prohibited the governors from giving any fiscal commissions to the expert Jews, Governor Volkov dispatched his expert Jew to supervise the collection of the *korobochnyi sbor* in the districts of Poltava province. Moreover, in defiance of the confidentiality prescribed by the "Secret Regulation," the governor publicized the mission of the expert Jew. In 1860 by order of Volkov, Tseitlin's findings and recommendations on Jewish tax collecting practices were published in the *Poltavskie gubernskie vedomosti*, the official periodical of the provincial administration.[51]

In general, expert Jews carried out the two essential missions assigned to them by the provincial and central administration of the MVD on their inspection trips. First, they collected complete and accurate information about the Jews, a vital resource for both everyday administration and long-term policymaking.[52] Second, despite their inherent lack of administrative power, expert Jews served as extensions of the administration, reaching the remote districts of the Pale of Settlement. They successfully accomplished these missions largely due to their personal involvement and positive attitude. While working on their assignments, they demonstrated due diligence and great enthusiasm.

Investigations and Legal Proceedings

Investigations and legal proceedings were largely conducted by expert Jews during the first and second periods of their service history, from the 1850s to the 1870s. While these assignments constituted a minor portion of their workload, they were by no means marginal.

The investigations carried out by expert Jews mainly focused on Jewish "fanaticism," perceived as the main impediment to the social integration of the Jews. The "Secret Regulation" of 1850 gave a typology of fanaticism, including its religious (anti-Christian) and social (anti-government) forms, and suggested that the governors use their expert Jews to investigate "fanaticism" in the Jewish population. As a rule, the governors followed this recommendation.

In 1853, the governor-general of Vitebsk, Mogilev, and Smolensk provinces, Pavel Ignat'ev, reported on a clandestine Hasidic printing press in the Kopys' district of Mogilev province.[53] By order of the governor-general, expert Jew Moisei Berlin was commissioned to assist in the investigation of that case "beyond his regular service duties," that is, unofficially, as prescribed by the "Secret Regulation." According to Berlin, his work on the case consisted of "collecting information, providing translation and expertise," and cost him "considerable time, effort and expense."[54] Due to the unofficial nature of the assignment, the expenses of the expert Jew were covered by the limited resources of his salary and were only partly reimbursed.[55] However, Berlin's contribution to the investigation was noted by the governor-general, who obviously planned to use the expert Jew in similar cases. As a result, Ignat'ev secured the MVD's approval of funds in the amount of 200 silver rubles annually, allocated for travel and other official expenses of the expert Jew.[56]

In 1859, by confidential order of the vice-governor of Poltava province Veselkin, expert Jew Aaron Tseitlin was dispatched to the town of Lokhvitsa to unofficially monitor the investigation of counterfeiting by the Jews.[57]

The case of Mikhail Apatovskii involved both Hasidism and counterfeit money, representing both the religious and social aspects of Jewish "fanaticism." Vladimir Fedorov, expert Jew under the governor-general of Kiev, Volhyn, and Podolia provinces, was commissioned to verify the testimony of the key witness in the case.

In 1857, Kiev resident, doctor of medicine, and converted Jew Mikhail Apatovskii submitted his memorandum, "On Religion and Morals in the Life of the Russian Jews,"[58] to the MVD. At the same time, he reported the illegal activity of the Jews—counterfeiting and distribution of official credit notes—to the Ministry of Finance and to the governor-general of Kiev, Podolia, and Volhyn provinces.[59] In accordance with official bureaucratic procedure, the Minister of Internal Affairs, Sergei Stepanovich Lanskoi, and the governor-general, Prince Illarion Illarionovich Vasil'chikov, initiated an investigation.

Apatovskii's memorandum was sent for examination to the DDDII. The head of the second division within the second section of the department dealing with the religious affairs of the Jews, collegiate assessor Nikolai Gradovskii, considered Apatovskii's conclusions superficial and irrelevant.

Apatovskii argued that Jewish "fanaticism" was the major obstacle to rapprochement between Jews and Russians. This "fanaticism" and general devotion to the Talmud was spreading among Jews due to the growing Hasidic sect, labeled by Apatovskii the "moral gangrene" of Russian Jews. Therefore, Apatovskii proposed eradicating this sect completely and, thus, uprooting Jewish "fanaticism" in Russia.[60]

Gradovskii pointed out that from 1824 to 1852, various agencies of the Russian government had thoroughly examined and solved the Hasidic problem. Hasidism was deemed an insignificant religious deviation from traditional Judaism. The government viewed the social and religious rift caused by this schism as a positive factor, since it contributed to the fragmentation and disintegration of the Jewish community and, thus, enabled the social integration of the Jews into imperial society. Hasidim were subject to the general legislation and regulations concerning the Jews, since separate legislation would eventually lead to the unlikely institutional recognition of the Hasidic sect. Moreover, the religious administration for the Russian Jews was ordered to suppress the illegitimate institutes of the Hasidic sect.[61] Therefore, Apatovskii's memorandum, suggesting a solution to an already solved problem, was simply ignored.

Likewise, according to Governor-general Prince Vasil'chikov, his own investigation of counterfeiting by the Jews demonstrated that the evidence presented by Apatovskii was unfounded. The governor-general reported to the MVD that he had "assigned his trusted official to engage in secret contact with Apatovskii to determine the identity of the suspects."[62] However, Apatovskii had failed to provide any plausible information apart from his "equivocal and vague statements and explanations" and his obvious disdain for Kiev merchants Rapoport and Brodskii.[63] Evidently, this undisclosed "trusted official" assigned with unofficial contact with Apatovksii was the collegiate assessor Vladimir Fedorov, expert Jew under the Governor-general Prince Vasil'chikov.[64] Gradovskii's conclusions and Vasil'chikov's report were approved by the director of the DDDII Count Emmanuil Sivers and archived.

Legal proceedings were not mentioned among the standard missions of expert Jews in the "Secret Regulation" of 1850 or in any other official documents. However, governors did not hesitate to commission them with official arbitration in disputes between Jews on a regular basis. The shelved institution of the provincial rabbinate left a structural vacuum and procedural gap between the authority of the lower Jewish religious courts, *batei din* and district rabbinate, and the Jewish religious supreme court of appeals, the Rabbinical Commission. Thus, expert Jews, essentially a provisional substitute for provincial rabbis, filled the vacuum and bridged the gap as a surrogate intermediary echelon of the Jewish religious court system.

In the 1860s, according to expert Jew Aaron Tseitlin, the governor of Poltava province, Aleksandr Volkov, frequently assigned him "examination of claims and arbitration in disputes between Jews, if at least one side had officially appealed to the governor. In most cases [the expert Jew] managed to bring the sides to a settlement."[65] An order of the governor of Poltava province, Mikhail Martynov, commissioning expert Jew Tseitlin "to satisfy the petitioner on the subject of divorce from her husband,"[66] is an example of the kind of disputes brought to the arbitration of expert Jews. According to Tseitlin, this practice prevailed until 1864, when the universal public court system was introduced to Poltava province. However, according to the governor, in 1866, when reformed courts were established throughout Poltava province, Tseitlin's successor, expert Jew Lev Zaidiner, continued to "resolve disputes between Jews, about 20 cases per year" on a regular basis.[67] In 1873, the governor-general of the Baltic provinces reported the same commission given to his expert Jew, Fillip Keil'man. According to the governor-general, "due to the significant increase of the Jewish population in Riga, the number of disputes between Jews settled by the expert Jew increased accordingly."[68]

In full compliance with the "Secret Regulation" of 1850, the provincial authorities used the unofficial assistance of expert Jews when investigating manifestations of religious and social "fanaticism" of the Jews. Expert Jews collected and examined the evidence and were used as trusted agents, assigned to have unofficial secret contacts with Jews under investigation. The expert Jews themselves did not consider such assignments to be a legitimate part of their official mandate and displayed little enthusiasm when on these missions. Apparently, the investigation assignments were perceived by the Jewish bureaucrats as pure police tasks, which had nothing to do with their service ethos and overall mission aimed at the civil improvement of Russian Jews.

The involvement of expert Jews in legal proceedings, lacking any basis in the "Secret Regulation," was in high demand within the provincial administration. The provincial authorities assigned the arbitration of disputes between Jews to Jewish bureaucrats on a regular basis, before and after the Court Reform of 1864. Thus, expert Jews were a surrogate small claims court for the Jews, an intermediary echelon of the Jewish religious court system, and in some cases even a replacement for the reformed public courts.

Legal, Religious, Ethnographic, and Historical Expertise

The MVD used the official expertise of expert Jews extensively during the whole span of their service history. The authorities demanded and digested tons of information describing and explaining the social, economic, religious, and political lives of the Russian Jews. This pursuit of information began in the 1850s with the need for basic knowledge about Jewish ritual (from everyday prayers and local customs to the fine points of talmudic law), which the government attempted to "restore" in order to comply with "pure Mosaic Law distorted by the Talmudists."[69] Later, in the 1860s and 1870s, the implementation of government policies of social integration of the Jews required more in-depth studies of the social, religious, and legal structures of the traditional Jewish communities that the government sought to reform. Finally, in the 1880s and 1910s following the growing expansion of Russian bureaucracy into the lives of imperial subjects including the Jews, the number of areas of Jewish life that were of interest to the government grew exponentially. During the early phases of the service history of expert Jews, their work could be considered a solid academic-level historical and ethnographic study of the Jews. However, during the later phases when expert Jews had to cope with large amounts of data representing the vast spectrum of contemporary Jewish life, the output of Jewish officials tended to be more dry, formal and purely bureaucratic.

At the beginning of their service history, the expert work of Jewish bureaucrats satisfied the initial hunger for information of the Russian administration for adequate and reliable data on the everyday lives of the Jews and their "fanaticism." The government's appetite was all-encompassing. Thus, the administrators demanded the knowledge of Jewish bureaucrats on minor details of Jewish ritual as well as on mass social and religious movements among the Jews.

In 1854, on the order of Pavel Ignat'ev, governor-general of Vitebsk, Mogilev, and Smolensk provinces, expert Jew Moisei Berlin compiled "a scholarly article" on ritual prayers by moonlight, *kiddush levana*. In his article, the expert Jew explained the origins of this ritual and pointed out "obscene (*nepristoinye*) phrases incorporated within the liturgy."[70] Apparently, these "obscene" (i.e., subversive) phrases showed the general messianic undertones of this ritual. Therefore, Berlin's expertise implicitly classified the ritual of *kiddush levana* as a display of Jewish fanaticism, since the messianic hopes of the Jews, "preventing them from obtaining permanent settlement," were explicitly qualified as a component of religious fanaticism by the "Secret Regulation" of 1850.[71]

In 1853, Governor-general Ignat'ev commissioned expert Jew Berlin to "compile a history of the development of the Hasidic sect among the Jews in general and its expansion to Belorussia in particular, to provide the authorities with a clear understanding of this phenomenon."[72] The realization of this academic project proved to be a complicated and even perilous enterprise for the expert Jew. As Berlin wrote: "I conscientiously completed this important assignment, and despite the due confidentiality, my project did not go unnoticed by adverse members of the [Hasidic] sect. Thus I became subject to offences by these people, whose violent fanaticism and ignorance were exposed by me to the government."[73] The followers of the Lubavicher Rebbe, Menachem Mendel Shneerson, subjectively portrayed by the expert Jew, attempted to discredit Berlin's expertise and destroy his reputation with the authorities.[74] As a result, the career of the expert Jew was almost ruined. However, Berlin's history of Hasidism won "official recognition and the highest praise" of the governor-general,[75] and was well received in the highest echelons of the MVD.[76] Moreover, the study of expert Jew Moisei Berlin was a landmark achievement in the development of Russian Jewish historiography.[77]

In 1861, the director of the DDDII, Count Emmanuil Sivers, requested the expert opinion of Moisei Berlin, then expert Jew at the central offices of the MVD, on the *eruv*, "the Jewish custom of putting up wire connections between houses on Saturdays."[78] Count Sivers needed this information for official resolution of a case brought by a petition of Jews from the town of Vladimir in Volhyn province, complaining that the local authorities had prohibited them from making an *eruv*. The expert Jew explained that the custom of the *eruv* "was established to make it easier for Jews to observe the strict Mosaic regulations regarding the Sabbath, which absolutely prohibited any work for these *inorodtsy* [the Jews]. Therefore, the act of connecting the houses with wire is nothing more than a clever shortcut allowing them to circumvent the rules. Without these connections, on the Sabbath no pious and observant Jew could extend a helping hand to his neighbor outside his home, even in the case of an accident, such as a fire."[79] Berlin pointed out that this custom was practiced not only by Russian Jews, supposedly fanatical and ignorant, but also by the Orthodox faction within civilized German Jewry, as confirmed by information from the credible German periodical *Algemeine Zeitung des Judentums* appended by the expert Jew to his report. Thus, Berlin concluded, the *eruv* should not be qualified as fanaticism, and should not be subject to administrative persecution since "this custom currently holds sway only among the ignorant populace, and with time and the progress of the enlightenment its sway will inevitably fade."[80]

The compatibility between Jewish religious law and imperial legislation, both in general and exclusively related to the Jews, was an important concern of the Russian government. In the 1850s, the government sought to determine the extent and authority of Jewish religious law and its institutions. In particular, the government needed reliable information to decide whether *halacha* (Jewish religious law) and the *batei din* (rabbinical courts) contributed to Jewish fanaticism and increased the social isolation of the Jews.

In 1856, the MVD solicited the opinions of the governor-generals regarding the Jewish religious court, *beit din*. A MVD circular directive highlighted an ambiguous situation where the general thrust of imperial policy embodied by the reforms of the 1840s aimed at the elimination of Jewish communal autonomy, but was apparently disregarded by legislation[81] granting legal authority to the *beit din*, an obvious vestige of the kahal autonomy. The MVD requested basic information from the governor-generals about the structure and functions of the *batei din* in their provinces. Provincial administrators were also instructed to report to the Ministry on whether the proceedings of the Jewish courts breached the jurisdiction of the general courts, and whether the *batei din* were helpful or detrimental to the MVD policies of social integration of the Jews.[82]

In response to the directive, the governor-general of Novorossiia and Bessarabiia, Aleksandr Stroganov, mobilized the support of his subordinate administrators, including the city governors of Odessa and Taganrog, and the governors of Kherson and Ekaterinoslav provinces, in order to collect information for the MVD. The governor-general also commissioned his expert Jew, Markus Gurovich, to compile an analysis of the history and the contemporary role of the *beit din*. The reports of the Russian officials and of their Jewish colleague unanimously upheld the loyalty and practical use of the *batei din*.

The Russian administrators pointed out the bureaucratic advantage of the Jewish religious court, which, due to its informal and efficient procedure, significantly lightened the burden of their daily workload. They defined the *beit din* as a dynamic institution with fluid staff and flexible functions and procedures, unencumbered by excessive paperwork. This structure enabled the *beit din* to resolve the majority of cases by settlement, without the usual procrastination and petty formalities of the Russian courts and bureaucratic chancelleries. Moreover, according to the provincial administrators, the agenda of the *beit din* never exceeded the limits of politically safe matters, such as marital issues, ritual slaughter, annual participation in the ritual of *Kol Nidre*, and the swearing into office of government rabbis and Jewish military recruits.[83] The official from the provincial chancellery of Bessarabia maintained that the *beit din* was absolutely useful, since "it helped decrease the number of small claims in the general courts and freed the provincial chancelleries from the burden of cumbersome correspondence."[84]

Expert Jew Gurovich complemented the opinions of his Russian colleagues by arguing that historically the *beit din* had emerged as an institution independent from any supreme Jewish or non-Jewish authority. Thus, the expert Jew concluded, the long history and unofficial status of the *beit din* made it a trustworthy source of arbitration and an indispensable feature of Jewish life.

Finally, based on these reports from the Russian administrators and the conclusions of the expert Jew, the governor-general reported his official opinion to the MVD. According to Stroganov's report, the existence of the *beit din* was fully justified by the religious and economic needs of the Jews. Furthermore, this institution "did not encourage fanaticism, and did not serve the interests of any harmful sect."[85]

After Russian judicial reform was launched in 1864, the problem of the basic compatibility of Jewish religious law and imperial legislation grew more significant, and was linked to the general official policy of rapprochement between Jews and Russians. The government defined this policy mainly in judicial terms as the civil and legal equality of Jews with the rest of imperial subjects by gradual extension of general legislation to the Jews.[86] Thus, the government's interests in this area encompassed both the minor aspects of legal procedure and its fundamental principles and institutes.[87] Official Jewish oaths, an important civil ritual and a key legal procedure, were of special interest to the government for three decades, from the 1850s through the 1880s.

In 1859, Emperor Alexander II approved the formulae of special Jewish oaths, including a universal oath of allegiance and service, an oath for court witnesses, for the government rabbi, for the members of the Jewish religious board, and for Jewish military recruits.[88] Unlike the *juramentum more Judaico*, the dominant special Jewish oaths in medieval Christian Europe, the Russian oaths did not debase the Jews. Moreover, these oaths were entirely based on formulae used by all subjects of the empire, and had plain and flexible procedures. Thus, if a Jew was unable to take the oath in Russian, he could easily take it in Yiddish using the officially approved translation.[89] In 1871, on assignment for the Ministry of Internal Affairs and the Ministry of Justice, the government rabbi of St. Petersburg and the acting expert Jew at the MVD, Avraam Neiman, compiled additional Jewish oaths necessitated by the implementation of the Judicial Reform of 1864. Neiman compiled oaths for the judge, the attorney (*prisiazhnyi poverennyi*), the bailiff (*sudebnyi pristav*), jurors (*prisiazhnyi zasedatel'*), and court witnesses. The expert Jew supplemented the formulae with a "formal order," the detailed rites of swearing the oaths.[90] These rites required that a Jew be sworn with his head covered and in front of the open book of the Hebrew Bible. Jews should not be sworn on Saturdays or during Jewish holidays. They should be sworn in any proper place, and, if the government rabbi was unavailable, a Jew could be sworn in by a non-Jewish official.[91] Neiman's formulae and rites were approved by the government and signed into law by the emperor.

The fair-minded attitude of the government toward the legitimacy of the Jewish oath was largely based on official consensus corroborated by expert Jews. The opinions of expert Jews diverged on both the formulae and procedural details of the oaths. Some expert Jews supported the unification and standardization of the oath while others insisted on the preservation of a special Jewish format. However, all expert Jews agreed that the institute and act of the oath should be sacred for Jews and have full legal power for universal public justice. A minority of expert Jews believed that the special Jewish oath should be even more Jewish and authentic both in its language and formulae. According to these expert Jews, the authentic features of the Jewish oath would ensure its binding power among Jews and legitimacy in the general courts.

In 1854, by request of the MVD and on assignment from Belorussian governor-general Ignat'ev, expert Jew Moisei Berlin prepared a memorandum entitled "Treatise on Jewish Oaths." The treatise provided a comprehensive historical survey and juridical analysis of the institute of the Jewish oath, testifying to the "sanctity of the oath for Jews." However, Berlin pointed out some relatively easy techniques which "by omitting certain details the binding power of the oath could be eliminated," and proposed means for the prevention of such abuses.[92]

In 1869, Blavshtein, expert Jew under the governor of Podolia province, acting on his own initiative, submitted a proposal to the MVD to replace the "official (*kazennaia*)," Jewish oath, with the "popular (*narodnaia*)" oath, the only "genuine and valid" form recognized by the Jews.[93]

In the practical experience of the expert Jew, which also included seven years as government rabbi in the town of Kamenets of Podolia province, he found that "despite strong rabbinical admonitions, for Jews taking the oath at the demand of the authorities, this official Jewish oath had no credibility."[94] According to Blavshtein, since the oath was a civil act based on religious faith, the Jewish oath should be based on Jewish religious ritual and law. Only then would it become truly significant and sacred for the Jews. The expert Jew submitted to the MVD his Russian translation and transliteration of the authentic formulae of the traditional Jewish oath, and described its rites. According to the expert Jew, the text of the oath should be written down and should include the specific details of the case for which the oath was being taken. In particularly important cases, the rites of Yom Kippur applied. Thus, a Jew should be wrapped in a *talit*, a prayer shawl, and should stand barefoot while taking the oath.[95]

The MVD took Blavshtein's proposal seriously, although without much enthusiasm. The MVD officials repeatedly discussed the recommendations of the expert Jew with the Ministry of Justice and planned to include the issue in the agenda of the Rabbinical Commission in 1879 and the Highest Commission on Re-examination of the Laws on the Jews in 1883. However, Blavshtein's idea was never under full official consideration and was ultimately postponed, since the government chose the approach to Jewish oaths advocated by the majority of expert Jews. The majority of Jewish bureaucrats believed that the universal formulae and procedures of the Jewish oath, approved by the government in 1859 and 1871, were more in harmony with the political goals of the government aimed at the social integration of the Jews. According to the opinion of these expert Jews, the procedure of the oath should be minimal, and only in accordance with the most crucial rules of *halacha*, which prevented Jews from taking the oath on the Sabbath and on Jewish holidays.

In 1863, German Barats, expert Jew under the governor-general of Kiev, Volhyn, and Podolia provinces, submitted to the Ministry of Internal Affairs a memorandum entitled "On the Legitimacy of the Jewish Oath in General, and on the Regulations of Jewish Religious Law Concerning Witness Testimony against Informers in Particular."[96] Barats presented a comprehensive historical and legal overview of the institution of the Jewish oath and its evolution over several centuries, from Emperor Justinian's prohibition of Jewish testimony against Christians, to the humiliating practices of the *juramentum more Judaico*, to the contemporary decision of the French court, which ruled that "the sole legitimate guarantee against perjury is the human conscience; thus, constraining and auxiliary procedures are mere formalities which afford no additional power to the ceremonial act of the oath."[97] The expert Jew also reviewed the Russian legislation on Jewish oaths. According to Barats, Russian laws were "well ahead of contemporary European laws in their humane approach to this issue."[98] In the beginning of the nineteenth century, the Russian Senate ruled that courts and administrative institutions throughout the empire should treat Jewish witnesses on an equal basis with the rest of imperial subjects, Christian or non-Christian, and should accept the testimonies of Jews in all proceedings, including disputes between Christians and cases against Christians.[99] Thus, Russian law and the Russian government considered the oaths and testimonies of Jews fully legitimate and tended to simplify and unify the formalities for these procedures.

At the same time, according to the expert Jew, the issue of legitimacy of the Jewish oaths continued to surface in the practical work of the bureaucratic chancelleries, "due to the denunciations of Jews themselves, who, out of malice toward their co-religionists or some other dishonorable motives, sought to discredit the truthfulness of the Jewish oath in the eyes of the government."[100] Soon after, this observation was perfectly supported by the activity of Iakov Brafman, acting expert Jew at the DDDII. In his books "The Jewish Brotherhoods, Local and Universal" (Vilna, 1868) and "The Book of Kahal" (Vilna, 1870), Brafman argued that *Kol Nidre*, the annual ritual of absolution from oaths, essentially undermined the legitimacy of the Jewish oaths.[101] However, Brafman's opinions did not affect the official approach to the Jewish oaths, mostly due to heavy criticism of his own credibility as an expert in the contemporary Jewish press, and consequent skepticism about his findings and conclusions within Russian officialdom.[102]

In 1874, Lev Bornshtein, government rabbi in the town of Dubno of Volhyn province, was absent at the court session held during the regular convention of justices of the peace (*s'ezd mirovykh sudei*) of Dubno district, where he would have officially sworn in the Jewish witnesses summoned by the court. Prior to the court session, Rabbi Bornshtein reported to the chairman of the convention that he would be unable to officiate at the swearing, since it was on the Jewish holiday of Rosh

Hashana, and referred to Jewish religious law, citing article 602, *Hilchot Rosh Hashana*, of *Shulchan Aruch*, the major halachic compendium, which prohibited Jews from taking oaths during the ten days of repentance, beginning with Rosh Hashana and continuing through Yom Kippur. Moreover, Bornshtein cited the Russian law stipulating that a non-Jewish official could swear in Jews in the absence of a rabbi. As a result, the court session was postponed, and the disappointed chairman of the convention asked the governor of Volhyn province, Petr Gresser, to investigate the alleged misconduct of Rabbi Bornshtein.[103] Consequently, in 1875 the governor told his expert Jew Lev Binshtok to clarify the issue. Expert Jew Binshtok confirmed that the article of *Shulchan Aruch* cited by Bornshtein did prohibit oaths during the ten days of repentance. However, Binshtok pointed out that according to the authoritative commentaries on the *Shulchan Aruch*, such as *Magen Avot, Magen Avraham,* and *Ture Zahav,* "in the interval between Rosh Hashana and Yom Kippur the courts should be open and justice should be served."[104] The expert Jew argued that the prohibition of oaths during the days of repentance was not found elsewhere "in the entire religious codex of the Jews," except in the article of *Shulchan Aruch* cited by Bornshtein. Thus, Binshtok concluded that Jewish witnesses could be sworn in by the courts without difficulty during the days of repentance.[105]

Due to the disagreement between the opinions of Rabbi Bornshtein and expert Jew Binshtok, Governor Gresser forwarded the entire case to the MVD for further examination and resolution by the Rabbinical Commission. However, the case was not included in the agenda of the Commission's session in 1879, and was instead assigned to Illarion Kaufman, acting expert Jew at the Ministry of Internal Affairs. Based on his meticulous analysis of *halacha* and contemporary Russian laws, expert Jew Kaufman claimed that the controversial issue of the possibility of Jewish oaths during the days of repentance had great political significance. Kaufman pointed out that article 602 of *Hilchot Rosh Hashana*, the focus of contradictory interpretations by Bornshtein and Binshtok, was not a straight prohibition, but "advice and guidance" provided by the authoritative fifteenth-century rabbi known as Maharil. The expert Jew explained that traditionally such guidance, albeit not technically halachic law, still "had great authority among Orthodox Jews and was strictly

Illarion Kaufman (Aleksandr Polovtsov, ed. Russkii biograficheskii slovar' [St. Petersburg: Tipografiia I.N.Skorokhodova, 1896–1918], at www.rulex.ru/01110736.htm, accessed on December 20, 2015)

observed."[106] Thus, when a rabbi was forced to disregard such guidance, his piety would be significantly challenged.[107] Violation of pious conduct constituted outright sin. Therefore, by forcing a rabbi to officiate at the swearing of oaths during the days of repentance, the authorities were ultimately forcing him to commit a sin. As a result, such actions of the government would undermine the authority of the Russian administration among the Jews, since, according to the expert Jew, "such coercion would make a very grim impression among Orthodox Jews, i.e., the largest part of the Jewish population."[108] Furthermore, Kaufman argued that contemporary Russian legal practice allowed the chairman of the court to swear in witnesses of non-Christian denominations, even if a member of the clergy of this non-Christian faith was present in the court chamber. According to the expert Jew, this "flexibility of the contemporary law, and the general spirit of religious tolerance implicit in the imperial legislation," did not allow for spiritual leaders of the Jews, the rabbis, to be coerced to commit sinful acts.[109] Therefore, Kaufman proposed that the administrators and the court authorities refrain from forcing rabbis to officiate at oath swearings in the interval between Rosh Hashana and Yom Kippur.[110]

Based on the conclusions of the expert Jew, the MVD instructed the governor of Volhyn province that although "neither the Bible nor Talmud prohibited oaths during the interval between Rosh Hashana and Yom Kippur, nevertheless, based on the latest religious rulings (*Shulchan Aruch*) obligatory for observation by Jews, it was prohibited to swear in Jews during these days." The opinion of expert Jew Kaufman and the MVD directive signified an important shift in the confessional policy of late imperial Russia. In the middle of the nineteenth century, the government considered "the latest religious rulings"—the Talmud and *Shulchan Aruch*—to be misinterpretations of pure Mosaic law and the basis of Jewish fanaticism, subject to eradication by the joint forces of Russian and Jewish bureaucrats. However, by the end of the century, the government compromised on this approach to Judaism and other foreign faiths for support among the traditional masses and conservative religious leadership, in order to sustain conservative domestic policy aimed at containment of radical political activity and revolution.[111]

However, the paradigmatic shift in general confessional policy did not produce an immediate change in established policies on various religious groups and implementation of these policies.[112] Thus, in the 1870s and the 1880s, the eradication of Jewish fanaticism was still on the agenda of the MVD and expert Jews. At this point, however, the government increasingly defined "fanaticism" as a political and national rather than religious attribute of Jewish social isolation. Thus, the MVD targeted the institutional base of "fanaticism," such as *chavurot*—unofficial voluntary associations and charitable societies—largely unaffected by previous policies and administrative regulation. Jewish burial societies, *chevre kadi-sha*, were of special interest to the government.

According to a confidential DDDII memorandum entitled "On Jewish Charitable Organizations in the Empire," the Russian government first learned about Jewish burial societies in 1819 from a Jewish petition denouncing abuses by the leadership of a local *chevra kadisha*.[113] The government's first impression was therefore a negative one. The negative attitude continued toward these societies, which were believed to wield considerable financial and even administrative authority among the Jews, disguised by their pious and charitable agenda. The DDDII memorandum referred to the burial societies as a stronghold of Jewish fanaticism, since "besides charitable purposes, they pursued the goal of strengthening Jewish faith through the preservation of its rituals; using their power and influence, felt by every Jew, [the societies] were keeping the Jewish masses in slavery, a detriment to their civic development."[114]

The government's attention to Jewish burial societies translated into numerous assignments for expert Jews. While on their inspection missions, expert Jews routinely examined local Jewish charitable organizations with special attention to burial societies. Thus, in 1853, the inspection report of expert Jew Moisei Berlin on Jewish religious, communal, and charitable organizations in the city of Mogilev included a "special section on the main charitable organization, the so-called sacred brotherhood (*chevra kadisha*), or burial society."[115]

In 1854, in his inspection report on the Jewish organizations of Novorossiia, expert Jew Markus Gurovich "provided a largely negative portrayal of the activities of Jewish burial societies."[116] According to Gurovich, the existence of burial societies did not violate the law, which permitted these voluntary organizations.[117] In theory, these societies were innocuous "associations of people who take upon themselves, for religious motives, the sacred duty of burying the dead, which has very important meaning for the Jews."[118] However, according to the expert Jew, burial societies "were not under any official authority and did not follow any rules stipulated by law."[119] Thus, Gurovich declared the lack of government regulation to be a source of alleged and actual abuse by the burial societies.

The governor-general of Novorossiia and Bessarabiia, Aleksandr Stroganov, assigned his expert Jew Markus Gurovich to develop measures aimed at the protection of the "poor Jewish masses" from widespread "exploitation and robbery" by Jewish burial societies.[120] The expert Jew prepared draft regulations applicable to all Jewish burial societies in Russia, which were approved by the governor-general and submitted to the DDDII. According to this draft, the activities of the burial societies had to be strictly limited to their charitable mission of taking care of burial rites. The societies could not have any authority over finances, properties and other Jewish assets, in order to prevent access of these organizations to any means of administrative control. Furthermore, burial societies should be placed under the supervision of the government rabbinate.[121] Despite the fact that Gurovich's draft was approved by the Rabbinical Commission in 1862, these regulations for Jewish burial societies were never implemented.[122]

Apparently, in accordance with the emerging policies of centralization and unification of the imperial administration, the government refrained from establishing another separate Jewish institution, even one that would be officially recognized and regulated. Some Russian administrators pushed these policies to extremes in their approach to the problem of Jewish burial societies. In 1868, the Special Commission for Examination of the Problem of Jewish Burial Societies under the governor-general of Vilna, Kovno, and Grodno provinces, Aleksandr L'vovich Potapov, concluded that burial societies, which perpetuated Jewish fanaticism and social isolation and used force and illegal authority to collect money from Jews, should be dissolved. Jewish burial procedures should instead be conducted in accordance with the rules established by law for all subjects of the empire.[123]

The proceedings of the commission were based on extensive reference materials prepared by expert Jews Moisei Berlin, Iakov Brafman, and Samuel Joseph Fuenn.[124] The expert Jews under the governor-general of Vilna, Kovno, and Grodno provinces, Osip Gurvich and Sheftel' Kliachko, were members of the commission. However, the opinions of these expert Jews varied greatly. Thus, expert Jew Gurvich pointed out the unlawful practice of burial societies encouraging Jews to bury their dead immediately after death, according to *halacha*, in order to observe the full seven days of mourning period traditionally counted from the day of burial. As a result, Jews, unable and unwilling to lose any time due to economic reasons, were forced to violate the three-day interval between death and burial set by the law for the purposes of police control and maintenance of public health.[125] Expert Jew Kliachko, on the other hand, was the only member of the commission who voted against the dissolution of Jewish burial societies.[126]

Based on the conclusions of the commission and the near unanimous vote of its members, the governor-general dissolved all Jewish burial societies in Vilna, Kovno, and Grodno provinces by a circular directive of 1868.[127] The MVD ultimately supported this initiative in 1872, when the Special Council for the Development of an Administrative Agenda on the Jewish Question under the Minister of Internal Affairs concluded that Jewish burial societies represented "one of the main plagues of Jewish society, which, based on their enormous financial resources and their fanaticism and intolerance, exerted the most harmful influence on their co-religionists."[128]

The MVD extended its approach toward Jewish burial societies to all secular and religious Jewish voluntary societies and associations regardless of their agenda. Thus, in 1872, the MVD did not approve the bylaws of the Odessa society for dissemination of vocational training and elementary education among Jewish girls from poor families, although they were recommended and backed by the city governor of Odessa. The MVD based its decision on its general approach to all similar initiatives, which "absolutely should not be allowed," since they reinforced Jewish social isolation in general, and, in particular promoted the exclusion of Jews from participation in general charitable initiatives "not limited in their scope and outreach to particular religious groups."[129]

At the beginning of the twentieth century, the MVD's demand for information on the Jewish subjects of the empire grew considerably. According to Moisei Kreps, expert Jew at the DDDII from 1907 to 1917, he "submitted countless memoranda and reports to the MVD on various matters and cases pertaining to Jewish religion, society, politics and everyday life."[130] A mere listing of these matters and cases took two pages of Kreps's official autobiography, densely covered with writing. Most of the items involved traditional aspects of imperial Jewish policy and its institutions, including the rabbinate, schools, marriages and divorces, oaths, and charitable organizations. However, according to the list, the MVD gradually adjusted its focus according to the new realities. Thus the list included such issues as the "role of the Jewish chaplains (*voennye ravviny*) in the satisfaction of the spiritual and ritual needs of Jewish soldiers," "the release of Jewish clergy from military service," "the establishment of a Jewish university and upper school of Jewish studies," and "legalization of marriages and divorces done by Russian Jews abroad."[131] The new agenda of official Jewish policy was also visible in this list, represented by such items as "the problems of Jewish emigration," "factions within the Zionist movement," "international efforts on behalf of Jewish emancipation in Russia," and "nationalist and political movements among Jews."[132]

In the last years of the empire, the knowledge base of official Jewish policy, mostly compiled by expert Jews, was still far from complete. The dynamic changes in the social, economic, and political life of Russian Jews, combined with the MVD's thrust to place this life under total bureaucratic control, reinforced the administrative demand for the expertise of Jewish bureaucrats.

Policymaking and Implementation of Administrative Measures

The "Secret Regulation" of 1850 absolutely prohibited governor-generals from delegating administrative authority of any kind to their expert Jews. However, both provincial governors and the central offices of the MVD frequently commissioned expert Jews with tasks linked to unambiguous administrative functions involving some bureaucratic authority. This was for the most part unavoidable due to the *maloliudstvo*, an endemic shortage of competent cadres of Russian administrators. Still, in many cases the governors and the MVD intentionally assigned administrative tasks to expert Jews.

Expert Jews were the most professional and loyal group among the religious administration for Russian Jews. At the same time, these Jewish bureaucrats were an integral component of general Russian officialdom. Expert Jews therefore enjoyed the full trust of the administration and served as authorized government agents vested with considerable bureaucratic authority. However, in each particular case, this authority was distinctly circumscribed by MVD regulations and executive orders of the governors. Such assignments ranged from the improvement of the district government rabbinate to the censorship commissions within the provincial administration to the all-embracing policymaking proceedings within the Rabbinical Commission in St. Petersburg.

The period of the most extensive and effective administrative involvement of expert Jews was during the years of the Great Reforms, the 1850s through the 1870s. Starting in the 1880s, administrative assignments almost disappeared from the Jewish bureaucrats' agenda. However, from the 1890s through the 1910s, the last period of the service history of expert Jews, supervisory tasks aimed at verification of the confessional conformity and political loyalty of the newly formed Jewish religious associations were sporadically assigned.

In 1861, the governor of Poltava province, Aleksandr Volkov, appointed his expert Jew, Aaron Tseitlin, to the office of government rabbi in the town of Kremenchug. Based on the assignment of the governor, the expert Jew, acting as government rabbi, "reestablished and improved the practices of keeping metrical books, totally neglected during the term of the previous government rabbi."[133] Tseitlin worked as government rabbi in Kremenchug for eight months in 1861 and for the whole year in 1863. In 1862 the governor also appointed him acting government rabbi in the city of Poltava.[134] The lack of adequate cadres thus compelled provincial administrators to fill the formally elected office of government rabbi with appointed Jewish bureaucrats.

In some cases this practice created ambiguous situations. In 1884, the governor of Chernigov province, Sergei Vladimirovich Shakhovskoi, reported to the MVD that his expert Jew, Efrem Freidin, also serving as elected government rabbi of Chernigov and Gorodnia districts, was prosecuted in the capacity of government rabbi for violating procedures of keeping metrical books.[135] According to the governor, paradoxically, the investigation of these violations was formally the domain of the same Freidin in the capacity of expert Jew, who was "supposed to provide assistance in this case."[136] Therefore, the governor requested the MVD's approval for Freidin's dismissal from the office of expert Jew.

In 1857, the governor-general of Novorossiia and Bessarabiia, Aleksandr Stroganov, assigned his expert Jew, Markus Gurovich, a censorship mission. By order of the governor-general, the expert Jew was officially told to assess the editorial program and bylaws of the Russian-language Jewish journal *Rassvet*, presented by Odessa Jews Osip

Rabinovich and Joachim Tarnopol for authorization by the provincial administration and approval by the MVD. Gurovich provided the governor-general with a positive review of the editorial agenda and pointed out that, in general, the goals of *Rassvet* were parallel to "the benevolent goals of the government."[137] According to the expert Jew, *Rassvet* would significantly contribute to the promotion of the Russian language among Jews and to the general official policy of rapprochement, since the journal's editorial policy was aimed at "bringing unity to the education and views" of Jews and Russians.[138] Gurovich attested that the publishers, Rabinovich and Tarnopol, "were educated people and knew the spirit and needs of their people very well."[139] Gurovich's tactful yet principled critique of the journal's editorial program clearly reflected the official standpoint of the MVD. The editorial program proposed the regular publication of current imperial laws and government regulations pertaining to the Jews, supplemented by an editorial perspective on the legislation, urging Jews to observe the law. Expert Jew Gurovich pointed out that the sole publication of legal acts, without any supplementary explanations, would suffice. He argued that propagation of loyalty through the Jewish press was unnecessary since obedience to the law was an implicit civil duty of all subjects of the empire including Jews. Moreover, the explanation and interpretation of laws pertaining to the Jews was the official domain of bureaucracy in general, and of the government rabbinate in particular. Thus, Gurovich proposed requiring the publishers to supply complementary copies of *Rassvet* to each government rabbi in the empire.[140] The publishers also intended to provide coverage of the contemporary status of Jewish communities, schools, agricultural colonies, and to "expose, delicately and with great caution, their shortcomings, and to seek means of improvement."[141] The expert Jew argued that such shortcomings could be and should be exposed if they did not involve any flaws in the government administration of the Jews, since "it's completely inappropriate for private parties to criticize the actions of the government."[142] However, according to Gurovich, the shortcomings of Jews who "did not appreciate the protective care of the government" should be reported by *Rassvet* in order to motivate Jews to seek self-improvement.[143]

Based on the conclusions of the expert Jew, the governor-general authorized the editorial program and bylaws of *Rassvet* and submitted them for final approval to the MVD along with his report, in which he extensively quoted the recommendations and conclusions of the expert Jew.[144]

In 1866, the Minister of State Domains Aleksandr Aleksandorovich Zelenoi, acting in coordination with the chairman of the Patronage Committee for Foreign Settlers in Southern Russia, V. N. Ettinger, and the governor-general of Novorossiia and Bessarabiia, Pavel Kotsebu, assigned an administrative mission to expert Jew Markus Gurovich. The expert Jew was told to develop and implement administrative measures aimed at the "gradual and stress-free transformation of the current system of private education for Jewish children by melamdim in their private homes, with the main goal of eradicating harmful religious fanaticism and superstitious customs among Jewish farmers."[145]

Gurovich carefully examined the current status of Jewish elementary education in the Jewish agricultural colonies of Kherson province, selected as experimental ground for the reorganization of the Jewish school system, and submitted his draft reform project to the administration. The expert Jew took into account the results of the Jewish school reform implemented by the government in the western provinces of the Pale of Settlement in the 1840s. According to his analysis, the radical anti-traditional thrust of these reforms provoked much distrust and resistance in the Jews, especially the melamdim, whose interests were seriously affected by the government initiatives. Thus, the reforms had proven unsuccessful, as evidently demonstrated by the current "miserable" conditions of the government-sponsored Jewish schools in the western provinces of the empire.[146] Gurovich's plan proposed preserving the melamdim, an integral institute of Jewish communal life. He argued that "the Jews were used to melamdim" and thus the institution of young teachers, graduates of secular Jewish schools and Russian gymnasia, would only push Jews away from the new schools.[147] Gurovich proposed a unique design for a Jewish elementary school, which he called the "two-class melamed's room (dvukhklassnaia melamedskaia komnata)." This new type of school, to be set up in each Jewish agricultural colony, not only made use of the traditional terminology in its name,[148] but also retained the personnel and the curriculum of the traditional cheder. According to Gurovich's plan, the faculty of each "room" would include two melamdim, instructors in religion and Hebrew language. They would be officially appointed by the Patronage Committee for Foreign Settlers and funded by the students' parents. In addition to the melamdim, the faculty would also include one teacher of secular subjects, including Russian and German languages, funded by the government. Each "room" would be under the supervision of the school council, which would include the local government rabbi and two instructors, equally represented by melamdim and teachers.[149]

In 1868, with the support of V. N. Ettinger, the chairman of the Patronage Committee for Foreign Settlers, expert Jew Gurovich started implementing his reform project in the Jewish agricultural colonies of Kherson province. As a result of his efforts, twelve "rooms" (ten for boys and two for girls) were opened in ten Jewish agricultural colonies. Moreover, with the financial support of the Patronage Committee, Gurovich supplied these schools with brand-new classroom furniture. The expert Jew personally inaugurated the schools in the colonies of Novyi Berislav and L'vova.[150] His actions while on this mission far exceeded the limits set by the "Secret Regulation" of 1850, since Gurovich not only communicated with the authorities and the Jews directly, but also administered the reform in the full capacity of a government official. However, the expert Jew was also exerting his moral influence, strongly encouraged by the "Secret Regulation," since, in many cases, Gurovich verbally promoted the reform, arguing for the practical utility of modern education to the Jewish colonists.

The expert Jew provided a firsthand account of this mission. He wrote: "For the execution of this important and difficult mission, I traveled to the colonies of Kherson province and, sparing neither energy nor effort, I influenced the preconceptions of the Jewish colonists through indirect means. My goal was to win their trust and support for the caring measures of the government, and, upon the approval of the decisions of a communal meeting [on the opening of the new schools] by the local administrative boards, to initiate opening the schools immediately. I dare say that as a result of my edifying addresses to the communal meetings of colonists, the colonists not only agreed to open the schools, but also allotted significant resources from the communal budget to fund them."[151]

For the successful completion of this mission, Ettinger, the chairman of the Patronage Committee, and Governor-general Kotsebu nominated expert Jew Gurovich for an award. He was decorated with the Order of Saint Stanislav of the third degree, a special imperial order for non-Christian officials, and awarded a bonus in the amount of 500 silver rubles.[152]

In the 1860s, expert Jews significantly contributed to the work of the Rabbinical Commission, the central organ of the religious administration for Russian Jews. The Jewish bureaucrats provided data and analyses for the Commission's proceedings, and participated in these proceedings directly as members of the Commission. In 1861, expert Jews made up the majority of the Rabbinical Commission.

According to the law, the proceedings of the Rabbinical Commission were collective in nature, with a transparent decision-making process. Therefore, the law called for bureaucratic procedures that supported these basic principles: the only working language of the Commission was Russian, and all discussions had to be documented by detailed minutes, including members' opinions, their final decision, and the precise basis for it.[153] The proceedings of the Rabbinical Commission therefore reveal the policymaking practices of the MVD and the role of expert Jews in this process. The work of the Rabbinical Commission of 1861 was a radical departure both from traditional Russian politics based on authoritarian "ministerial power" and the traditional Jewish politics of *shtadlanut* conducted behind closed doors. This open yet essentially bureaucratic procedure involving the Jewish bureaucratic elite constituted a new kind of Jewish politics—a legitimate and loyal branch of Russian bureaucratic politics.

The third session of the Rabbinical Commission convened in St. Petersburg from November 15, 1861, to March 13, 1862. The contribution of this session to official Jewish policy included several landmark decisions in key areas, while the composition of the participating members encompassed the whole spectrum of key institutes of this policy. Thus, the Rabbinical Commission of 1861 embodied the institutional maturity of the religious administration for Russian Jews and of the Russian Jewish bureaucratic elite.

In 1861, membership of the Commission was expanded to ten members. Six of them were elected by representatives of the Jewish communities and approved by the MVD.[154] The four additional members were put on the Commission by various Russian ministries in order to discuss the issues put on the agenda by those ministries.[155] Three of the six elected members—Avraam Neiman, German Barats, and

Avraam Madievskii—were expert Jews under provincial governors and governor-generals. Two of the four other members—Il'ia Zeiberling and Samuel Joseph Fuenn—were expert Jews under the superintendents of the educational districts, and one—Moisei Berlin—was under the DDDII. For the first time, the membership of the Rabbinical Commission included a representative of the emerging acculturated Jewish economic elite—Evzel' Gintsburg. Gintsburg's participation in bureaucracy signified a breakthrough in the formal acknowledgment of the elite social status of the growing Russian Jewish bourgeoisie.[156]

The draft agenda of the Commission, prepared by the DDDII and approved by its director, consisted of fourteen questions.[157] This agenda clearly demonstrated the comparative roles of the government agencies in official Jewish policy. Three of the fourteen questions were initiated by the emperor and his personal chancellery, one by the Russian Senate, and the remaining ten questions "by order of the Ministry of Internal Affairs,"[158] the principal bureaucratic agency encompassing major areas of official Jewish policy. Six of the fourteen questions were framed by expert Jews' opinions and administrative proposals.[159] Two more questions, initiated by the administration, dealt with the current and prospective bureaucratic roles of expert Jews.[160]

The thematic scope of the Commission's agenda reflected both its bureaucratic approach to the problems of Jewish social, religious, and family life, and the general bureaucratic character of official Jewish policy.[161] Thus, five questions on the agenda of the Rabbinical Commission of 1861 involved issues of administration, regulation, and organization of Jewish communal life.[162] Four questions were on the regulation of Jewish religious ritual.[163] Two questions addressed the traditional Jewish family.[164] The last two questions dealt with government-sponsored Jewish education.[165]

The political contribution of the Rabbinical Commission of 1861, largely guided by expert Jews,[166] included bureaucratic measures for the advancement of a general imperial policy toward Jews, aimed at the comprehensive regulation of religious life and its institutions. These measures included bringing order to the traditional Jewish religious and communal organization by regulation of its institutional structure, budget, and personnel; bringing order to traditional Jewish religious ritual by introducing "civilized" European models such as rabbinical sermons, orderly worship supplemented by choir music, and confirmation of Jewish boys; and bringing order to traditional Jewish society and lifestyle through eradication of "fanaticism" and prejudices embedded in the customs, family values, and language of the Jews.[167]

The ultimate goal of these policies was to place all major aspects of Jewish life under the institutional control of the Russian ministerial system and its Jewish bureaucrats, expert Jews. The great significance of these bureaucratic procedures and institutions was that they constituted a major alternative to the authoritarian approach of "ministerial power," represented by the political debacles of the 1840s and the 1850s, such as the largely unsuccessful Jewish school reform and the never-implemented sorting (*razbor*) of the Jews. Thus, the bureaucratic framework of official Jewish policy, established in the 1850s and 1860s, set the limits of the administrative bent of Russian officialdom.[168] Moreover, this development was fully in line with the general thrust of the Russian Great Reforms, which promoted the primacy of institutions and bureaucratic procedures in the general domestic policy of the imperial government.[169]

In general, the Rabbinical Commission of 1861 recommended preserving the basic elements of Jewish religious life. However, the Commission advocated the adaptation of these elements to contemporary government policies aimed at the modernization of the empire. In the spirit of the Great Reforms, the measures proposed by the Commission did not rely on administrative repression and police enforcement. Instead, the implementation of these recommendations was based on the improvement of institutions which administered the Jewish subjects of the empire, and the enhancement of bureaucratic procedures which regulated various aspects of Jewish life, including education, the rabbinate, and the structure of religious and communal organization.[170]

In sum, the Rabbinical Commission of 1861, the majority of which was expert Jews, discussed an agenda for the most part devised by these expert Jews, and based its decisions on their expert materials and preliminary conclusions. Ultimately, each issue discussed and each solution recommended by the Rabbinical Commission became part of official Jewish policy. However, the agenda and decisions of the Rabbinical Commission did not automatically translate into imperial legislation or administrative directives of the MVD. As a rule, the deliberations and recommendations of the Commission were taken into account and implemented indirectly, through the everyday official discourse and bureaucratic practice of the imperial administration.[171]

During the last period of the service history of expert Jews, the 1890s through the 1910s, their administrative involvement lacked the dynamics and scope of the previous decades. In the later years, the service missions of expert Jews supported the MVD's domestic policy aimed at the preservation of the autocratic regime and containment of all kinds of subversive activity in the empire.[172] These missions largely reflected the ultra-conservative approach of contemporary MVD policy.

In 1909, the director of the DDDII, Aleksei Nikolaevich Kharuzin, assigned expert Jew Moisei Kreps to attest to the confessional conformity and political loyalty of the newly formed Jewish reformist congregation of St. Petersburg. An official attestation of the expert Jew was required for the pending approval of the congregation by the city governor of St. Petersburg, Daniil Vasil'evich Drachevskii.

According to its founder, philologist and littérateur Dr. Naum Abramovich Pereferkovich, the goal of the congregation, made up of himself and "fifty-six like-minded people belonging to the assimilated Russian-speaking Jewish intelligentsia," was "the establishment of a family *minyan* for us and our children, so we can create an environment in which our children could learn the Torah and Jewishness, and in which our wives could pray along with their husbands and children."[173]

Kreps examined the bylaws and program of the congregation presented for official approval, and pointed out the radical spirit of the reformist initiative, which, according to the expert Jew, was based on rejection of the "sacred and essential tenets accepted by the rest of religious Jews, since [the reformist congregation] does not accept the authority of Talmudic discourse."[174] Kreps argued that, in the opinion of the Jews of St. Petersburg, Pereferkovich's initiative was not only completely baseless, but extremely dangerous. According to the expert Jew, the leadership of the St. Petersburg Choral synagogue requested that the principals of the private Jewish schools where Pereferkovich taught at the time ban him from teaching, since he had "abandoned the faith of our fathers."[175] Moreover, in 1908, the leadership of the St. Petersburg Jewish community removed Pereferkovich's candidacy from the ballot for the office of government rabbi of the capital city, since he "did not share the fundamental religious tenets of the majority of the Jews."[176] Consequently, in his

УЧЕНЫЙ
ЕВР. ПРИ
МИНИСТЕРСТВѢ
Вн. Дѣлъ.
9 Октября 1909 г.
№ 259

Его Превосходительству
Г. Директору Департамента
Дух. Дѣлъ Инастр. Исповѣд.

Вслѣдствіе порученія Вашего Превосходительства имѣю честь объ образующейся въ Петербургѣ еврейской реформатской общинѣ доложить нижеслѣдующее.

Основателемъ имѣющей организоваться еврейской реформатской общины является Наумъ Абрамовичъ Переферковичъ, іудейскаго вѣроисповѣданія, кандидатъ восточныхъ языковъ СПБ. университета, проживающій нынѣ здѣсь по Матвѣевской ул. д. № 20 на Петербургской сторонѣ. Родомъ онъ изъ Ставрополя, гдѣ окончилъ гимназію. Теперь ему лѣтъ 40; года 1½ тому назадъ женился на еврейкѣ изъ Риги, имѣетъ отъ ней дочь. Занимался все время литературными трудами, преподавалъ законъ еврейской вѣры въ разныхъ учебныхъ заведеніяхъ. Года 3 тому назадъ провелъ почти цѣлый годъ въ Америкѣ (Ныо-Іоркъ). — Въ прошломъ году выступалъ въ качествѣ кандидата на постъ петербургскаго общественнаго раввина, съ каковой цѣлью приносъ въ молитвенномъ облаченіи проповѣдь въ мѣстной главной синагогѣ, послѣ чего выяснилось, что онъ не имѣетъ шансовъ на избраніе на упомянутую должность

1906

Moisei Kreps's official report on St. Petersburg reform Jewish congregation, October 9, 1909 (RGIA, f. 821, o. 8, d. 331, l. 95)

official report to the director of the DDDII, the expert Jew declared the reformist congregation a "sect, separated from mainstream Judaism."[177]

Kreps's conclusion apparently signaled alarm to the authorities, who denied official registration to the reformist congregation, labeled by the expert Jew as a "dangerous sect." This decision demonstrated the overall ultra-conservative bias of the late imperial administration, which in the 1900s and 1910s, while suppressing the reform initiative, officially permitted six private Jewish congregations, largely Orthodox, in St. Petersburg in addition to the main Choral synagogue.[178]

Hence, the evolution of policymaking and administrative missions of expert Jews demonstrates the progressive bureaucratization of their service along with the shifting objectives and approaches of general imperial policy toward the Jews. If in the 1860s, the official missions of expert Jews Berlin and Gurovich targeted Jewish religious fanaticism as the main obstacle to the social integration of the Jews, in the 1900s the official mission of expert Jew Moisei Kreps was to safeguard the "sacred and essential tenets accepted by religious Jews," formerly defined as religious fanaticism, from any innovation.

Official Translation and Chancellery Work

The "Secret Regulation" of 1850 prohibited expert Jews from keeping any official records documenting their work. The strictly confidential reports of expert Jews to their superiors, including governors, governor-generals, and the Minister of Internal Affairs, were the only allowed legitimate form of documentation of their work. In addition, due to their status as officials for special missions, expert Jews were exempt from chancellery routines and dull bureaucratic paperwork. However, since the "Secret Regulation" put expert Jews fully at the disposal of their superiors, both the provincial administration and central offices of the MVD consistently assigned Jewish bureaucrats tedious chancellery tasks, including monitoring and digesting the current press, as well as registration, legalization, and translation of official documents. As a rule, expert Jews felt such assignments to be a burden, and considered them irrelevant and marginal in their bureaucratic agenda.

In 1853, the governor-general of Vitebsk, Mogilev, and Smolensk provinces assigned his expert Jew Moisei Berlin translation work for a police investigation of illegal Jewish printing press in the Kopys' district. Berlin considered this assignment burdensome and absolutely unrelated to his official responsibilities.[179] He also complained that another assignment, the Yiddish translation of instructions for Jewish farmers, while "apparently insignificant," according to the expert Jew, took a lot of his effort, since it required an accurate rendering of the Russian laws in a vernacular accessible to "people of little education."[180] Moreover, according to expert Jew Berlin, in 1854 his service included many more "unimportant assignments, such as translations, etc."[181]

From 1907 to 1917, expert Jew under the DDDII Moisei Kreps provided monthly digests of the Jewish press in Russian, Hebrew and Yiddish (in the form of newspaper and journal clippings accompanied by a few comments and translations) to the MVD and Ministry of National Enlightenment.[182]

From 1856 to 1908, during his entire tenure as expert Jew under the governor of Mogilev province, Arnold Mandel'shtam was used as "interpreter of foreign languages" by the provincial chancellery.[183] In his petition to the Minister of Internal Affairs, Mandel'shtam complained that this assignment was absolutely unrelated to his responsibilities as expert Jew; however, he dutifully carried out this mission "by the order of the Governor and without any compensation."[184] The expert Jew pointed out that his workload in the capacity of official interpreter had considerably grown during the 1900s due to the increasing demand for travel documents and passports. According to the expert Jew, the governor Dmitrii Fedorovich Gagman assigned him the task of issuing passports to the Jews, and the expert Jew had to work overtime and even hire a personal assistant, whom he paid out of his own pocket. Mandel'shtam petitioned the MVD to release him from this burdensome duty, which significantly interfered with his principal official agenda. Ironically, the DDDII rejected this petition on the basis of the "Statute on Expert Jews," which stipulated that expert Jews were to be used at the discretion of the governors.[185]

Chancellery work was routinely assigned to expert Jews during the entire span of their service history. However, during the last decades of this history, the growing proportion of bureaucratic chancellery assignments among the service missions of expert Jews virtually buried them under mountains of paperwork.

Service of Expert Jews and the Continuity of Official Jewish Policy

In addition to the general bureaucratization of the MVD and imperial domestic policy, the service of expert Jews was influenced by the arbitrariness of the governors, who chose when and where to use their Jewish officials, or whether to use them at all. Factors of location and time, such as regional differences in the objectives and methods of expert Jews and the length of their service terms, also played an important role. The time factor was of particular significance since the stability of the office of expert Jew ensured the overall institutional stability of official Jewish policy, and the individual longevity of the serving expert Jews safeguarded the continuity of that policy.

Mikhail Vorontsov, Aleksandr Stroganov, and Pavel Kotsebu, the top Russian bureaucrats who served as the governor-generals of Novorossiia and Bessarabia from the 1850s to the 1870s, routinely assigned bureaucratic cases in many areas of official Jewish policy to their expert Jew, Markus Gurovich. At the same time, a comparable number of cases related to Jewish matters were processed by the chancellery of the governor-general without the involvement of the expert Jew.

In the early 1850s, expert Jew Markus Gurovich was a novice bureaucrat at the chancellery of Governor-general Vorontsov. His work was integrated in bureaucratic practices gradually and slowly.[186] He was not initially assigned cases obviously related to his official expertise, such as the project of appointing retired Jewish soldiers to the lower supervisory positions (*sotskie i desiatskie*) within the district land police (*zemskaia politsiia*) in areas densely populated by Jews,[187] and the project of reducing the number of district rabbis and synagogues and abolishing private prayer assemblies as sources of Jewish fanaticism.[188]

In the late 1850s and 1860s, however, the institute of expert Jew came of age and became an integral part of the provincial bureaucracy, and the incumbent Jewish official Markus Gurovich had acquired significant bureaucratic experience and earned the trust of his superiors. However,

Governor-general Stroganov, apparently following the "Secret Regulation" of 1850, barred the expert Jew from cases related to the legal status of the Jews, their taxation, and direct administration. Thus, Gurovich was not assigned to such cases as the determination of rights of the *krymchaki* (Jews of Crimea) to purchase land in 1860;[189] the introduction in Odessa of a property tax for Jews in addition to the *korobochnyi sbor* in 1857;[190] and the establishment of societies for the promotion of agriculture among Jews under the patronage of the Ministry of State Domains in 1858.[191]

In the 1870s, Governor-general Kotsebu apparently believed that Russian bureaucracy had acquired enough experience in Jewish matters to deal with them directly without the help of Jewish bureaucrats. Thus, in the words of Fedor Girs, Governor-general Kotsebu presumed that he could "influence the Jews through his chancellery and his [Russian] officials,"[192] at least in simple matters that did not require the special knowledge and bureaucratic experience of the expert Jew. In particular, the governor-general did not assign to Gurovich the examination of the bylaws of the Odessa society for dissemination of vocational training and elementary education among Jewish girls from poor families in 1872.[193]

The factor of location caused significant differences in both the service of expert Jews in the western and southern provinces of the Pale of Settlement and in the chancelleries of the provincial administration and central offices of the MVD in St. Petersburg.

Government policy in the western provinces was aimed at the comprehensive obliteration of the social and political legacies of the independent Polish state. As a result, the imperial authorities were consistently expanding their spheres of direct control over these territories through policies of unification and centralization of the administration and cultural Russification of the population.[194] However, the government implemented these policies with extreme caution, fearing mass unrest and resistance, a real danger, as demonstrated by the two Polish uprisings of 1830 and 1863. The government used the same caution in its approach to the traditional Jewish population of the western provinces, which included a significant proportion of Hasidim, considered by the authorities the most subversive element within Russian Jewry. Therefore, in the western provinces of the empire the Russian government used its bureaucratic instruments of intervention and control over the society selectively and cautiously. Thus, in the Kingdom of Poland, the principal provinces of the former independent Poland, the institute of expert Jews was never implemented. In the western provinces, the former parts of the Polish commonwealth—Belorussia and Lithuania—Russian governor-generals largely used expert Jews for auxiliary missions, such as inspections and unofficial investigations, which were carefully concealed from the Jewish population. From 1853 to 1855, one-third of the assignments given by the governor-general of Vitebsk, Mogilev, and Smolensk provinces to expert Jew Moisei Berlin were secret missions, documented by the strictly confidential reports of the expert Jew in which he "provided the administration with secret evidence of the illegal activity of the Jews."[195] In the same period, half of Berlin's assignments were confidential inquiries into various areas and issues of Jewish religion, history, society and economy.[196]

In the southern provinces of the Russian empire, as Fedor Girs put it, "there [was] no Polish question, but there [was] another plague—the Jewish question."[197] Compared to the Jewish population of the western provinces, the Jews of southern Russia were a less numerous yet more dynamic segment of Russian Jewry.

The Jews of the southern provinces, including the Jewish farmers of Novorossiia and the Jewish entrepreneurs, merchants, and artisans of Odessa, were far less traditional and far more integrated into general imperial society than Jews in the western provinces. Thus, southern Russia became an experimental ground for imperial Jewish policy. As a result, the first secular Jewish school and the first Jewish agricultural colonies emerged in these provinces. The service of Markus Gurovich, expert Jew under the governor-general of Novorossiia and Bessarabiia, was also an example of this special situation. The administration never assigned the expert Jew any confidential investigations or secret missions. Conversely, Gurovich's service consisted of innovative projects, substantial field work, administrative assignments, and extensive direct communication with the Jews and the authorities. The progressive nature of these missions reflected the general vitality of Jewish life in the southern provinces of the Russian empire.

The MVD's corps of expert Jews had a flat organizational structure. There were no hierarchical relationships between expert Jews, so the status of expert Jew under the DDDII at the central offices of the MVD was not formally superior to that of expert Jew under governors in the provinces. In fact, expert Jews under the DDDII frequently served as the higher expert authority in Jewish matters, providing final judgment when the opinions of provincial Jewish bureaucrats diverged. Thus, in 1880 the acting expert Jew under the DDDII, Illarion Kaufman, resolved the issue of Jewish oaths raised by the controversial opinions of Lev Binshtok, expert Jew under the governor of Volhyn province, and Lev Bornshtein, government rabbi of Dubno district.[198] Moreover, expert Jews at the central offices of the MVD were assigned tasks applicable to all Jewish subjects of the empire, which were never given to expert Jews in the provinces. For example, in 1871, expert Jew under the DDDII Avraam Neiman adapted the formulae and procedures of Jewish oaths to the new standards introduced by the Russian Court Statutes of 1864. Neiman's adaptation became part of Russian legislation relevant to all Russian Jews.[199]

Generations of top MVD officials and provincial administrators relied on the expertise of their Jewish aides for policymaking and implementation. Thus, long-serving expert Jews not only supported their superiors but also harmonized many incongruent administrative measures and policies, making them one consistent whole: a government policy for the Jews.[200] In a way, expert Jews were the institutional memory of that policy.

There is interesting yet anecdotal evidence about the expert Jews' role in the governors' awareness about matters of official Jewish policy. According to expert Jew Shmarya Levin, his superior "Prince Sviatopolk-Mirsky [Prince Petr Dmitrievich Sviatopolk-Mirskii (1857–1914), governorgeneral of Vilna, Kovno, and Grodno provinces from 1902 to 1904, Minister of Internal Affairs from 1904 to 1905] . . . an extraordinary man, the governor of a province with a large Jewish population, had no idea . . . of the disabilities under which the Jews labored. He did not know that there were so many special laws designed to make Jewish life intolerable. At every new revelation [of the expert Jew] he would open eyes as if to say: 'Is that really so?' "[201]

From the 1850s to the 1910s, the average service term of expert Jews was twelve years, while for Russian governors it was four years. Moreover, half these governors occupied their offices for less than two years, while half the expert Jews remained in the same office for more than twenty years.[202] The service of several expert Jews far exceeded these limits and spanned dozens of terms of their superiors. Among these veteran expert Jews were Arnold Mandel'shtam, who served under the governor of Mogilev province for fifty-two years, 1856–1908,[203] and Ruvim Shnitkind, who served under the governor of Kovno province for forty-three years, 1868–1911.[204] During his fifty years of service, 1861–1911, expert Jew Grigorii Shkliaver worked with seventeen governor-generals of Vilna, Kovno, and Grodno provinces.[205] This longevity of the expert Jews was largely due to the fact that, as a rule, they were appointed to their offices for life.

No other institution of the religious administration for Russian Jews could compete with the structural, political, and cadre stability of expert Jews. Membership in the Rabbinical Commission was inconsistent and depended on the pragmatic necessities of the moment rather than fundamental political principles. Due to the extended intervals between sessions of the Commission, its membership was rarely made up of the same delegates. The cadres of the government rabbinate were even more fluid, since rabbis were elected by the Jewish communities for short three-year terms. The heterogeneous personnel of the government rabbinate encompassed the entire social spectrum of Russian Jews, and therefore lacked any political consistency or significance.

Thus, the continuity of official Jewish policy was for the most part maintained by the cadres of expert Jews, who occupied their offices for decades and were united by common education, culture, service ethos, and, as the following chapter shows, a common ideology.

5

Literature and the Table of Ranks

Intelligentsia, Bureaucracy, and "False Transparency"

Unlike the Russian bureaucracy, the Russian intelligentsia was not an estate or social class, but rather an amorphous "self-proclaimed social subculture"[1] with permeable boundaries and shifting social features, structurally divided by diverse ideological, political, and social affiliations. In the first half of the nineteenth century, the diverse ideological groups within Russian intelligentsia became visible through the articulation and implementation of their ideologies, social values and political platforms in the public sphere, mostly in informal and often illegal political, social, and cultural organizations. The anti-liberal political climate of mid-nineteenth century Russia and its endemic social fragmentation, especially the wide gap between the bureaucracy and the rest of society, promoted the political radicalization of the Russian intelligentsia, which used every available channel to popularize its dissident opinions. Thus, university pulpits, literature, and the press became important platforms for public concerns and criticism of the bureaucracy, which persistently avoided open and direct dialogue with society.[2]

In the 1850s at the onset of the Great Reforms era, the ideological divide between bureaucracy and intelligentsia narrowed. The new generation of Russian officials, enlightened bureaucrats, and the Russian intelligentsia had common roots in the rational ideas of the European Enlightenment. Bureaucracy and intelligentsia had close social ties, shared common education and culture, and even collaborated in the government chancelleries.[3] During the era of the Great Reforms, relationships between the government and members of various groups of the intelligentsia intensified. The government sought the support of the intelligentsia—a major source of public opinion in Russia and an unofficial political rival of the bureaucracy—for the development and implementation of political initiatives. However, the government, especially the MVD, used this support cautiously and kept it under control, using the bureaucratic technique known as "false transparency" (*iskusstvennaia glasnost'*). Thus, Russian ministries would often initiate open public discussions in the press in order to find out the opinions and attitudes of a particular social group targeted by new policies and legislation.[4] Since the intelligentsia, for the most part, took it seriously and thought that the government was really interested in hearing, publicizing, and openly discussing diverse opinions, the government used the opinions of the intelligentsia with caution and on a selective basis. According to Andrei Parfenovich Desiatovskii, a typical Russian enlightened bureaucrat, "The assistance of private persons at their own will could be very useful and valuable for the government; however, these private persons should fully support [the goals and methods of] the government."[5]

Thus, in the 1860s–1880s, the government actively used periodicals as a main arena in which to publicize its political ideology and promote its practical policies. However, only those members of the intelligentsia and of the larger Russian society who fully supported the government and, ideally, members of the bureaucracy were allowed to be government spokesmen and to debate official policies in the press. As bureaucrats, such spokesmen were supposed to demonstrate exemplary loyalty to the monarch and empire, by which the loyalty of all other subjects was measured.

Publications by Expert Jews on Social and Political Issues

In 1888, a collection of historical documents on Jewish life in seventeenth- and eighteenth-century Poland, compiled by Iona Gurliand, Russian Jewish scholar-cum-bureaucrat, was published in Krakow.[6] The publication printed Gurliand's formal portrait along with a full list of his official titles, including the rank of collegiate councilor. An anonymous reviewer of the book pointed out its mediocre quality and sarcastically suggested that Gurliand "pay more attention to history and literature, and less to the Table of Ranks."[7]

As if heeding this advice, the MVD paid very serious attention to literature as a means of implementation of its Jewish policy. The MVD considered the press an important tool for the moral exhortation and civil improvement of the Jews. Thus, a Jewish variety of "false transparency" emerged. In 1888, a DDDII memorandum included the statement that in order to overcome Jewish fanaticism, "the emerging Russian-language Jewish press was a more influential and powerful tool" than expert Jews.[8] However, the Jewish press was such a powerful tool mostly due to the publications of expert Jews, who were for the most part expressing official opinions and promoting government policies toward the Jews.

The publications of expert Jews, regularly appearing in the Russian-language Jewish press, represented the official side in the controlled dialogue between the government and the Jews. Thus, expert Jews extended their service into the realm of public discourse, including journalism and literature. As bureaucrats, they often articulated their opinions in the official press (*ofitsioz*), sponsored and controlled by the Russian ministries and the provincial administration. Expert Jews rarely used pseudonyms and signed publications with their full names and official titles, lending additional strength to their arguments, which promoted official policies. The subject matter of their publications encompassed for the most part topics within the official scope of Jewish bureaucrats and major aspects of official Jewish policy.

The following analysis of publications by expert Jews is based on a representative selection[9] of forty examples of journalism and scholarship, translations, and public addresses published from 1861 to 1911 by thirteen Jewish bureaucrats in sixteen Russian-language periodicals. Ten of these periodicals were Jewish newspapers and journals, six of them Russian. Five out of six Russian periodicals were official mouthpieces of the MVD (e.g., *Severnaia pochta*) and Russian provincial administrations (e.g., *Volynskie gubernskie vedomosti*). Four out of ten Jewish periodicals were semi-official organs, which published new government decrees and legislation on the Jews and backed the official Jewish policy (e.g., *Rassvet* and its successor *Tsion*). One Jewish periodical, the monthly journal *Evreiskie zapiski,* was founded and run by expert Jew Aron Pumpianskii in Riga.[10] The analyzed publications also include nine monographs—books and pamphlets.

The largest group, thirteen of the forty publications by expert Jews, has to do with the institutes of official Jewish policy, from the Rabbinical Commission and rabbinical seminaries to the administration of prayer houses and community libraries. Several publications of this group simply cover the routine work of these institutes, such as the 1861–1862 session of the Rabbinical Commission,[11] and commencement ceremonies at the rabbinical seminaries of Vilna (1865)[12] and Zhitomir (1868).[13] Some publications popularize the goals and important functions of institutions in the religious administration for the Jews. For example, such publications argue that the government rabbinate brought law and order into the religious and social life of Russian Jews,[14] and that censorship of Jewish religious literature promoted religious tolerance because it prevented expressions of nationalistic hatred in the press.[15] The publications of expert Jews often exposed defects in the institutional structure of official Jewish policy and suggested bureaucratic solutions for improvement. For example, they maintained that the role and influence of the Rabbinical Commission could be significantly enhanced by publicizing its proceedings among Jews and by recruiting new members who would represent Russian Jews living beyond the Pale of Settlement, in the capital cities of St. Petersburg and Moscow and in the provinces of central Russia.[16] Expert Jews also believed that the government rabbinate could incorporate traditional, "spiritual," rabbis. However, in order to qualify for the office, aspiring candidates had to have exposure to secular academic disciplines, which could be introduced into the curriculum of the largest and most influential traditional *yeshivot* in Russia.[17] Expert Jews argued that inadequate financial reporting by the Jewish communities could be fixed by placing it under the direct supervision of the local municipal authorities.[18] For the most part, expert Jews in these publications promoted institutional and bureaucratic approaches to the social problems of Russian Jews. They believed that the establishment of public libraries of secular books in Russian and Jewish languages in synagogues would significantly contribute to the advancement of modern education among the Jews.[19] Furthermore, they suggested that the institution of special communal charitable committees, beyond the traditional framework of Jewish charitable organizations, would eliminate Jewish vagrancy and beggary.[20]

A considerable number of publications—eight of the forty—focus on problems of secular Jewish education and pedagogy. These materials reflect the personal and professional experiences of expert Jews who were, for the most part, graduates, teachers, and inspectors of the rabbinical seminaries and government-sponsored Jewish schools. Expert Jews pointed out the major goals of secular Jewish education in Russia, including the intellectual and civil development of the Jews, necessary for the "creation of a new life."[21] Expert Jews considered government-sponsored Jewish schools the "breeding-ground of the enlightenment," and strongly supported compulsory enrollment of Jewish children in these schools.[22] Many acknowledged the poor condition of government-sponsored Jewish schools, caused by the limited budget and "reluctance of traditional Jews to public education."[23] However, Jewish bureaucrats believed that these schools still had great potential as the basis for the elementary secular education.[24] They argued that the special Jewish status of these schools was not an impediment to rapprochement between Jews and Russians, since "rapprochement was only possible between educated people."[25] They highlighted the central role of the Russian language in the education and social integration of the Jews, and consequently the lack of knowledge Russian constituted a serious "civil disability."[26] Expert Jews considered the education provided by the curriculum of Jewish elementary schools, including the basics of Russian language and secular subjects, a necessary but insufficient requisite for the social integration of the Jews. Thus, Jewish youth should complete their education in the Russian gymnasia and universities where all subjects, including Jewish religion, were taught in Russian.[27]

The next group of publications by expert Jews focuses on another important aspect of the social integration of Russian Jews: military service. Expert Jews argued that in contrast to the selective and unfair practices of the Nikolaevan military drafts, universal military service, imposed on an equal basis on all imperial subjects including Jews during the military reform of 1874, should be perceived by Russian Jews as the equivalent "of granting [them] the rights of citizenship."[28] Expert Jews demonstrated that the relatively high number of draft dodgers among Jews did not signify their refusal to accept the rights and perform the duties of Russian citizens, but instead cited the important religious and family reasons forcing Jews to evade military service and suggested changes to the legislation and regulations that would help them adjust to and appreciate military service as an upgrade of their citizenship status.[29] In particular, expert Jews suggested extending the release from service during the Jewish holidays, already granted to Jewish soldiers on active duty, to Jewish army reservists.[30]

A small yet very important group of publications by expert Jews focused on the pogroms of 1881. Trying to unearth the roots of the anti-Jewish violence, expert Jews blamed neither the Russian government nor Russian Jews. Instead, they held Russian society and its negative attitude toward the Jews, cultivated by Russian journalists and "scandalous press," fully accountable for the pogroms.[31] Russian public opinion, they argued, was greatly influenced by the press, which created a negative image of Jews based on both century-old (ritual use of Christian blood) and modern (covert kahal government and economic exploitation of Russian peasants) prejudices.[32] Thus, according to expert Jews, hostility toward the Jews was forced on the Russian people, and therefore "pogroms were provoked artificially, and were organized" by enemies of the Jews in Russian society, who "exploited the pogroms to impel the government to impose severe limitations on their civil rights, so they would finally leave the country."[33] At the same time, expert Jews pointed out the deeper roots of the pogroms, which lay in the overall economic, social, and political "crisis of the Russian state."[34] In the economic sphere, this crisis was intensified by the general poverty of the Russian population exacerbated by economic competition with the equally poor masses of Jews. In the social and political spheres, the division of the population into native and non-native subjects made the "civil development" and social integration of the *inorodtsy*, including the Jews, virtually impossible.[35] Under such circumstances, expert Jews did not appeal to Russian public opinion, but suggested that the pressing issues raised by the pogroms be settled between the Jews and the government. The majority of the solutions proposed by expert Jews were conservative and essentially bureaucratic. They maintained that, since Russia had hospitably accepted the "wandering [Jewish] people" and put them under the protection of the law, Russian Jews, despite the pogroms, should not breach Russian laws.[36] At the same time, the government should develop new laws to restore order and resolve the problems generated by the pogroms.[37] However, a few expert Jews went farther and argued that the government should "take measures to remove the limitations restricting residence of Jews in Russia, since these measures would ultimately contribute to the economic development and political stability of Russia."[38]

Several publications by expert Jews included materials directly related to their own service. These publications included social, economic, and statistical research by expert Jews, such as an analysis of the death rate among the Jews of the city of Zhitomir from 1851 to 1866,[39] a comparative analysis of population statistics and economic productivity of Jewish agricultural colonies in Ekaterinoslav province,[40] and an analysis of data on Jewish artisans in Kovno province, collected in 1887 during the census conducted by the district government rabbis.[41]

A number of publications by expert Jews reflected their scholarly pursuits in the field of Jewish historiography. Many of these publications were translations of German Jewish authors, augmented by commentaries and supplements by expert Jews. They translated general histories of the Jews and supplemented them with their original surveys of Jewish history in Russia.[42] These supplements featured self-portraits of Jewish bureaucrats in historical context, such as the history of the Jews in the Baltic provinces by Aron Pumpianskii, which included the author's account of his work as expert Jew and government rabbi of Riga.[43]

The publications by expert Jews also included translations of classical Jewish religious texts and liturgy. In 1859, reviewing the editorial program of *Rassvet*, expert Jew Markus Gurovich argued that a Russian-language Jewish journal that ignored theological issues could not be popular among Jews, who were essentially a religious people. Gurovich pointed out that "it's not enough to use the press to talk to Jews only about reforms and improvements." The expert Jew strongly supported the founders of *Rassvet*, who intended to publish "discourses on Jewish theology" on a regular basis.[44] However, contemporary regulations of the Russian Orthodox Church prohibited literal translation of the Bible into modern Russian. Therefore, Gurovich recommended that quotations be kept to a minimum, and, when necessary, the Orthodox Old Slavonic canon be used for rendering biblical text.[45] Coincidentally, in the same year of 1859, the Holy Synod finally sanctioned a modern Russian translation of the Bible, which was completed only in 1876.[46] In the 1870s, expert Jews translated some texts of the Hebrew Bible into modern Russian, including the Psalms of David.[47] In 1870, expert Jew Osip Gurvich published his Russian translation of the Jewish prayer book, accompanied by the original Hebrew text.[48] This publication was praised by an anonymous Russian reviewer as the first attempt "at sincere and serious rapprochement between Jews and Russians."[49]

In sum, the publications of expert Jews expressed the loyal and moderate position of Jewish bureaucrats, supporting the government on all major issues of official Jewish policy. This position was firm and consistent through the whole history of expert Jews. However, while their position did not evolve conceptually or ideologically, it tended to expand on new and emerging problems and areas of Jewish life such as pogroms, universal military service, and many others. Thus, the ideological stability of expert Jews reflected the continuity of official Jewish policy as well as the mounting bureaucratization of this policy, whose goal was to put the multitudes of Jewish life under bureaucratic control.

Russian Wissenschaft des Judentums and Its Bureaucratic Beginnings

Missions to provide information in support of official Jewish policy constituted a sizable proportion of the service assignments of expert Jews, since their superiors, Russian enlightened bureaucrats working at the MVD, considered accurate and complete information about local conditions in the provinces an essential basis for policymaking. Russian enlightened bureaucrats emphasized and promoted modern scientific methods of collecting, processing, and analyzing this information.[50] Consequently, the reports and memoranda of expert Jews embodied this approach and resembled academic scholarship.[51]

Scholarship is an ongoing conversation, real or imagined, between scholars of different generations, disparate backgrounds, and diverse views. From one such dialogue—between the German founders of the science of Judaism (Wissenschaft des Judentums) and their Russian adherents, students, and colleagues, including expert Jews—a whole academic field of Jewish studies in the Russian language, including historiography, philology, and religious and legal studies, emerged during the 1850s through the 1870s.

The modern science of Judaism began in nineteenth-century Germany in the midst of the social transformation and intellectual revolution that accompanied the emancipation of the German Jews. Emancipation shaped the research agendas, methods, and social mission of nascent Jewish scholars. Wissenschaft des Judentums never crystallized into a standardized school of thought and research but developed as an ever-expanding circle of scholars of Jewish history and literature. Through this ongoing scholarly conversation, Wissenschaft des Judentums continued to attract fresh new minds into its intellectual orbit. The common ethos of the Wissenschaft des Judentums scholars shaped the distinct features of the emerging field of Jewish studies. It was a field dominated by Jews, whose scholarship challenged the anti-Jewish stereotypes of medieval Christian scholarship on Judaism, as well as the ahistorical mode of traditional Jewish scholarship. Wissenschaft des Judentums scholars recognized the social consequences of their studies; they shared a twofold mission—to promote understanding and social acceptance of Jews among non-Jews, and to invigorate the modernization of the living Jewish community and tradition. The right of free inquiry was essential to Wissenschaft des Judentums scholarship. Daring questions answered with the help of new methods and sources allowed for a rich and nuanced picture of the Jewish past. This approach validated non-traditional forms and genres of Jewish literature, non-Jewish sources, and non-Jewish components of Jewish culture as a legitimate source base of the field. A conceptual mode of thinking was fundamental to Wissenschaft des Judentums creativity. Any single historical text was subordinate to its larger historical context. Thus, Wissenschaft des Judentums scholars addressed larger issues of Jewish history through their thematic and synthetic treatment.

In 1818, Leopold Zunz, a founder of Wissenschaft des Judentums, published an essay entitled "On Rabbinic Literature,"[52] in which he devised a research program for his newly formed *Verein für Kultur und Wissenschaft der Juden*. Zunz called for a scholarly assessment of the Jewish historical experience preceding the era of emancipation. He argued that only a historian armed with modern knowledge and methodology could accomplish this enormous task, which required the examination of the full sweep of Jewish literary creativity. Thus, according to Zunz, history was to replace the exegesis and philosophy of traditional Jewish scholarship, and would become both "expositor and arbiter of Judaism."[53] In the decades from the 1830s to the 1870s, major breakthroughs of Wissenschaft des Judentums scholarship occurred. Zunz himself published a monumental study of the synagogue as the remarkable institution responsible for the historical continuity of Judaism.[54] Heinrich Graetz, Abraham Geiger, and Zecharias Frankel in their studies and critical editions of rabbinic literature expounded on the concept of the historical development of Judaism, a key thesis of Wissenschaft des Judentums.[55] Peter Beer, Isaak Markus Jost, and Julius Furst pioneered scholarship on Jewish sectarianism, exploring different historical developments and influential intellectual currents within Judaism, such as Karaism, Jewish mysticism, and messianic movements.[56] Moritz Steinschneider's study revealed the cultural contribution of medieval Spanish Jews, who served as mediators in the transmission of the classical Greco-Roman heritage from the Muslim East to the Christian West.[57] By the 1870s, the main parameters of Wissenschaft des Judentums—its ideology, methodology, and institutional base—also took shape. Conceptually, due to its "Spanish bias," Wissenschaft des Judentums emphasized the achievements of Sephardic Jewry during their "Golden Age" in Spain, and largely ignored the underachieving Ashkenazi Jews of Eastern Europe. Cultural history—the dominant methodology of Wissenschaft des Judentums, essentially the study of literature—left little space for the development of alternative methods, such as political and social history. Wissenschaft des Judentums never became part of German academia, and therefore its principal institutional base—semi-academic Jewish theological seminaries—formed strong bonds between the scholars and the modern rabbinate. New sources, interests, and concerns eventually expanded Wissenschaft des Judentums into an international movement, spreading as far as France, England, the United States, and Russia.

Russian Jewish historians, nurtured as modern Jews in the German cultural tradition, worked in the broader context of the German-centered Wissenschaft des Judentums, which used the civil emancipation and cultural integration of the Jews to reshape Jewish historical memory. The nineteenth-century development of Russian Jewish historiography was largely inspired by German Wissenschaft and, at the same time, radically challenged it. Although German Wissenschaft rejected traditional Ashkenazic Judaism, above all in its pietistic Eastern European forms, the scholars who created Russian-language Jewish studies used Wissenschaft models of thought in order to prove precisely the opposite, namely that a rational scholarly approach was perfectly applicable to the Eastern European, Russian, and Polish world. Thus, Russian Wissenschaft emerged.

The term "Russian Wissenschaft" describes an influential segment of Jewish scholarship in the Russian language, by academic and semiacademic scholars of Jewish history and literature who were university-educated and professionally employed by Russian academia and the Russian government. These Russian scholars were directly connected to Wissenschaft des Judentums as students, esteemed colleagues, or open adherents of German scholars of the movement, from the renowned Abraham Geiger to the humble Peter Beer. The scholars of Russian Wissenschaft also shared a thematic focus, source base, and methodology in their research. Their interests encompassed the early medieval period of Russian Jewish history, the cultural cross-fertilization of Slavic and Judaic traditions, and the history of Jewish sects. They used cutting-edge methodology, including sophisticated philological and historiographic analysis of multi-lingual texts. What's more, the scholars of Russian Wissenschaft conceived of their work within a shared conceptual framework and saw their scholarship as the fulfillment of a social mission. They sought to integrate Russian Jewish history into the shared past of the multi-ethnic and multi-confessional Russian empire, and to remake Russian Jews, seen by contemporary Russians as a strange and dangerous minority, into an organic part of the Russian imperial state and society. Unlike its German source and counterpart, however, Russian Wissenschaft was in large part nurtured by the Russian government and its need to build the empire.

Russian Wissenschaft's interest in Russian Jews was shared and shaped by the Russian imperial bureaucracy. This interest created the unique institutional base of Russian Wissenschaft.[58] State-sponsored rabbinical seminaries in Zhitomir and Vilna nurtured such scholars as German Barats and Abraham Harkavy.[59] The provincial bureaucratic chancelleries and imperial ministries in St. Petersburg employed such historians and literary scholars as Moisei Berlin and Naum Pereferkovich as government experts in Jewish matters. Government offices and official academic institutions also sponsored the first Russian publications in Jewish history, archaeology, and ethnography.[60]

Russian Wissenschaft emerged in the early 1850s, when ambitious social—rather than religious, as was the case of the classical German Wissenschaft—reforms of traditional Jewish life made the Russian government a major sponsor as well as a major consumer of historical scholarship on the Jewish past. Not surprisingly, Russian Jewish bureaucrats serving the government as expert Jews were among the pioneers of Russian Jewish historiography.

Thus, expert Jew Moisei Berlin's studies, including his "History of Hasidism" (1854) and "Essay on the Ethnography of the Jewish Population in Russia" (1861), are examples of the embryonic Russian Jewish historiography. Berlin's works built upon the research and methodology of German Wissenschaft and anticipated the research interests, concepts, and approaches shared by Russian Jewish historians of the succeeding generations.

Moisei Berlin compiled his "History of Hasidism" in 1854 as an official memorandum ordered by his superior Pavel Ignat'ev, governor-general of Vitebsk, Mogilev, and Smolensk provinces.[61] In his introduction, Berlin wrote: "I added an essay [on Kabbalah] as an introduction to the history of Hasidism. One cannot understand the essence and genesis of Hasidism without knowledge of Kabbalah and its historical development."[62] According to Berlin, his introduction built upon the findings of the "impartial scholars of Jewish literature," an obvious reference to the German Wissenschaft des Judentums.[63] Berlin demonstrated how "rabbis . . . in order to preserve the confidence and respect of the masses and maintain their power and control over the Jews," were able to contain the social potential of Jewish mysticism for centuries.[64] The status quo exploded in the seventeenth century during the "uprising of the fanatical kabbalist," Sabbatai Tzevi.[65] Based on the history of Sabbateanism, Berlin singled out patterns—such as charismatic leadership and the extreme polarization of the Jewish community—found in other Jewish sectarian movements, such as Hasidism in Poland and Russia in the eighteenth and nineteenth centuries. Berlin negatively portrayed the whole gallery of Hasidic leaders—from the legendary founder of Hasidism, Israel ben Eliezer (the Besht), to Berlin's contemporary the Lubavicher

Копія, исправленная въ слогѣ и изложеніи состоявшихъ при Витебскомъ Генералъ-Губернаторѣ Полковникомъ Петро[в]скимъ (нынѣ Витебскимъ Вице-Губернаторомъ), —

— Исторія Хасидизма.

Начало секты Хасидовъ. Основателемъ секты Хасидовъ (благочестивыхъ) былъ Валахскій Еврей Израиль Бешитъ, вовсе неученый и даже слабый Талмудистъ, но одаренный всѣми качествами отличнаго шарлатана: ловкостью, проницательностью, хитростью и пріятнымъ обхожденіемъ. Въ молодости онъ занимался ремесломъ помощника Меламеда (учителя евреевъ); потомъ, оставя это занятіе, арендовалъ корчмы, и живя между Валахами, перенялъ ихъ обманы въ леченіи болѣзней посредствомъ нашептыванія, талисмановъ, и всѣ другіе фокусы шарлатанства.

Въ второй половинѣ прошедшаго столѣтія Бешитъ явился въ г. Бродахъ (въ Австріи), женился тамъ на сестрѣ уважаемаго между соотечественниками Еврея Гершена Кутеварго, и началъ распространять свое имя сказаніями о мнимыхъ чудесахъ своихъ; но скоро очутился въ невозможности ослѣпить

Moisei Berlin's memorandum on history of Hasidism, 1854 (RGIA, f. 821, o. 8, d. 397, l. 40)

Rebbe, Menachem Mendel Shneerson—who, in the opinion of the expert Jew, exploited the ignorance and desperate condition of the Jewish masses and thus promoted Jewish social separatism. Berlin also argued that Hasidism triggered social conflict within the Jewish community, since its messianic appeal gained wide social support among the Jewish populace oppressed by the traditional rabbinical elite.[66] However, due to a common hostility to the ideas of the Jewish enlightenment, Haskalah, which emerged at the end of the eighteenth century, an unlikely alliance formed between the belligerent factions within traditional Jewry. According to Berlin, this development intensified the fragmentation of Jewish society and ultimately reinforced the position of Hasidism, which, by the mid-nineteenth century, had become a stronghold of Jewish Orthodoxy and a major obstacle to the historical progress of the Jews.[67]

Like a true bureaucrat, Berlin concluded his memorandum with questions to be addressed by his superiors: "Would it be useful for the government to diminish this sect [Hasidism]? Would restrictive or other measures be more instrumental for this purpose?"[68] And, like a true historian, Berlin concluded his "History of Hasidism" by pointing out that "it will be necessary to expand and complete this history."[69]

In 1859, Berlin seized the opportunity to continue this work in a more scholarly fashion. The ethnographic division of the Imperial Russian Geographic Society (*Imperatorskoe Russkoe Geograficheskoe Obshchestvo* [IRGO]) commissioned the expert Jew to prepare an ethnographic survey of the Jewish population in Russia for their larger survey of ethnic and religious groups residing in the empire. The resulting study—"Essay on the Ethnography of the Jewish Population in Russia"—written by Berlin and published by the IRGO, described the historical background and current status of two million Russian Jews for the educated Russian readership. The structure of the "Essay" made it a practical and accessible reference work designed for the general reader. It included chapters on the following topics: general appearance of the Jews; language; everyday life, including clothing, food, occupations, customs, and rituals; social life, including social categories and classes, communal administration, and professional and charitable associations; intellectual and moral skills, religion and education, including a brief survey of major subdivisions within Judaism; and folklore, including folk legends and songs. Berlin's work was based on extensive sources ranging from traditional Jewish texts to contemporary Russian legislation on the Jews.

In his "Essay," Berlin also reflected on Jewish history and historiography. He argued that "sources on this subject [the history of the Jews in Russia] are practically nonexistent.... However, the memory of this people is full of information about its historic past.... All historical events were recorded by [Jewish] literature. No people has such a distinctive historical tradition, from its very beginning to the present, as the Jews. It was not based on myths, but on the logical order of successive facts."[70] Berlin pointed out important materials, preserved by the Jewish communities, waiting for scholars of Jewish history. Among these materials were *pinkasim*, the minute books of the Jewish communities, which, according to Berlin, "frequently included interesting inscriptions and even historical chronicles; it's a pity that nobody has worked on them."[71] In 1861, the expert Jew's perspective on the significant role of archival sources anticipated the agenda of the emergent Russian Jewish historiographers, who, in the 1890s, considered the collection and exploration of historical sources their main priority.[72]

Berlin admitted that his own study was short on historical sources and, thus, incomplete. He called on future scholars of Russian Jewish history to study the subject "more in-depth, more comprehensively, and in a word, better."[73]

However, from the 1860s to the 1880s it was the Russian government's need for Jewish policies, rather than Berlin's wishes, that shaped the research agenda of the nascent Russian Wissenschaft.

Jewish History in the Curriculum of the Modern Jewish School

In the second half of the nineteenth century, the reform and modernization of traditional Jewish education was a key priority of Russian official policy toward the Jews, as well as one of the most controversial and divisive issues of internal Jewish communal politics. In the 1840s, the Russian Ministry of Popular Enlightenment under Count Sergei Uvarov launched an ambitious reform project resulting in the establishment of a network of state-sponsored Jewish elementary schools (*kazennye evreiskie uchilishcha*) and two secondary schools cum rabbinical seminaries in Zhitomir and Vilna. The traditional Russian Jews in the Pale of Settlement regarded these schools with distrust and even hostility. Jewish parents were afraid to enroll their children in the state-sponsored schools, believing that the primary goals of the official reform of Jewish education were the wholesale Christianization and Russification of the younger generation of Russian Jews. As a result, by the mid-1870s many of these schools, including the rabbinical seminaries, were officially deemed unsuccessful and closed. However, Count Uvarov's reform of Jewish education had an impact on a small yet important segment of Russian Jewry. The secular, Russian-language curriculum studied in the *kazennye evreiskie uchilishcha* allowed for the students' acculturation and social integration into the Russian intelligentsia and middle-class bourgeoisie.

Forty years later, Jewish education reform was revisited by the Russian government along with other important issues of official Jewish policy. In 1887, it was the focus of the inter-ministerial Highest Commission on the Re-examination of the Laws on the Jews (1883–1888), dubbed the Palen Commission after its chairman, Count Konstantin Palen. The government made a new attempt to reform and modernize traditional Jewish education. The new policy was no longer to be implemented through state-sponsored schools—alien and untrustworthy to most traditional Jews. Instead, the emphasis was on modernizing the academic curriculum of traditional Jewish educational institutions—*chadarim* and *yeshivot*—now to be officially recognized. This new curriculum was the focus of lengthy deliberations of the official Jewish experts invited by the Palen Commission.

These experts were drawn from the elite strata of Russian Jewish society. They included Baron Goratsii Gintsburg, Samuil Poliakov, and A. Varshavskii, leading entrepreneurs and the wealthiest Russian Jews; Dr. Avraam Drabkin, the government rabbi of St. Petersburg; and Nikolai Bakst and Adam Girshgorn, both medical doctors. In their opinion, the officially approved "minimal essential curriculum of special Jewish disciplines for elementary Jewish school [i.e., *cheder*]" should include Jewish history defined as either "biblical history," or "major phenomena of Jewish history."[74] The experts expressed a common belief that Jewish history should be one of the main subjects, along with Hebrew reading and writing, liturgy, Tanach (Hebrew Bible), and everyday and holiday ritual. The foundational subjects and key texts of traditional Jewish education, the Mishna and Talmud, did not make it into the "minimal essential curriculum," but, in the experts' opinion, they could be studied as elective subjects.[75] The experts' emphasis on the study of Jewish history to replace rabbinic literature in the core curriculum prompted an emotional response from traditional Russian Jews who were well aware of the experts' deliberations and did not hesitate to petition the Palen Commission. One such petition, signed by representatives of the Vilna Jews, called the alleged decision of the government a "grave mistake," which would "completely eliminate [the study of Talmud] and replace [it] with plain instruction in the biblical history of the Jewish people."[76] The petitioners argued that the study of the Talmud was fundamental for the maintenance and transmission of traditional Jewish values, including religious piety, respect for the law, and loyalty to the government. They concluded that "if there were no Talmud, Jews would long ago have become the worst kind of rationalists ... harmful socialists and political agitators."[77]

Apparently, the Commission seriously considered the opinions of both the experts and the petitioners. While the question of balance between Jewish history and Talmud in the core curriculum of elementary Jewish schools remained unresolved, the academic program of the planned rabbinical institute, adopted by the Palen Commission, included both "the Talmud (Babylonian and Jerusalem)" and "history of the Jews in relation to the history of Jewish literature and the Jewish religious outlook."[78]

The official Jewish experts of the Palen Commission also paid careful attention to the language of instruction and special textbooks for students of Jewish subjects. Baron Goratsii Gintsburg pointed out that the traditional Jewish educational system could hardly be regulated. In his words, "The Jewish faith had never been dogmatized, they [Jews] have neither catechism, nor school textbooks. The laws of the Jewish faith are studied using original sources. This type of instruction cannot be circumscribed by an [academic] program or limited by a certain amount of lectures and [study] hours."[79] Gintsburg believed that the problem could be solved through the publication of "original sources, [i.e.] Jewish religious books" with a Russian translation prepared by a "competent assembly" of academic experts.[80] Gintsburg also recommended the gradual replacement of "Jewish jargon [i.e., Yiddish]" with Russian as the principal language of instruction in the study of religion and other Jewish subjects.[81]

The first Russian-language works on Jewish history appeared in the 1860s and 1870s. These pioneering studies dealt with many aspects—anthropological, linguistic, and legal—of Jewish history in Russia from the eleventh to nineteenth centuries. Their authors—official expert Jew Moisei Berlin, collection curator of the Imperial Public Library Abraham Harkavy, and independent lawyer Il'ia Orshanskii—sought to introduce Jewish history and the current status of Russian Jews to the Russian reading public.[82]

In the 1880s, the pressing need to modernize Jewish education, felt by both Jews and Russian officialdom, required a new type of historical work: a universal Jewish history (whether academic or popular, original or translated) in Russian. Several histories meant to satisfy this demand, such as the synthetic works by government rabbi Mark Nemzer and expert Jew and government rabbi Solomon Minor to be examined in the following pages, were conceived of and prepared with the needs of modern Jewish schools in mind, as school textbooks, teaching aids, and material for self-education.

Wissenschaft des Judentums obviously helped the authors of Russian Jewish history textbooks by providing inspiration, scholarly standards, and an intellectual framework. The ideological foundations of Wissenschaft, including its academic ethos, critical approach to sources, and social mission, along with exemplary German textbooks and general accounts of Jewish history—from M. Elkan's "handbook" to Heinrich Graetz's monumental history—profoundly influenced Russian authors, shaping their conceptual thinking, research interests and methods.

Dialogue, either direct or indirect, between the Russian authors and their German teachers-cum-opponents, characterize the conceptions and narrative of the Russian textbooks on Jewish history analyzed below. Even when translating German works, Russian translators acted as if they were virtual co-authors, extensively commenting, amending, and editing the originals. Each textbook emphasizes a very different smaller yet important piece within the larger story of the Jewish people. Each small piece focuses on very different heroes—pietists or freethinkers, conservatives or reformers. Finally, the main hero of all these stories, namely, the Jewish people as a whole, is presented by each of the textbook authors differently, as either a race, an ethnicity, a nation, or a religious community.

One remarkable feature that these textbooks have in common is the close attention they pay to Russian Jews, largely ignored by German authors as a backward community, anachronistic culture, and even a historical anomaly. The Russian authors consistently emphasize the inseparability of the historical experiences of Western European and Eastern European Jewry. Thus, Russian translations of universal Jewish histories by German authors often contained amendments with original histories of the Jews in Poland and Russia written by the translators.

Patriotic History

One textbook, *History of the Jewish People (from the Jews' Migration to Babylon to the Destruction of the Second Temple) for Students of the Law of Jewish Faith in Gymnasia and Government-sponsored Jewish Schools*,[83] was compiled by Mark Osipovich Nemzer (1833–1912), graduate and former instructor of the Vilna Rabbinical Seminary, former government rabbi of Vilna, currently (in 1880, when his book was published) teacher at the women's gymnasium in Vilna, and future candidate for the position of expert Jew at the central offices of the MVD.[84] This modest book—152 pages in large, student-friendly typeface—is limited in chronological and thematic scope, and lacks an overt conceptualization of Jewish history.

The unpretentiousness of this *History* is especially apparent when compared to the first volume of the Russian translation of Heinrich Graetz[85] that appeared the same year. Graetz's massive volume (398 pages) covers a similar time period (just over 500 years); however, unlike Nemzer's account, it paints a rich picture of Jewish life—from its socioeconomic aspects to the development of Jewish literature and scholarship—against the broader background of major events and developments of early medieval non-Jewish history. Graetz's work also features the author's revolutionary conceptualization of the Jewish people and Jewish history. According to Graetz, the unity of "soul" (Jewish religion and tradition) and "flesh" (the Jewish people) cements the Jewish nation and shapes Jewish history. For centuries, the complex interplay of "soul" and "flesh" was a major driving force of Jewish history, which had always been conspicuously "national in character."[86] Thus the Jews, living on different continents among different peoples in different periods of time, never left their "spiritual fatherland."[87] The history of this "fatherland" was Graetz's principal focus. Jews and their non-Jewish hosts and neighbors might share historical space and time in the Diaspora, yet the core developments of Jewish society and culture always had a considerable degree of autonomy from non-Jewish societies and cultures. Hence, from the ninth to the twelfth century, during the European "Dark Ages," the Jews in Spain experienced their "Golden Age," marked by an unprecedented blossoming of Jewish civilization.[88]

Graetz's idea of a Jewish "fatherland" is one of the few conceptual problems discussed extensively in Nemzer's textbook. If Graetz's "spiritual fatherland" is essentially cosmopolitan because it did not bind Jews with loyalty to any specific polity, Nemzer's alternative could be best defined as "patriotic." Unlike Graetz, Nemzer does not bother to summarize his views. However, he integrates them into his narrative by emphasizing certain stories while downplaying and even concealing others. Nemzer frames his narrative with two catastrophic events—the Babylonian captivity in the sixth century BCE and the destruction of the Second Temple in the first century CE—that set the theological, political, social and institutional limits of the Jewish Diaspora for centuries to come. Nemzer's textbook links these events with a narrative—the story of the consolidation of the Jewish people in preparation for their historical ordeal—of *galuth*, indefinite exile from their homeland and life among other peoples. Core Jewish spiritual and political institutes, such as the Temple,[89] the Torah,[90] and the Great Assembly (*Sanhedrin*),[91] play a central role in Nemzer's account of the "preparatory" stage of Jewish history. His mostly negative portrayal of the kings of Israel and Judea and overly positive interpretation of the "learned men" of the *Sanhedrin* are also telling. The author thus condemns the disastrous historical role of the Jewish monarchy, bent on the preservation of its political sovereignty at any price, and contrasts it with the constructive, historical role of Jewish institutes and values, such as spirituality, justice, and civic consciousness, which unifies the people and ensures their national future. The actions of the Jewish kings and their generals who, like Flavius Josephus, put their personal ambitions before a "commitment to the people's cause and earnest love of their fatherland,"[92] led to the loss of the Jews' political independence along with "the loss of their national and religious center; since they [Jews] considered their fatherland any country where they lived, [where they] were born and raised."[93] Thus, the Jews were (and still are) divided by the borders of the many fatherlands to which they were obliged to be loyal and patriotic.

Nemzer appended a biographical index of a dozen of the most prominent Jewish historical figures featured in his narrative. Kings and military leaders are conspicuously absent from this appendix, entitled "Learned Men Who Lived during the Times of Syrian Rule and the Maccabees," but the rabbis Shammai and Hillel, Rabban Gamaliel, and other pillars of rabbinic Judaism are included.[94]

One contemporary reviewer sharply criticized Nemzer's "History," pointing out its lack of originality and the poor quality of its scholarship.[95] Nemzer promptly responded, painstakingly dismissing most of the criticism as irrelevant.[96] In fact, Nemzer's "History" is very well written, thought out, and structured, reflecting the author's solid Jewish learning[97] and his knowledge of contemporary scholarship in Jewish studies, including works by Russian Jewish historians.[98]

Didactic History

Solomon Minor's textbook—*Handbook for Teaching the History of the Jewish People from the Most Ancient to Modern Times with a Brief Survey of Palestine Geography for Jewish Schools. Brief Outline [of the history] of the Jews in Poland, Lithuania, and Russia*[99]—was published in 1881, along with Nemzer's book. Like Nemzer, Solomon (Zalkind) Minor (1826–1900) was a graduate and former instructor of the Vilna Rabbinical Seminary. He also served as expert Jew under the governor-general of Vilna, Kovno, and Grodno provinces from 1856 to 1859.[100] However, unlike Nemzer, Minor, a rabbi and public figure, was a prominent leader of the Russian Jews. He was government rabbi of Moscow, one of the largest Jewish communities in the late Russian empire, for several decades, from 1869 to 1892. He was the first Russian rabbi to deliver regular sermons in Russian.[101] Minor also wrote influential pamphlets and articles on pressing issues of Jewish life in Russia, such as antisemitism and the adaptation of Jewish tradition to modern realities.[102]

Minor's textbook comprises two parts. The first is his translation of a German textbook on Jewish history by M. Elkan, first published in the 1840s.[103] The second part is Minor's own study of Jewish history in Eastern Europe, aimed at improving on the German original by broadening its scope. Compared to Nemzer's work, Minor's textbook provides a wider and far more sophisticated perspective on Jewish history. Minor's narrative spans over four thousand years, from biblical times to the mid-nineteenth century. It provides an incredible panorama of Jewish life worldwide, including historical accounts of overlooked Jewish communities in China and India[104] and the marginalized community of Karaite Jews.[105] Minor's textbook also benefits from the overall quality and proven popularity of its authoritative German source. Minor used the sixth edition (1870) of Elkan's textbook, widely used "in all Jewish schools of Germany and . . . recently translated into Hungarian."[106] According to Minor, the first edition of his Russian translation of Elkan[107] was a comparable success in Russia, where it was "selling quickly" and officially approved by authorities in the Vilna educational district as "the textbook to be used for teaching the history of the Jewish people to Jewish students in the higher grades of gymnasia and realshules."[108] Thus, in Minor's words, he undertook this second edition of his textbook based on the success of the first, and also in order to fix "serious errors" found in both the original and the translation by his academic consultant, "our prominent scholar" professor Abraham Harkavy.[109] In fact, Minor's own supplementary outline of Jewish history in Poland, Lithuania, and Russia, humbly aimed at amending the authoritative German textbook, was a major breakthrough in Jewish history textbooks. By telling a new story, Minor added a whole new chapter to the established instructional narrative of Jewish history as in Elkan's book where the Jews of Eastern Europe were allotted just a few lines.[110] Technically, Minor's textbook was a huge step forward compared to Nemzer's work. Its narrative is complete with chapter summaries, lists of key phenomena, developments and concepts, and useful study aids, such as a "Geographic survey of Palestine,"[111] listing natural and historical places, and a timeline extending from the creation of the world in the year 3988 BCE to the civic emancipation of the Jews in Austria-Hungary in 1868.[112]

Unlike Nemzer, Minor explicitly articulates his conception of Jewish history as well as his ideas about the social mission of historiography. His narrative could best be described as a rationalist "didactic" history aimed at enlightening Russian Jews, who, due to their long isolation lacked "culture" and were alien to "esthetics" in the contemporary Western understanding of these terms. Jewish life in Russia was therefore not yet up to contemporary standards of a true national history, but Minor recognized the attempts of the Russian Jews, such as secular education and the introduction of a modern lifestyle, at living up to that standard. According to Minor, Russian Jews had first to "refresh their spirit with a stream of the past [i.e., history of the Western Jews]," and only then could they "consciously start [their true] national, social and spiritual life."[113] Minor's textbook established a close connection between the history of the Jews in Eastern Europe and the Jews in the rest of the world. His narrative, both the translated and original parts of the textbook, link Eastern and Western European Jews by establishing common features of Jewish life in the Diaspora, such as the "anti-esthetical" and "anti-social" role of the Talmud,[114] and by showing common historical developments, such as the inevitable civic emancipation of the Jews.[115] At the same time, Minor emphasizes the close historical connection between the fate of the Russian Jews and the "fate of the whole of Russia, the fate of its other citizens."[116] Minor believed that Jews should put all their efforts into self-improvement and work to the benefit of Russia in order to earn civil freedom and thus fully unite with their progressive brethren in the West. Minor concludes his textbook with an appeal to Russian Jews "to work and work honestly, work physically and work intellectually; then there is no reason to be afraid of the future—it will bring a certain freedom."[117]

Like Nemzer, Minor singled out the principal heroes of his own narrative and appended their lists, including biographies, major works, and achievements, to most chapters. Minor's heroes are mainly the pioneers and active proponents of "culture" and "esthetics" among the Jews, from the *paytanim* in medieval Spain[118] to the *maskilim* in modern Germany.[119]

A contemporary reviewer praised Minor's textbook, observing that its principal source, Elkan's book, is "the best textbook on Jewish history," because it "links the political and clerical history of the Jews." However, the reviewer failed to recognize Minor's own achievement, the survey of the history of Eastern European Jews, noting that it was "an exposition of an article on Jews by Polish author [Tadeusz] Czacki."[120] In his response, Minor pointed out that he "significantly improved on Czacki."[121]

Actually, Minor's account of Eastern European Jewish history had been seriously researched using his own previous publications,[122] a study by Alexander Krauszar,[123] numerous publications of primary sources,[124] and other materials in addition to Czacki's work.[125]

Thus, in the 1880s, authors of Russian Jewish history textbooks set out to resolve a host of immediate as well as imminent problems of Russian Jews. First and foremost, they sought to introduce Jewish history to the curriculum of modern Jewish schools as one of the core subjects. In the long term, they envisaged the study of Jewish history as a major tool of Jewish national revival. The stories and heroes of Nemzer and Minor's textbooks had achieved some of these challenging objectives. In addition to making the subject of Jewish history integral to modern Jewish education, they contributed to making the Jewish historical past integral to the consciousness of generations of Russian Jews.

The development of Russian-language Jewish history textbooks was linked to the Russian Wissenschaft and the overall development of Russian Jewish historiography in the late nineteenth century. The main contributions of Russian Jewish scholarship to academic Jewish studies first appear in these textbooks, including the history of the Jews in Eastern Europe as a whole new field of study.

Conclusion

As demonstrated in this book, the institution of Russian Jewish bu-reaucracy was the primary means of the making and implementation of Russian imperial policy toward the Jews.

In the 1840s, the ambitious government program of social transfor-mation of the Russian Jews necessitated fundamental rebuilding of the framework of traditional Jewish religious and communal institutions. In this process, the Jewish bureaucracy emerged as the principal institutional base for imperial Jewish policy. The French Jewish consistories, estab-lished in the 1800s, provided the Russian government with the prototype of a comprehensive bureaucratic institution affecting all spheres of Jewish life. In the words of an official memorandum, "One of the incentives for the establishment of the Rabbinical Commission was the government's desire to form a highest agency of control for religious affairs of the Jews, which would supervise and guide the lowest echelon—the provincial and district rabbinate. With the aid of expert Jews [at the provincial level], the government sought to advance, among the ignorant Jewish masses, a rapprochement between the Jews and the native population."[1] In fact, the constituent institutions of Russian religious administration for the Jews performed quite independent functions. The Rabbinical Commis-sion acted as the Jewish supreme court in religious matters. The provin-cial expert Jews were charged with helping the government to identify and overcome Jewish "fanaticism" (i.e., social isolation of the Jews). The district rabbinate took over police functions, including registration of Jewish taxpayers and recruits.

This book demonstrates that expert Jews were never fully integrated into the hierarchy of the Jewish religious administration, including the government rabbinate and Rabbinical Commission. Instead, they became an integral part of the Russian bureaucratic structure of the Ministry of Internal Affairs, as officials for special missions under the provincial governors. Expert Jews had no administrative authority and acted on the orders of their superiors. The expert Jews' fellow Jewish bureaucrats—government rabbis—were overloaded with technical work and had limited access to Russian officials, while the members of the Rabbinical Commission had direct contact with top imperial bureaucrats but convened rarely and sporadically. Expert Jews, on the other hand, were trusted experts working alongside official Russian decision makers on an everyday basis. Thus, the office of expert Jew became the Jewish back office of the Russian government, a bureaucratic hub connecting various policies and administrative measures, consolidating official policy toward the Jews.

The bureaucratic cases and documents examined in this book single out the eradication of so-called Jewish "fanaticism" as a key official assignment on the service agenda of expert Jews. In the 1830s, before Jewish bureaucracy was institutionalized, Russian authorities had very limited knowledge of their Jewish subjects. The government relied more on its enlightened perceptions of the Jews and Judaism than on empirical observation. This perspective was further biased by self-appointed Jewish experts-cum-informers, often pursuing personal interests. Thus, in the words of Yohanan Petrovsky-Shtern, "the regime came to consider the Jews a mob of ignorant and gullible fanatics, worshippers of the anti-Christian Kabbalah and the offensive medieval Talmud."[2] Jewish "ignorance" and "fanaticism" were perceived as the main impediment to the social integration of the Jews into imperial society. In the 1850s, the Ministry of Internal Affairs defined and targeted two major forms of "fanaticism": religious (anti-Christian) and social (anti-government). The government limited the expert Jews' bureaucratic scope to the exposure of Jewish religious "fanaticism" and its eradication through moral influence on the Jewish population. Eradication of Jewish "fanaticism" remained a priority of the Russian government for most of the late imperial period. Eventually, due to the bureaucratic input of expert Jews, the authorities revisited the meaning and role of "fanaticism" in a more positive light and adjusted their policy toward the Jews. If in the 1860s the official missions of expert Jews Moisei Berlin and Markus Gurovich targeted Jewish religious fanaticism as the main obstacle to the social integration of the Jews, in the 1900s the official mission of expert Jew Moisei Kreps was to safeguard the sacred and essential tenets of Judaism, formerly defined as Jewish religious "fanaticism," from any type of innovation. Thus, expert Jews contributed to conservative domestic policy aimed at the preservation of the autocratic regime and containment of any kind of subversive activity in the empire.

The work of expert Jews to expose and eradicate Jewish "fanaticism" won them a bad reputation among the Jews. In the popular imagination, expert Jews were government spies, ruthless informers and ultimately traitors of their people. Paradoxically, in the eyes of ordinary Jews the expert Jew was also a powerful and influential figure invested with political authority through his proximity to the Russian authorities and appropriation of the traditional Jewish political roles of *shtadlan*, social critic, and informer.[3] Thus, many ordinary Jews believed it was at the expert Jew's discretion (or a matter of his moral choice) whether to intercede on behalf of his fellow Jews or to harm them. At the same time, in the eyes of expert Jews' Russian superiors they were first and foremost loyal servants of the state. Governors and other Russian officials trusted the impartiality of Jewish bureaucrats in Jewish matters because of their Jewish religion and education, their oath of service, and their belonging to the ranks of Russian officialdom.

The documents on the service of expert Jews analyzed in this book reveal very little about the direct impact of their work on the everyday lives of Russian Jews. Compared to their fellow Jewish bureaucrats, the government rabbis, expert Jews had much less exposure to ordinary Jews and their individual problems. Instead, on an everyday basis expert Jews worked alongside their fellow Russian bureaucrats. Their bureaucratic work was mostly that of making, rather than implementing, official Jewish policy. In the rare cases when expert Jews encountered the Jewish population face to face as part of their service missions, they did not let

Jewish petitioners into the chancellery, as government rabbis usually did. Like their Russian superiors, expert Jews visited the Jewish communities to inspect them or to implement administrative measures firsthand. Expert Jews' field trips, like those of their Russian superiors, could either be secret, in order to expose Jewish crimes and abuses (like Moisei Berlin's inspection trips to Belorussia in the 1850s), or well publicized, in order to mobilize the Jewish population for some urgent task (like Markus Gurovich's trip to the Jewish agricultural settlements of Novorossiia in the 1860s).

The biographical material on expert Jews examined in this book testifies to the high official status of these Jewish bureaucrats. Their official and social status was on par with that of their Russian bureaucratic colleagues, while the educational and general intellectual profile of expert Jews was much higher. Their specialized modern education intellectual engagement and esprit de corps that was nurtured in the rabbinical seminaries gave expert Jews their strong service ethos, emulating that of the Russian enlightened bureaucrats who modernized Russia in the 1860s. Thus, generations of expert Jews were motivated by the political ideals of the Great Reforms era, including the belief in progress and the transformational potential of state bureaucracy.

The literary output of expert Jews reviewed in this book, including journalism and especially historiography, reveals a unique bureaucratic as well as genuinely Jewish perspective on the Jewish past, present, and future in Russia. This book demonstrates that expert Jews should be counted among the pioneering historians of Russian Jews. They saw their scholarship as the fulfillment of a social mission. They sought to integrate Russian Jewish history into the shared past of the multi-ethnic and multi-confessional Russian empire and to refashion Russian Jews, seen by contemporary Russians as a strange and dangerous minority, into an organic part of the Russian imperial state and society. The scholarly work of expert Jews was in large measure sponsored by the Russian government in its need to build the empire. However, according to their own testimony, Jewish bureaucratic historians worked "for the sake of the historical nation to which [they] belong."[4]

In the end, this book brings expert Jews to the fore as an important elite group within Russian Jewry in the process of modernization. In striking contrast to other modern Russian Jewish elites—such as the leadership of traditional, wealthy, liberal, nationalist, and revolutionary factions—these Russian Jewish bureaucrats were firmly integrated within imperial officialdom and entrusted with vital policymaking tasks by the state. Essentially loyal state servitors, expert Jews were motivated by their unique bureaucratic service ethos, which combined a devotion to the Jewish people with a strong commitment to its change.

Epilogue

One dream, one big dream follows me in my life,
it lives in me, like my heart and my song:
When I remain on my own with the naked earth,
when the Jewish cemetery takes my old bones,
I hope a passer-by, noticing my fence
and seeing the grass which grows from my body,
will tell the living wind:
—He was a mensch, he served his people!
> —*Itzik Fefer, Epitaph*
> (translated from Yiddish by Gennady Estraikh)

The passing of expert Jew German Barats on March 26, 1922, in Kiev went unnoticed by the contemporary Soviet Russian press. However, Barats's death produced a considerable response among his friends and colleagues who had emigrated to Europe and America after the fall of the Russian empire. The obituaries in the Russian émigré press reflected aspects of Barats's long and successful career, linked to every major development in the history of the Jews in late imperial Russia.

Barats was remembered as a bureaucrat who, based on his ethos, toiled both for the sake of the government and for the sake of the Jews. According to the prominent Yiddish linguist Nochum Shtif, Barats "occupied a key office, thus, he was on a slippery road and had to maneuver between the Jews and the authorities, all of whom were suspicious of the expert Jew. It was a miracle that Barats remained in office for 30 years, held in high repute by both sides. He earned trust and honor, of which no other Jewish bureaucrat could boast. He was a man of principle, never flattered anyone, and always spoke the truth boldly. He did not want to curry favor with the Jews and did not seek peace or sympathy from those Jews whom he disliked. However, he strongly believed in the necessity of the reforms, and, as a bureaucrat, always supported the initiatives of the government (especially in the field of Jewish education). He knew the attitudes of his superiors well and strongly supported government-sponsored Jewish schools. One must read his arguments [presented in Barats's official memoranda and journalism] and feel his passionate tone in order to comprehend Barats's commitment to the goals of the Jewish enlightenment, which sometimes jeopardized his official status and career."[1] According to philosopher Boris Gurevich, "Barats, a shy maskil, tirelessly called on the Jews to enroll in Russian schools; he immediately resigned when a governor-general who supported the pogroms took office [as Barats's superior]; he persistently struggled for Jewish interests in the administrative commission, which declared the Jews responsible for the pogroms; in this commission, starting from the defense [Barats] turned to the offense."[2]

Barats was remembered as a lawyer whose exemplary work and attitude embodied the spirit of the Great Reforms. According to attorney and former member of the Rabbinical Commission Moisei Mazor, Barats "belonged to a minority of Russian attorneys for whom their profession was, first and foremost, a calling and a public service aimed at the preservation of the established rule of the law. Barats approached his work with love, devotion and professionalism; his court appeals were always successful. A tiny minority of Russian attorneys remained faithful to the spirit of the Court Reform [of 1864], and Barats shone among them. Until the end, he was a genuine legal professional who embodied the spirit of the Great Reforms, the last courageous soldier of the glorious army of attorneys, drafted by the reform of 1864."[3]

Barats was remembered as a historian who, while focusing on Russian antiquity, pursued a significant contemporary mission aimed at "explaining how Kiev, where at the time Jews were banned from residing, had been a major center of Jewish culture a thousand years before. Barats argued that Russia is a complex chemical conglomerate, fused by the centuries [of its history], where we [the Jews] are a significant proportion. This shy maskil strongly reminded the oppressors of the Jews of this simple truth during the darkest days of the reaction."[4] According to the dean of Russian historians, Simon Dubnow, Barats "worked to bridge the gap between the Palestinian and Babylonian Jewish academies and the Kiev Caves Monastery, and between the Midrash and the chronicles of Nestor. His scholarship established the important historical fact that Jewish literature (via Byzantium) significantly influenced [the culture] of the Kievan Rus."[5]

When his service came to an end along with the agonizing end of the *ancien régime*, expert Jew German Barats remained faithful to his mission. Simon Dubnow, eulogizing Barats, described the grand finale of the long career of the expert Jew, who "accomplished an important mission, establishing the Jewish roots of ancient Russian literature and culture. Barats continued his monumental work until his death. He wrote his last pages amid the cannonades of the Russian Civil War and died in his study, his scholarly place of duty. The eighty-year-old scholar, sifting through historical charters of ancient Rus in its very historical cradle [i.e., Kiev]— was he not a vivid historical symbol?"[6] According to Nochum Shtif, who saw Barats during his last days, the old expert Jew pleaded: "Dear friends, remember me in the Jewish way, and please, make sure the Jews do not forget my name."[7]

This book ensures that the names of German Barats and his fellow expert Jews will never be forgotten again.

Appendix

Table 1. Expert Jews' Terms of Government Office in the Pale of Settlement and the Ministry of Internal Affairs, 1850–1917

Governor-general of Baltic Provinces, Governors of Lifland and Kurland Provinces	
Neiman, Avraam	1850–1877
Vagengeim, Samuil	1852–1873
Keil'man, Filipp	1870–1876
Kaplan, Vasilii	1870–1876
Pumpianskii, Aron	1877–1893
Pukher, Solomon	1894–1898
Mikhel'son, Isidor	1900–1907
Kreps, Moisei	1907–1917

Governor of Chernigov Province	
Shikin, Leiba	1857
Freidin, Efrem	1870–1892
Kaminer, Isaak	1892–1901
Gormiz, Mordukh	1901

Governor of Ekaterinoslav Province	
Levin, Shmarya	1901–1906
Tavrovskii, Markus	1904

Governor of Grodno Province	
Katsenel'son, Grigorii	1914–?

Governor-general of Kiev, Podolia, and Volhyn Provinces

Fedorov, Vladimir	1857– [1863]
Gal'perin, Izrail'	[1858]
Barats, German	1862–1881, 1902–1915
Tseitlin, Aaron	1872–1887
Cherner, Gersh	1884–1901

Governor of Kovno Province

Shnitkind, Ruvim	1868–1911

Governor of Minsk Province

Shatskin, Saul	1857–1860
Katsenelenbogen, Samuil	1876–1879
Gurvich, Osip	1880–1904, 1906–1914
Sheindel's, Boris	1914–?

Governor of Mogilev Province

Mandel'shtam, Arnold	1856–1908

Governor-general of Novorossiia and Bessarabiia

Gurovich, Markus	1852–1874
Schwabacher, Simon	? –1874

City governor of Odessa

Dynin, Iakov	1904–1912

Governor of Podolia Province

Blavshtein	1868–1872

Governor of Poltava Province

Madievskii, Avraam	1856–1859
Tseitlin, Aaron	1859–1870
Zaidiner, Lev	1872–?
Perel'man	1893–1900

Appendix

Governor-general of Vilna, Kovno, and Grodno Provinces

Minor, Solomon	1856–1859
Gershtein, Iona	1856–1891
Kagan, V. L.	1858–1860
Shkliaver, Grigorii	1861–1911
Vol'per, Mikhail	1891–1912
Tsuntser, Abram	1906–1912

Governor of Vilna Province

Kliachko, Sheftel'	1902–?

Governor-general of Vitebsk, Mogilev, and Smolensk Provinces

Berlin, Moisei	1853–1856
Zel'tser, Litman	1853–1856

Governor of Vitebsk Province

Gittel'son, B. A.	1881–?

Governor of Volhyn Province

Binshtok, Lev	1867–1882
Kulisher, Iser	1908–1916
Uger, Semen	1916

Department of Spiritual Affairs of Foreign Faiths in the Ministry of Internal Affairs

Berlin, Moisei	1856–1866
Kaufman, Illarion	1875
Brafman, Iakov	1879
Pumpianskii, Aron	1877–1893
Pukher, Solomon	1894–1898
Mikhel'son, Isidor	1900–1907
Kreps, Moisei	1907–1917

Table 2. Rabbinical Seminaries of Expert Jews

Name	Institution	Year of graduation
Barats, German	Zhitomir Rabbinical Seminary	1859
Binshtok, Lev	Zhitomir Rabbinical Seminary	1858
Freidin, Efrem	Vilna Rabbinical Seminary	1860s
Gershtein, Iona	Vilna Rabbinical Seminary	1850s
Gurvich, Osip	Vilna Rabbinical Seminary	1860
Kagan, V. L.	Vilna Rabbinical Seminary	1850s
Katsenel'son, Grigorii	Vilna Jewish Teachers' Institute	1870s
Mandel'shtam, Arnold	Vilna Rabbinical Seminary	1853
Mikhel'son, Isidor	Vilna Rabbinical Seminary	1850s
Minor, Solomon	Vilna Rabbinical Seminary	1850s
Perel'man	Vilna Rabbinical Seminary	1870s
Pukher, Solomon	Vilna Rabbinical Seminary	1858
Pumpianskii, Aron	Vilna Rabbinical Seminary	1859
Sheindel's, Boris	Vilna Jewish Teachers' Institute	1877
Shnitkind, Ruvim	Vilna Rabbinical Seminary	1860s
Tseitlin, Aaron	Vilna Rabbinical Seminary	1856
Zaidiner, Lev	Zhitomir Rabbinical Seminary	1862

Table 3. Official Rank, Awards, and Social Status of Expert Jews

Name	Official rank	Social status	Awards
Barats, German		attorney	
Brafman, Iakov	provincial councilor		
Cherner, Gersh	collegiate councilor		
Dynin, Iakov		honorary citizen	
Fedorov, Vladimir	titular councilor		
Gurovich, Markus		honorary citizen	2 orders, 4 medals
Gurvich, Osip		honorary citizen	3 medals, diamond ring
Katsenel'son, Grigorii		honorary citizen	
Kulisher, Iser		honorary citizen	
Mandel'shtam, Arnold		honorary citizen	
Mikhel'son, Isidor	collegiate councilor		
Perel'man	collegiate councilor		
Shkliaver, Grigorii		honorary citizen	
Shnitkind, Ruvim		honorary citizen	1 medal
Tavrovskii, Markus		honorary citizen	
Tsuntser, Abram		honorary citizen	

Table 4. Other Bureaucratic Appointments of Expert Jews

Name	Term of service as expert Jew	Terms of other appointments	Other appointments
Barats, German	1862–1881, 1902–1915	1861, 1870–1901, 1893	member of the Rabbinical Commission, censor of Jewish literature
Berlin, Moisei	1853–1856, 1856–1866	1861–1864	official expert of the emperor's personal chancellery
Binshtok, Lev	1867–1882	1867–?	editor of the official provincial newspaper
Blavshtein	1868–1872	1868–1872	government rabbi, Kamenets
Brafman, Iakov	1879	1871–?	censor of the Jewish literature
Fedorov, Vladimir	1857–?	1856	censor of Jewish literature
Freidin, Efrem	1870–1892	1870–1892	government rabbi, Chernigov
Gal'perin, Izrail'	[1858]	1858	member of the Rabbinical Commission
Gershtein, Iona	1856–1891	1860	secretary of the Rabbinical Commission
Gittel'son, B. A.	1881	1881	member of the provincial commission on Jewish question
Gurovich, Markus	1852–1874		inspector of government-sponsored Jewish school
Gurvich, Osip	1880–1904, 1906–1914	1881–?, 1881	teacher in government-sponsored Jewish school, member of the provincial commission on the Jewish question

Name	Term of service as expert Jew	Terms of other appointments	Other appointments
Kagan, V. L.	1856– [1860]	1857, 1860	secretary of the Rabbinical Commission
Kaminer, Isaak	1892–1901	1892	district doctor
Katsenelenbogen, Samuil	1876–1879	1876	teacher in government-sponsored Jewish school
Kliachko, Sheftel	1902	1877–1892	member of the municipal council
Kreps, Moisei	1907–1917	1910–1917, 1910	government rabbi, Kherson; member of the Rabbinical Commission
Levin, Shmarya	1901–1906		government rabbi, Ekaterinoslav; member of the State Duma
Madievskii, Avraam	1856–1859	1856–?, 1861	government rabbi, Zen'kov; member of the Rabbinical Commission
Mandel'shtam, Arnold	1856–1908		teacher in government-sponsored Jewish school
Mikhel'son, Isidor	1900–1908		government rabbi, Riga
Minor, Solomon	1856–1859	1859–?, 1869–?	government rabbi, Minsk; government rabbi, Moscow
Neiman, Avraam	1850– [1877]	1854–1863, 1857, 1860, 1863–?	government rabbi, Riga; member of the Rabbinical Commission
Perel'man	1893–1897		government rabbi, Simferopol
Pukher, Solomon	1894–1898	1893–1898	government rabbi, Riga

Name	Term of service as expert Jew	Terms of other appointments	Other appointments
Pumpianskii, Aron	1877– [1893]	1871–1893	government rabbi, Riga
Schwabacher, Simon	? –1874		government rabbi, Odessa
Sheindel's, Boris	1914–?	1892–?	teacher in government-sponsored Jewish school
Shikin, Leiba	1857	1857	teacher in government-sponsored Jewish school
Shnitkind, Ruvim	1868–1911	1868–?	government rabbi, Kovno
Tseitlin, Aaron	1859–1870, 1872– [1887]	1856–?	instructor in the rabbinical seminary; government rabbi, Kremenchug; censor of Jewish literature
Tsuntser, Abram	[1906–1912]		teacher in government-sponsored Jewish school
Vol'per, Mikhail	1891– [1912]	1904–?	inspector of the Jewish teachers' institute
Zaidiner, Lev	1872–?	1863–1872	government rabbi, Poltava

Table 5. Compensation of Expert Jews

Name	Year when initial salary was set	Initial salary (silver rubles per annum)	Year when salary was reassessed	New salary
Barats, German	1869	900	1905	900
Berlin, Moisei	1853	900		
Binshtok, Lev	1867	900		
Blavshtein	1868	260		
Bliumenfel'd, Faitel'	1880	600		
Cherner, Gersh	1884	900		
Fedorov, Vladimir	1858	900		
Gershtein, Iona	1856	450	1856	400
Gormiz, Mordukh	1901	600		
Gurovich, Markus	1852	900		
Gurvich, Osip	1880	900	1910	1,500
Kagan, V. L.	1856	300	1856	650
Kaminer, Isaak	1892	600		
Kaplan, Vasilii	1870	350		
Katsenel'son, Grigorii	1914	900		
Katsenelenbogen, Samuil	1876	700		
Keil'man, Fillip	1870	350	1873	600
Kliachko, Sheftel'	1902	800		
Kreps, Moisei	1907	1,800	1917	3,000
Levin, Shmarya	1901	900		
Mandel'shtam, Arnold	1856	400	1908	600
Mikhel'son, Isidor	1900	600		
Minor, Solomon	1856	450	1856	400
Neiman, Avraam	1850	600		
Perel'man	1893	600		
Pukher, Solomon	1894	600		
Pumpianskii, Aron	1877	600		
Schwabacher, Simon	1874	600		
Shatskin, Saul	1857	700		

Appendix

Name	Year when initial salary was set	Initial salary (silver rubles per annum)	Year when salary was reassessed	New salary
Shikin, Leiba	1857	250		
Shkliaver, Grigorii	1861	900		
Shnitkind, Ruvim	1868	900		
Tseitlin, Aaron	1859	600	1872	900
Vagengeim, Samuil	1852	600		
Vol'per, Mikhail	1892	600	1912	900
Zaidiner, Lev	1872	260		

Table 6. Service Terms of Expert Jews

Name	Years in office
Barats, German	32
Berlin, Moisei	13
Binshtok, Lev	15
Blavshtein	4
Cherner, Gersh	17
Dynin, Iakov	8
Freidin, Efrem	22
Gershtein, Iona	35
Gurovich, Markus	22
Gurvich, Osip	32
Kagan, V. L.	4
Kaminer, Isaak	9
Kaplan, Vasilii	6
Katsenelenbogen, Samuil	3
Keil'man, Fillip	6
Kreps, Moisei	10
Kulisher, Iser	8
Levin, Shmarya	5
Madievskii, Avraam	3
Mandel'shtam, Arnold	52
Mikhel'son, Isidor	8
Neiman, Avraam	27
Perel'man	4
Pukher, Solomon	4
Pumpianskii, Aron	16
Shatskin, Saul	3
Shkliaver, Grigorii	50
Shnitkind, Ruvim	43
Tseitlin, Aaron	26
Tsuntser, Abram	6
Vagengeim, Samuil	21
Vol'per, Mikhail	21

Notes

Introduction

The epigraph is taken from Shmarya Levin, *Forward from Exile* (Philadelphia: Jewish Publication Society of America, 1967), 186–87.

1. I am grateful to late professor John Doyle Klier (1944–2007) for helping me with coining this term.
2. Dar'ia Dontsova, *Striptiz Zhar-ptitsy* (2008), http://dontsova-knigi.narod.ru/001_20_5.html, accessed September 2, 2015.
3. Proximity with superiors also meant special confidence and personal relationships. Thus patronizing superiors addressed their closest subordinates as *golubchik* (lit., little dove; deary). See ibid.
4. Grigorii Kanovich, *I net rabam raia* (Moscow: Sovetskii pisatel', 1989), 184.
5. Grigorii Kanovich, *Slezy i molitvy durakov* (Vilnius: Vaga, 1987), 89.
6. Ibid., 244.
7. Ibid., 39–40.
8. Ibid., 233.
9. Grigorii Kanovich, *I net rabam raia* (Moscow: Sovetskii pisatel', 1989), 70.
10. Ibid., 150.
11. Andreas Kappeler, *The Russian Empire: Ethnicity and Nationalism* (Harlow: Longman, 2001), 158–69.
12. Besides the "unsettled" lifestyle of the Jews, government policies targeted their traditional "un-productive" and "harmful" occupations, such as innkeeping, moneylending, and petty trade. Thus, the Russian government isolated the Jews as a socially alien group (*inorodtsy*, aliens) and subjected them to vigorous administrative measures (*sblizhenie*, rapprochement) aimed

at the social integration of the Jews within the general Russian population. See ibid., 273–74.

13. ChaeRan Freeze, *Jewish Marriage and Divorce in Imperial Russia* (Hanover, N.H.: University Press of New England, Brandeis University Press, 2002), 83.

14. In recent years many scholars have paid serious attention to these developments. See Elena Campbell, "The Autocracy and the Muslim Clergy in the Russian Empire (1850s–1917)," *Russian Studies in History* 44, no. 2 (2005): 8–29; Robert D. Crews, *For Prophet and Tsar: Islam and Empire in Russia and Central Asia* (Cambridge, Mass.: Harvard University Press, 2006); Mikhail Dolbilov, *Russkii krai, chuzhaia vera: Etnokonfessional'naia politika imperii v Litve i Belorussii pri Aleksandre II* (Moscow: Novoe literaturnoe obozrenie, 2010); Anders Henriksson, *The Tsar's Loyal Germans: The Riga German Community, Social Change and The Nationality Question, 1855–1905* (Boulder: East European Monographs; New York: Columbia University Press, 1983); Kappeler, *The Russian Empire*; Agnes Kefeli, *Becoming Muslim in Imperial Russia: Conversion, Apostasy, and Literacy* (Ithaca, N.Y.: Cornell University Press, 2014); Adeeb Khalid, *The Politics of Muslim Cultural Reform: Jadidism in Central Asia* (Berkeley: University of California Press, 1999); Alexei Miller, *The Ukrainian Question: The Russian Empire and Nationalism in the Nineteenth Century* (Budapest: Central European University Press, 2003); Paul Werth, *At the Margins of Orthodoxy: Mission, Governance, and Confessional Politics in Russia's Volga-Kama Region, 1827–1905* (Ithaca, N.Y.: Cornell University Press, 2002); Paul Werth, *The Tsar's Foreign Faiths: Toleration and the Fate of Religious Freedom in Imperial Russia* (Oxford: Oxford University Press, 2014).

15. The emergence of modern bureaucracy in nineteenth-century Russia, including politics, institutions, and personnel, has been thoroughly examined by historians. See Ilya V. Gerasimov, *Modernism and Public Reform in Late Imperial Russia: Rural Professionals and Self-Organization, 1905–30* (London: Palgrave Macmillan, 2009); Yanni Kotsonis, *States of Obligation: Taxes and Citizenship in the Russian Empire and Early Soviet Republic* (Toronto: University of Toronto Press, 2014); W. Bruce Lincoln, *In the Vanguard of Reform: Russia's Enlightened Bureaucrats, 1825–1861* (DeKalb: Northern Illinois University Press, 1982); Daniel Orlovsky, *The Limits of Reform: The Ministry of Internal Affairs in Imperial Russia, 1802–1881* (Cambridge, Mass.: Harvard University Press, 1980); Walter Pintner and Don Rowney, eds., *Russian Officialdom: The Bureaucratization of Russian Society from the Seventeenth to the Twentieth Century* (Chapel Hill: University of North Carolina Press, 1980); Francis W. Wcislo, *Tales of Imperial Russia: The Life and Times of Sergei*

Witte, 1849–1915 (Oxford: Oxford University Press, 2011); Francis W. Wcislo, *Reforming Rural Russia: State, Local Society and National Politics, 1855–1914* (Princeton, N.J.: Princeton University Press, 1990); Richard Wortman, *The Development of a Russian Legal Consciousness* (Chicago: University of Chicago Press, 1976); Richard Wortman, *Scenarios of Power: Myth and Ceremony in Russian Monarchy, Volume One: From Peter the Great to the Death of Nicholas I* (Princeton, N.J.: Princeton University Press, 1995); Petr Zaionchkovskii, *Pravitel'stvennyi apparat samoderzhavnoi Rossii v XIX v.* (Moscow, 1978).

16. ChaeRan Freeze, *Jewish Marriage and Divorce*, 94–95.

17. An ordinary shtetl Jew in a fictional account of Jewish life in late imperial Russia dreamed that "if every [Russian] official would have a favorite Jew [whom he trusts] then nothing would trouble [the Jews]. The empire has enough officials [for every Jew]." See Grigorii Kanovich, *I net rabam raia* (Moscow: Sovetskii pisatel', 1989), 173.

18. See, for example, a study of the Jewish bureaucracy in France: Phyllis Albert, *The Modernization of French Jewry: Consistory and Community in the Nineteenth Century* (Waltham, Mass.: Brandeis University Press; Hanover, N.H.: University Press of New England, 1977). See also comparative studies on state administration of the Jews and policies of their social integration in the nineteenth-century France, Russian, and Ottoman empires: Sarah Abrevaya Stein, *Making Jews Modern: The Yiddish and Ladino Press in the Russian and Ottoman Empires* (Bloomington: Indiana University Press, 2004); Aron Rodrigue, *French Jews, Turkish Jews: The Alliance israélite universelle and the Politics of Jewish Schooling in Turkey, 1860–1925* (Bloomington: Indiana University Press, 1990).

19. Robert D. Crews, *For Prophet and Tsar*, 9–10. For a comparative perspective on Jewish bureaucracy and confessional politics of Western modern states, such as France, and Eastern empires such as Ottoman Turkey and Russia, see Rodrigue, *French Jews, Turkish Jews*, 32–34.

20. Michael Stanislawski, *Tsar Nicholas I and the Jews: The Transformation of Jewish Society in Russia, 1825–1855* (Philadelphia: Jewish Publication Society of America, 1983), 51–54.

21. Crisis of traditional shtadlanut and emergence of Jewish bureaucracy were reflected by Russian literature. In the 1870s, during police investigation of the blood libel in a fictional Lithuanian shtetl, wealthy and influential Jewish lumber merchant Markus Fradkin was able to buy personal protection from the local Russian authorities. However, all his money was unable to save his fellow Jews charged with alleged crime. At the same time, official status of attorney at law guaranteed other Jew, Miron Dorskii, both personal

immunity (he is welcomed as equal by police authorities and even spared by violent antisemitic Lithuanian peasants) and legal intercession in investigation and court procedures. See Grigorii Kanovich, *I net rabam raia* (Moscow: Sovetskii pisatel', 1989), 173.

22. For elaborate discussion of using the term "emancipation" pertaining to the Jews in a Russian setting see Benjamin Nathans, *Beyond the Pale: The Jewish Encounter with Late Imperial Russia* (Berkeley: University of California Press, 2002), 77–80.

23. Eli Lederhendler, "Modernity without Emancipation or Assimilation? The Case of Russian Jewry," in *Assimilation and Community: The Jews in Nineteenth-Century Europe*, ed. Jonathan Frankel and Steven Zipperstein (New York: Cambridge University Press, 1992), 325–43.

24. This was the viewpoint of the first Russian Jewish historians, writing in the late nineteenth and early twentieth centuries, Simon Dubnow (1860–1941) and Iulii Gessen (1871–1939). In general, they characterized the history of Russian Jews in the first half of the nineteenth century as an "utter tragedy." See Simon Dubnow, "Evrei v Rossii v epokhu evropeiskoi reaktsii (1815–1848)," *Evreiskaia starina* 5 (1912): 274–89; 6 (1913): 23–50, 308–24; Simon Dubnow, "Sud'by evreev v Rossii v epokhu zapadnoi pervoi emasipatsii (1789–1815)," *Evreiskaia starina* 5 (1912): 3–25, 113–43; Iulii Gessen, *Istoriia evreev v Rossii* (St. Petersburg, 1914).

25. This view is found in the following works by Israel Tsinberg (1873–1939), Pesakh Marek (1862–1920), and Israel Sosis (1878–1967): Israel Tsinberg, "Isaak Ber Levinzon i ego vremia," *Evreiskaia starina* 3 (1910): 505–41; Pesakh Marek, "Bor'ba dvukh vospitanii. Iz istorii prosveshcheniia evreev v Rossii (1864–1873)" in *Perezhitoe* (St. Petersburg, 1909), vol. 1, 106–43; Israel Sosis, "Obshchestvennye nastroeniia epokhi Velikikh Reform," *Evreiskaia starina* 6 (1914): 21–41, 182–97, 342–64.

26. Michael Stanislawski devised a typology of Russian bureaucrats, whose distinctive views and approaches influenced state policy from 1825 to 1855, including those who sought the gradual social transformation of Russian Jews through moderate reforms. See Stanislawski, *Tsar Nicholas I and the Jews*, 9–10, 183, 185. For Hans Rogger, Russian ministries were the chief policymaking agencies in the late Russian empire. He deliberately excluded the last two Russian monarchs, Alexander III and Nicholas II, from his analysis of bureaucratic attitudes toward the Jews because, according to Rogger, despite the proven judeophobia of the tsars, it was the Russian ministerial system's bureaucratic leadership and conservative conception of *raison d'état* that were the key factors in policies related to the Jewish subjects of the empire.

See Hans Rogger, *Jewish Policies and Right-Wing Politics in Imperial Russia* (Berkeley: University of California Press, 1986), 57.

27. Eli Lederhendler, *The Road to Modern Jewish Politics: Political Tradition and Political Reconstruction in the Jewish Community of Tsarist Russia* (New York: Oxford University Press, 1989), 95.

28. Eugene Avrutin, *Jews and the Imperial State: Identification Politics in Tsarist Russia* (Ithaca, N.Y.: Cornell University Press, 2010); Freeze, *Jewish Marriage and Divorce*; Nathans, *Beyond the Pale*; Yohanan Petrovsky-Shtern, *Jews in the Russian Army, 1827–1917: Drafted into Modernity* (Cambridge: Cambridge University Press, 2009).

29. Similar methodology was applied in studies of Russian bureaucracy, such as Daniel Orlovsky, "High Officials in the Ministry of Internal Affairs, 1855–1881," in Pintner and Rowney, *Russian Officialdom*, 250–82, and Petr Zaionchkovskii, *Pravitel'stvennyi apparat samoderzhavnoi Rossii v XIX v.*

30. As demonstrated by scholars of Russian intellectual history, already in the late eighteenth century Russian writers-cum-statesmen, such as Aleksandr Petrovich Sumarokov (1717–1777), considered their literary activities as part of their state service. This attitude proved essential for the eventual construction of the image of the Russian writer as an influential public figure. See Irina Reyfman, *Rank and Style: Russians in State Service, Life, and Literature* (Brighton, Mass.: Academic Studies Press, 2012), 7–15, 22.

31. Robert P. Geraci, *Window on the East: National and Imperial Identities in Late Tsarist Russia* (Ithaca, N.Y.: Cornell University Press, 2001), 9–10; Kappeler, *The Russian Empire*, 277–78.

32. Nathans, *Beyond the Pale*, 79.

33. Osip Lerner, *Evrei v Novorossiiskom krae: istoricheskie ocherki po dannym iz arkhiva byvshego Novorossiiskogo general-gubernatora* (Odessa, 1901).

34. Among them are the biographical materials of expert Jew German Barats at the archives of YIVO Institute for Jewish research (RG 309. Leon Baratz) and Sholem Aleichem's autobiographical novel "From the Marketplace" (1916).

35. For elaborate analysis of the nineteenth-century bureaucratic narratives as primary sources for Russian Jewish history, see Olga Litvak, *Conscription and the Search for Modern Russian Jewry* (Bloomington: Indiana University Press, 2006), 14–21.

Chapter 1

1. Osip Lerner, *Evrei v Novorossiiskom krae: istoricheskie ocherki po dannym iz arkhiva byvshego Novorossiiskogo general-gubernatora* (Odessa, 1901), 25, 26.

2. Ibid., 27

3. See well-documented analyses of these developments in Yohanan Petrovsky-Shtern, *Jews in the Russian Army, 1827–1917: Drafted into Modernity* (Cambridge: Cambridge University Press, 2009); Michael Stanislawski, *Tsar Nicholas I and the Jews: The Transformation of Jewish Society in Russia, 1825–1855* (Philadelphia: Jewish Publication Society of America, 1983); V. N. Nikitin, *Evrei zemledel'tsy. Istoricheskoe, zakonodatel'noe, administrativnoe i bytovoe polozhenie kolonii so vremeni ikh vozniknoveniia do nashikh dnei. 1807–1887* (St. Petersburg, 1887).

4. Daniel Orlovsky, *The Limits of Reform: The Ministry of Internal Affairs in Imperial Russia, 1802–1881* (Cambridge, Mass.: Harvard University Press, 1980), 1–3, 23–37.

5. Ibid., 9–12.

6. Ibid., 1–6.

7. Deliberations and political contribution of such committees were studied in Stanislawski, *Tsar Nicholas I and the Jews*; John Klier, *Russia Gathers Her Jews: The Origins of the "Jewish Question" in Russia, 1772–1825* (DeKalb: Northern Illinois University Press, 1986); Benjamin Nathans, *Beyond the Pale: The Jewish Encounter with Late Imperial Russia* (Berkeley: University of California Press, 2002); Maiia Vitenberg, "Vlast', obshchestvo i evreiskii vopros v Rossii v 80-e gody XIX veka," Ph.D. diss., St. Petersburg Institute of History, Russian Academy of Sciences, 2009.

8. Orlovsky, *The Limits of Reform*, 23–37, 145; Nikolai Eroshkin, *Ministerstva Rossii pervoi poloviny XIX veka—fondoobrazovateli tsentral'nykh gosudarstvennykh arkhivov SSSR* (Moscow, 1980), 19, 33.

9. Orlovsky, *The Limits of Reform*, 23–37. In 1810–1819 officials of this kind had been used by the short-lived Ministry of Police. They did not hold any official title, office, or formal responsibilities. They were dispatched by the minister to conduct inspections of the provincial administration "examining the proceedings of local departments and their effectiveness." According to the ministry's regulations, such officials had to have "the ability to perform police investigations and to do other kinds of police jobs." See Nikolai Varadinov, *Istoriia Ministerstva vnutrennikh del* (St. Petersburg, 1858–1863), vol. 2, part 1, 29.

10. Orlovsky, *The Limits of Reform*, 23–37; W. Bruce Lincoln, *In the Vanguard of Reform: Russia's Enlightened Bureaucrats, 1825–1861* (DeKalb: Northern Illinois University Press, 1982), 32–39, 67–70.

11. During the late imperial period, governor-generals were repeatedly reestablished and eliminated. This is a perfect illustration of the constantly changing balance between the principles of institutional and personal power within Russian bureaucracy.

12. Orlovsky, *The Limits of Reform*, 145.

13. Andreas Kappeler, *The Russian Empire: Ethnicity and Nationalism* (Harlow: Longman, 2001), 247–48, 254; Elena Campbell, "The Muslim Question in Late Imperial Russia," in *Russian Empire: Space, People, Power, 1700–1930* (Bloomington: Indiana University Press, 2007), 321–22; Paul Werth, *At the Margins of Orthodoxy: Mission, Governance, and Confessional Politics in Russia's Volga-Kama Region, 1827–1905* (Ithaca, N.Y.: Cornell University Press, 2002), 5–7; Robert D. Crews, *For Prophet and Tsar: Islam and Empire in Russia and Central Asia* (Cambridge, Mass.: Harvard University Press, 2006), 352–54; Darius Staliunas, *Making Russians: Meaning and Practice of Russification in Lithuania and Belarus after 1863* (Amsterdam-New York: Rodopi, 2007); Mikhail Dolbilov, *Russkii krai, chuzhaia vera: Etnokonfessional'naia politika imperii v Litve i Belorussii pri Aleksandre II* (Moscow: Novoe literaturnoe obozrenie, 2010).

14. For recent analysis of this division and general policy of tolerance of non-Orthodox and non-Christian subjects of Russian empire see Crews, *For Prophet and Tsar*, 9–10.

15. Gregory Freeze, "Handmaiden of the State? The Orthodox Church in Imperial Russia Reconsidered," *Journal of Ecclesiastical History* 36 (1985): 89–90, 93.

16. Werth, *At the Margins of Orthodoxy*, 3–5.

17. Ibid., 14–15.

18. Kappeler, *The Russian Empire*, 129.

19. Werth, *At the Margins of Orthodoxy*, 3–5; Crews, *For Prophet and Tsar*, 354–55.

20. Nikolai Varadinov, *Istoriia Ministerstva vnutrennikh del*, 123–36.

21. *Polnoe sobranie zakonov Rossiiskoi imperii. Sobranie pervoe. S 1649 po 12 dekabria 1825 goda* (St. Petersburg, 1830), vol. 31, no. 24307.

22. Varadinov, *Istoriia Ministerstva vnutrennikh del*, 473.

23. Ibid., 136.

24. Ibid., 361.

25. Nikolai Eroshkin, *Istoriia gosudarstvennykh uchrezhdenii dorevoliut-sionnoi Rossii* (Moscow, 1983), 141.

26. Ibid.

27. Ibid., 78.

28. Varadinov, *Istoriia Ministerstva vnutrennikh del*, 265, 414.

29. Ibid., 631.

30. For a concise survey and bibliography of the history of the MNPDD and RBO see Cynthia Whittaker, *The Origins of Modern Russian Education: An Intellectual Biography of Count Sergei Uvarov, 1786–1855* (DeKalb: Northern Illinois University Press, 1984), 71–72, and notes to these pages.

31. During his tenure as minister from 1817 to 1824, Prince Golitsyn simultaneously headed the RBO and the Synod. In addition, he was a personal associate and close friend of the emperor Alexander I.

32. Eroshkin, *Istoriia gosudarstvennykh uchrezhdenii*, 141.

33. The Statute's paragraphs 11–20; see Varadinov, *Istoriia Ministerstva vnutrennikh del*, 62–68.

34. Ibid., 67.

35. Orlovsky, *The Limits of Reform*, 196.

36. Eroshkin, *Istoriia gosudarstvennykh uchrezhdenii*, 141.

37. Kappeler, *The Russian Empire*, 251.

38. ChaeRan Freeze, *Jewish Marriage and Divorce in Imperial Russia* (Hanover, N.H.: University Press of New England, Brandeis University Press, 2002), 338.

39. The fourth and fifth sections were subject to special oversight by the Minister of Internal Affairs, who appointed his officials for special missions as heads of these sections. See Viacheslav Kotkov, *Voennoe dukhovenstvo Rossii* (St. Petersburg, 2004), 192–214.

40. Orlovsky, *The Limits of Reform*, 209–10.

41. Kotkov, *Voennoe dukhovenstvo Rossii*, 192–214.

42. Werth, *At the Margins of Orthodoxy*, 14–15.

43. John Klier, *Russia Gathers Her Jews: The Origins of the "Jewish Question" in Russia, 1772–1825* (DeKalb: Northern Illinois University Press, 1986), 107.

44. David Fishman, *Russia's First Modern Jews: The Jews of Shklov* (New York: New York University Press, 1995), 89–90.

45. Iulii Gessen, *Istoriia evreev v Rossii* (St. Petersburg, 1914), 96.

46. Ibid., 96–97; Fishman, *Russia's First Modern Jews*, 86, 87, 91–93.

47. A history of this institution is meticulously documented and analyzed in Olga Minkina, *"Syny Rakhili." Evreiskie deputaty v Rossiiskoi imperii. 1772–1825* (Moscow: Novoe literaturnoe obozrenie, 2011).

48. Klier, *Russia Gathers Her Jews*, 167–68; Iulii Gessen, "Deputaty evreis-kogo naroda pri Aleksandre I," *Evreiskaia starina* 2–3 (1909); S. Pen, "Dep-utatsiia evreiskogo naroda. K istorii evreev v Rossii v epokhu Aleksandra I," *Knizhki Voskhoda* 30–31 (1905).

49. For a concise yet informative discussion of *shtadlanim* and *shtadlanut* (practices of *shtadlanim*), see Eli Lederhendler, *The Road to Modern Jewish Politics: Political Tradition and Political Reconstruction in the Jewish Commu-nity of Tsarist Russia* (New York: Oxford University Press, 1989), 19–21.

50. Klier, *Russia Gathers Her Jews*, 124–25, 161, 167–68.

51. RGIA, f. 821, op. 8, d. 456, l. 156.

52. Steven Lowenstein, "Governmental Jewish Policies in Early Nine-teenth Century Germany and Russia: A Comparison" *Jewish Social Studies* 46–3/4 (1984): 303–15; Nathans, *Beyond the Pale*, 33.

53. Nathans, *Beyond the Pale*, 31, 368.

54. Ibid., 33; Pavel Kiselev, "Ob ustroistve evreiskogo naroda v Rossii," *Voskhod* 4, 5 (1901): 25–40, 3–21.

55. Nathans, *Beyond the Pale*, 368–69; Aleksandr Polovtsov, ed., *Russkii biograficheskii slovar'* (St. Petersburg: Tipografiia I.N. Skorokhodova, 1896–1918), vol. 1.

56. Nathans, *Beyond the Pale*, 369; Aleksandr Polovtsov, ed., *Russkii bi-ograficheskii slovar'*, vol. 3.

57. RGIA, f. 821, op. 8, d. 504, ll. 10b-2.

58. Ibid., l. 25.

59. Ibid., ll. 25–25 ob.

60. Phyllis Albert, *The Modernization of French Jewry: Consistory and Community in the Nineteenth Century* (Waltham, Mass.: Brandeis University Press; Hanover, N.H.: University Press of New England, 1977), 45.

61. Ibid., 122–50.

62. Ibid., 155–73.

63. Ibid., 240–82.

64. In 1859, the seminary was relocated from Metz to Paris.

65. Iulii Gessen, *Istoriia evreev v Rossii* (St. Petersburg, 1914), 106.

66. RGIA, f. 821, op. 150, d. 371, l. 2.

Chapter 2

1. Circular directive on the formation, on the highest order, of committees of provincial officials and trusted and educated Jews to prepare the project of

establishing posts of provincial rabbis supplemented by religious boards in Odessa, Kiev, Vitebsk, Poltava, and Mitava. Issued on May 17, 1840. Cited in full by Osip Lerner, *Evrei v Novorossiiskom krae: istoricheskie ocherki po dannym iz arkhiva byvshego Novorossiiskogo general-gubernatora* (Odessa, 1901), 25.

2. Ibid., 26.

3. Ibid., 31.

4. The Jewish community of Kherson, reacting to the news of the establishment of the Odessa committee, and following long-established Jewish tradition as well as the precedent of the deputies of the Jewish people, appointed the merchant Moisei Varshavskii as its deputy to the committee and dispatched him to Odessa. However, acting governor-general Fedorov dismissed Varshavskii and the whole initiative as an utter misunderstanding. See ibid., 28–29.

5. Ibid., 25.

6. Ibid., 31.

7. Ibid., 32.

8. Ibid.

9. Ibid., 30.

10. Ibid.

11. Ibid., 30–32.

12. Ibid., 58.

13. RGIA, f. 821, op. 8, d. 456, l. 157.

14. *Polnoe sobranie zakonov Rossiiskoi imperii. Sobranie vtoroe. S 12 dekabria 1825 po 28 fevralia 1881 goda* (St. Petersburg, 1850), vol. 25, no. 24298.

15. RGIA, f. 821, op. 8, d. 456, l. 157 ob.

16. Ibid.

17. Ibid., l. 158.

18. Ibid., l. 158 ob.

19. *Polnoe sobranie zakonov Rossiiskoi imperii* (St. Petersburg, 1891), vol. 11, part 1, no. 1136–39.

20. Only two traditional rabbis sought the appointment: Avraam Madievskii, who served as an expert Jew for the Poltava governor from 1856 to 1859, and Leib Tsirel'son, who unsuccessfully applied for the position of expert Jew at the DDDII in 1908. See RGIA, f. 821, op. 8, d. 397, ll. 90–90 ob.; RGIA, f. 821, op, 8, d. 472, ll. 72–82 ob. For a discussion of emerging interest of the Orthodox Jews in the bureaucratic institutes and policies of the government, see ChaeRan Freeze, *Jewish Marriage and Divorce in Imperial Russia* (Hanover, N.H.: University Press of New England, Brandeis University Press, 2002), 243–45.

21. RGIA, f. 821, op. 8, d. 504, l. 1.

22. RGIA, f. 821, op. 8, d. 218, l. 17.

23. RGIA, f. 821, op. 150, d. 362, ll. 145–45 ob.

24. *Polnoe sobranie zakonov Rossiiskoi imperii. Sobranie vtoroe*, vol. 11, no. 1083.

25. RGIA, f. 821, op. 150, d. 362, l. 178.

26. RGIA, f. 821, op. 150, d. 372, l. 83 ob.

27. Ibid., l. 84 ob.

28. Ibid., l. 85 ob.

29. *Evreiskaia entsiklopediia: svod znanii o evreistve i ego kul'ture v proshlom i nastoiashchem* (St. Petersburg, 1908–1913), vol. 15, 147–48.

30. Ibid.

31. Verena Dohrn, "Evreiskaia Riga," in *Evrei v meniaiushchemsia mire: Materialy chetvertoi mezhdunarodnoi konferentsii: Riga, 20–22 noiabria 2001 g.* (Riga: Fond "Shamir" im. M. Dubina, 2002), 246.

32. As stipulated by the first article of the Statute on expert Jews. See RGIA, f. 821, op. 8, d. 456, l. 158 ob.; *Polnoe sobranie zakonov Rossiiskoi imperii* (St. Petersburg, 1891), vol. 11, part 1, no. 1136.

33. Vladimir Dal', *Tolkovyi slovar' zhivogo velikorusskogo iazyka* (St. Peresburg, 1880–1882), vol. 4, 1120.

34. *Polnoe sobranie zakonov Rossiiskoi imperii. Sobranie vtoroe*, vol. 11, no. 1070; RGIA, f. 821, op. 150, d. 371, l. 4.

35. *Evreiskaia entsiklopediia*, vol. 15, 147–48.

36. Ibid.

37. Ibid.

38. Ibid.

39. Ibid.

40. Ibid.

41. Ibid.

42. Ibid.

43. RGIA, f. 821, op. 133, d. 701, ll. 185–88 ob.

44. *Polnoe sobranie zakonov Rossiiskoi imperii* (St. Petersburg, 1892), vol. 11, part 2, no. 262, 429.

45. Verena Dohrn, "Rabbinical Schools as Instruments of Socialization," *Polin* 14 (2001): 104.

46. Phyllis Albert, *The Modernization of French Jewry: Consistory and Community in the Nineteenth Century* (Waltham, Mass.: Brandeis University Press; Hanover, N.H.: University Press of New England, 1977), 122–50.

47. Paragraphs 1, 10, 11, 14. See RGIA, f. 821, op. 8, d. 456, ll. 159, 160.

48. Ibid., l. 160.

49. Paragraphs 2, 3. See ibid., l. 159.

50. Paragraphs 4, 5. See ibid.

51. Paragraphs 6, 7, 9, 12, 13. See ibid., ll. 159 ob.–160.

52. Paragraphs 8, 10. See Ibid.

53. RGIA, f. 821, op. 8, d. 469, l. 127.

54. Ibid.

55. This is a common view found in such works as Michael Stanislawski, *Tsar Nicholas I and the Jews: The Transformation of Jewish Society in Russia, 1825–1855* (Philadelphia: Jewish Publication Society of America, 1983), 53–54; Eli Lederhendler, *The Road to Modern Jewish Politics: Political Tradition and Political Reconstruction in the Jewish Community of Tsarist Russia* (New York: Oxford University Press, 1989), 91, 96–97; Benjamin Nathans, *Beyond the Pale: The Jewish Encounter with Late Imperial Russia* (Berkeley: University of California Press, 2002), 38–39, 58–60, 68–69.

56. See Appendix.

57. These include six members of the Rabbinical Commission, twenty expert Jews under the MVD, 1,360 government rabbis (some eighty rabbis per province in the Pale of Settlement, based on the average number of districts in each province), three to five censors, and two to three expert Jews under the MNP.

58. The ranks of Russian officials were constantly increasing through the nineteenth century: from one official per 2,250 people in 1796, to one official per 929 people in 1851, and to one official per 335 people in 1897. See Petr Zaionchkovskii, *Pravitel'stvennyi apparat samoderzhavnoi Rossii v XIX v.*, 221.

59. This number grew from 74,300 officials in 1851 to 385,000 officials in 1897. See ibid.

60. Daniel Orlovsky, *The Limits of Reform: The Ministry of Internal Affairs in Imperial Russia, 1802–1881* (Cambridge, Mass.: Harvard University Press, 1980), 1–3.

61. Lerner, *Evrei v Novorossiiskom krae*, 25–27.

62. Ibid., 27–32.

63. Ibid., 58–59.

64. RGIA, f. 821, op. 8, d. 456, l. 157–58 ob.

65. The candidates were nominated by the governor-general of Vilna, Kovno, and Grodno, governor-general of Novorossiia and Bessarabia, governor-general of Riga, Lifland, Estland, and Kurland, and governors of Poltava and Mogilev. The general-governor of Kiev, Podolia, and Volhyn, and

governors of Chernigov, Minsk, and Vitebsk refrained from the nomination due to the reported lack of qualified candidates. See RGIA, f. 821, op. 8, d. 284, ll. 28–31 ob.

66. Ibid.

67. Ibid.

68. *Evreiskaia entsiklopediia*, vol. 13, 235.

69. RGIA, f. 821, op. 8, d. 397, ll. 181–82 ob.

70. RGIA, f. 821, op. 8, d. 456, l. 161 ob.

71. Ibid.

72. Ibid., l. 157 ob.

73. Ibid., l. 161.

74. Ibid., l. 160.

75. Ibid., l. 160 ob.

76. *Polnoe sobranie zakonov Rossiiskoi imperii. Sobranie vtoroe*, vol. 19, no. 18421.

77. RGIA, f. 821, op. 8, d. 456, l. 161.

78. RGIA, f. 821, op. 8, d. 227, l. 14.

79. Ibid., ll. 14–14 ob.

80. Ibid., ll. 15 ob–16.

81. Ibid., ll. 16–17.

82. RGIA, f. 821, op. 8, d. 456, l. 162.

83. Pavel Nikanorovich Shelgunov (in office from 1864 to 1868), Egor Aleksandrovich Kasinov (in office from 1868 to 1869), Vladimir Nikolaevich Tokarev (in office from 1869 to 1875). Short-term appointments of governors were characteristic for the Russian provincial administration. In the second half of the nineteenth century, the average governor spent four years in office. See Petr Zaionchkovskii, *Pravitel'stvennyi apparat samoderzhavnoi Rossii v XIX v.*, 144–45.

84. RGIA, f. 821, op. 8, d. 449, ll. 8–8 ob., 28, 111. The Jews of Minsk petitioned the MVD to dispute the appointment on the grounds of Katsenelenbogen's inadequate qualification, including lack of sufficient expertise and authority among the Jews. As in the case of the similar appeal by the Jews of Chernigov in 1857, the MVD ignored the petition. See RGIA, f. 821, op. 150, d. 362, ll. 30–31.

85. RGIA, f. 821, op. 8, d. 456, l. 164.

86. RGIA, f. 821, op. 8, d. 437, ll. 7–13 ob.

87. Ibid.

88. Ibid., ll. 1–6, 14–23.

89. Ibid., ll. 50–55, 64–77.

90. RGIA, f. 821, op. 150, d. 362, ll. 114–15.

91. Fedor Girs (1824–1891) was head of the chancellery of the gover-nor-general of Novorossiia and Bessarabiia from 1854 to 1863. In 1865, he was made chairman of the MVD Commission on the study of the Kyrgyz life, which developed the statute on the administration of Turkestan and the Steppes. In the 1880s, he was dispatched on inspectorial missions to the far-flung provinces of the empire, including Turkestan in 1882 and the Cau-casus in 1888, where he worked with the Armenian Gregorian clergy and supervised the education of the Armenians. In 1891, he was appointed as chairman of the General Evangelical-Lutheran Consistory in St. Petersburg. See Aleksandr Polovtsov, ed., *Russkii biograficheskii slovar'* (St. Petersburg: Brokgauz-Efron, 1896–1918), vol. 4, 238.

92. RGIA, f. 821, op. 150, d. 362, ll. 114–15.

93. Steven Zipperstein, *The Jews of Odessa: A Cultural History, 1794–1881* (Stanford, Calif.: Stanford University Press, 1985), 121–24.

94. RGIA, f. 821, op. 150, d. 362, ll. 114–15.

95. Ibid.

96. RGIA, f. 821, op. 8, d. 456, l. 161.

97. Ibid., l. 183.

98. RGIA, f. 821, op.8, d. 152, l. 39.

99. On Brafman's impact on official Jewish policy see Steven Zipperstein, *The Jews of Odessa*, 115, 179.

100. RGIA, f. 821, op.8, d. 152, l. 39.

101. RGIA, f. 821, op. 8, d. 456, ll. 183–83 ob.

102. *Trudy Gubernskikh komissii po evreiskomu voprosu* (St. Petersburg, 1884), vol. 2, 567, 617.

103. *Trudy Gubernskikh komissii*, vol. 1, 35; vol. 2, 102, 109, 710, 711, 1108.

104. John W. Slocum, "Who, and When, Were the Inorodtsy? The Evo-lution of the Category of 'Aliens' in Imperial Russia," *Russian Review* 57 (1998): 184.

105. RGIA, f. 821, op. 150, d. 371, l. 2.

106. RGIA, f. 821, op. 8, d. 456, l. 163 ob.

107. Ibid., l. 184.

108. The official Jewish experts of the Palen Commission included mem-bers of the Expert Council of the Ministry of National Enlightenment, Dr. Nikolai Bakst, Baron Goratsii Gintsburg, and Dr. Adam Girshgorn, the St. Petersburg government rabbi Avraam Drabkin, and the entrepreneurs A. Varshavskii and Samuil Poliakov. See RGIA, f. 821, op. 8, d. 246, ll. 84–146.

109. Orlovsky, *The Limits of Reform*, 50–51.

110. RGIA, f. 821, op. 8, d. 456, l. 184.

111. Ibid., ll. 64–65.

112. RGIA, f. 821, op. 133, d. 701, ll. 48, 124–24 ob.

113. RGIA, f. 821, op. 8, d. 472, l. 21.

114. Ibid., ll. 21–21 ob.

115. Ibid., l. 21 ob.

116. The expert Jew Osip Gurvich was dismissed in 1904 by the governor Aleksandr Aleksandrovich Musin-Pushkin (in office from 1902 to 1905) due to a conflict between the expert Jew and the local chief of gendarmes. Under the next governor, Pavel Grigor'evich Kurlov (in office from 1905 to 1906), the office of expert Jew remained vacant. See RGIA, f. 821, op. 8, d. 456, ll. 103–7, 132–55.

117. RGIA, f. 821, op. 133, d. 701, l. 25.

118. RGIA, f. 821, op. 8, d. 456, ll. 111–111 ob.

119. Nathans, *Beyond the Pale*, 39, 66, 72; Freeze, *Jewish Marriage and Divorce*, 275–76.

120. RGIA, f. 821, op. 8, d. 472, l. 21 ob.

121. RGIA, f. 821, op. 133, d. 701, ll. 130–130 ob.

122. Ibid., l. 130 ob.

123. RGIA, f. 821, op. 133, d. 393, ll. 185–88 ob.

124. Ibid., l. 185.

Chapter 3

1. Sholem Aleichem, *Sobranie sochinenii* (Moscow: Gosudarstvennoe izdatel'stvo khudozhestvennoi literatury, 1960), vol. 3, 567.

2. Ibid., 574–76.

3. Ibid., 577.

4. Ibid.

5. Ibid., 578.

6. Ibid.

7. Sholem Aleichem pointed out a special feature of the Jewish elite in Kiev—an incontestable preponderance of entrepreneurs and lawyers ("Brodskiis" and "Kuperniks") over bureaucrats and rabbis. The representation of Kiev province in the Rabbinical Commission illustrated this point well; the Jews of Kiev were represented in this organ by merchant I. E. Landau (in 1861), entrepreneur and banker Baron Goratsii Gintsburg (in 1879), attorney German Barats (in 1893), and attorney M. S. Mazor (in 1910).

See *Evreiskaia entsiklopediia: svod znanii o evreistve i ego kul'ture v proshlom i nastoiashchem* (St. Petersburg, 1908–13), vol. 13, 234.

8. Leo Tolstoy, *Anna Karenina* (Petrozavodsk: Gosudarstvennoe izdatel'stvo, 1960), 124.

9. Ibid., 315–16.

10. Ibid., 159.

11. This scholarship includes W. Bruce Lincoln, *In the Vanguard of Reform: Russia's Enlightened Bureaucrats, 1825–1861* (DeKalb: Northern Illinois University Press, 1982); Daniel Orlovsky, *The Limits of Reform: The Ministry of Internal Affairs in Imperial Russia, 1802–1881* (Cambridge, Mass.: Harvard University Press, 1980); Walter Pintner and Don Rowney, eds., *Russian Officialdom: The Bureaucratization of Russian Society from the Seventeenth to the Twentieth Century* (Chapel Hill: University of North Carolina Press, 1980); Richard Wortman, *The Development of a Russian Legal Consciousness* (Chicago: University of Chicago Press, 1976); Petr Zaionchkovskii, *Pravitel'stvennyi apparat samoderzhavnoi Rossii v XIX v.* (Moscow, 1978).

12. Wortman, *The Development of a Russian Legal Consciousness*, 3–5, 202, 204, 207–34.

13. Lincoln, *In the Vanguard of Reform*, 32–39, 42–51, 71–76.

14. Orlovsky, *The Limits of Reform*, 200.

15. According to archival sources, sixteen of twenty-eight expert Jews, for whom information on their education exists, graduated from the rabbinical seminaries (thirteen in Vilna, three in Zhitomir). See Table 2 in Appendix. The following studies examine general history, teaching staff, students, curriculum, and the relationship with the traditional Jewish society of the rabbinical seminary in Vilna: Judah Slutsky, "Beit ha-Midrash le-Rabbanim be-Vilna," *He'avar* 7 (1960): 29–48; Mordechai Zalkin, "The Vilna Rabbinical Seminary: Image and Reality," *Gal-Ed* 14 (1995): 59–72.

16. *Evreiskaia entsiklopediia*, vol. 13, 261.

17. Dohrn, "Rabbinical Seminaries as Instruments of Socialization," 101–2.

18. *Evreiskaia entsiklopediia*, vol. 13, 260.

19. Verena Dohrn, "Russkoe v evreiskom"; Dohrn, "Rabbinical Seminaries as Instruments of Socialization," 87–91.

20. Dohrn, "Rabbinical Seminaries as Instruments of Socialization," 100–103; Verena Dohrn, "Russkoe v evreiskom," 75, 77. According to Dohrn's study, Stoiunin's approach was based on his belief that the Russian educational system should cultivate humanitarian and civil values and produce good citizens rather than loyal bureaucrats. However, Russian instructors

of the rabbinical seminaries applied Stoiunin's ideas and methods in the setting of elite educational institutions aimed at the cultivation of elite bureaucratic cadres.

21. Ibid., 79, 80, 83. The authors of these textbooks included many Jewish bureaucrats, such as Osip Gurvich, Lev Levanda, Abram Paperna, and Iona Gershtein. For a full bibliographic description of these books, see ibid., 86.

22. Dohrn, "Rabbinical Seminaries as Instruments of Socialization," 104.

23. Freeze, *Jewish Marriage and Divorce*, 99, 101, 116.

24. *Evreiskaia entsiklopediia*, vol. 13, 260.

25. Ibid.

26. RGIA, f.821, op. 8, d, 437, ll. 7–10 ob.

27. Ibid.

28. Ibid.

29. Ibid.

30. RGIA, f. 821, op. 8, d. 456, l. 164.

31. RGIA, f. 821, op 8, d. 437, ll. 7–10 ob.

32. Ibid., ll. 11–23.

33. Ibid., ll. 46–49.

34. RGIA, f. 821, op. 8, d. 456, ll. 13–21.

35. *Evreiskaia entsiklopediia*, vol. 15, 788.

36. RGIA, f. 821, op. 8, d. 437, ll. 12–13 ob.

37. Ibid.

38. *Evreiskaia entsiklopediia*, vol. 15, 788.

39. RGIA, f. 821, op. 8, d. 437, ll. 2–40.

40. RGIA, f. 821, op. 8, d. 449, ll. 73, 87–88 ob.

41. RGIA, f. 821, op. 8, d. 456, ll. 34–35.

42. Ibid., ll. 25–29.

43. RGIA, f. 821, op. 133, d. 701, ll. 35–37 ob.; *Evreiskaia entsiklopediia*, vol. 5, 752.

44. RGIA, f. 821, op. 8, d. 456, ll. 73–75, 78–79.

45. RGIA, f. 821, op. 8, d. 472, ll. 72–82 ob.

46. RGIA, f. 821, op.133, d. 701, ll. 185–88 ob.

47. In contrast, the MVD's approach to the cadres of the government rabbinate was much more flexible. Only in the 1890s and 1900s, when the traditional Jewish religious elite of "spiritual" rabbis developed considerable interest in the political and administrative potential of the government rabbinate, did the MVD reluctantly support this tendency. The MVD's new approach to cadres of the government rabbinate aimed to bureaucratize the traditional rabbinate through official recognition of "spiritual" rabbis and

their appointment to the ranks of the government rabbinate. See Freeze, *Jewish Marriage and Divorce,* 244, 260–63.

48. This refers to a tentative typology based on archival and published sources about twenty-five expert Jews, for whom vital statistics and data on social background, education, and service exist.

49. These included five expert Jews born in the 1800s through the 1820s.

50. Ilia Lurie and Arkadii Zeltser, "Moses Berlin and Lubavich Hasidism: A Landmark in the Conflict Between Haskalah and Hasidism," *Shvut* 5 (1997): 42.

51. For a detailed account of Shklov's role in Russian Jewish history see David Fishman, *Russia's First Modern Jews: The Jews of Shklov* (New York: New York University Press, 1995).

52. Ilia Lurie and Arkadii Zeltser, "Moses Berlin and Lubavich Hasidism," 36.

53. Ibid.

54. Ibid.; *Evreiskaia entsiklopediia,* vol. 4, 271.

55. Lurie and Zeltser, "Moses Berlin and Lubavich Hasidism," 37.

56. Ibid., 42.

57. "Bedstiviia vremen. V pamiat' bedstvii, postigshikh evreev v 1648 i 1649 godakh v Ukraine, Podolii, Litve i Belorussii ot soedinennykh buntovshchikov pod nachal'stvom Bogdana Khmel'nitskogo. Sostavleno Egoshieiu, synom L'vovskogo ravvina, pravednika Davida iz Zamost'ia. Pechatano v Venetsii v 1656 godu. Perevedeno M. Berlinym," in *Chteniia Obshchestva istorii i drevnostei Rossiiskikh* (St. Petersburg, 1859), vol. 1.

58. Moisei Berlin, *Ocherk etnografii evreiskogo narodonaseleniia v Rossii* (St. Petersburg, 1861).

59. *Evreiskaia entsiklopediia,* vol. 4, 272; vol. 9, 389.

60. RGIA, f. 821, op. 8, d. 456, l. 161.

61. As a member of the Imperial Russian Geographical Society, Berlin could directly encounter Russian enlightened bureaucrats, since this organization was the locus of the socialization and consolidation of the Russian bureaucratic elite during the Great Reforms. See Lincoln, *In the Vanguard of Reform,* 91–101.

62. This refers to seventeen expert Jews born from the late 1820s to the early 1840s.

63. Tseitlin was appointed and served from 1859 to 1870, then reappointed from 1872 to 1887. See RGIA, f. 821, op. 8, d. 437, ll. 1–49; RGIA, f. 821, op. 8, d. 456, ll. 13–21. Barats was appointed from 1862 to 1881, then reappointed from 1902 to 1915. See RGIA, f. 821, op. 133, d. 701, ll. 189–94; YIVO, RG 309.

Gurvich was appointed from 1880 to 1904, then reappointed from 1906 to 1914. See RGIA, f. 821, op. 8, d. 456, ll. 103–7, 132–55.

64. In 1870, expert Jew German Barats passed the qualification examinations at Kiev University and received a bachelor's degree in jurisprudence, which, besides the full benefits of government service, entitled him to an independent law practice. See YIVO, RG 309. Expert Jew Illarion Kaufman received a degree in jurisprudence with specialization in finance law from Kharkov University. See *Evreiskaia entsiklopediia*, vol. 9, 389.

65. Expert Jew Aaron Pumpianskii studied the history of the Jews in the Baltic provinces of the Russian empire. In 1881, Pumpianskii published his scholarship in the Russian-language Jewish journal edited by him in Riga. See Aaron Pumpianskii, "Evrei v Lifliandskoi i Kurliandskoi Guberniiakh. Istoricheskii ocherk," *Evreiskie zapiski* 1–6 (1881); *Evreiskaia entsiklopediia*, vol. 13, 117. For more information on Pumpianskii's historical scholarship see Dohrn, "Evreiskaia Riga," 250–51. Expert Jew Iona Gershtein compiled a Russian-language textbook for Jewish elementary schools, which was reprinted many times. See Iona Gershtein, *Pervye uroki russkoi gramoty* (Vilna, 1866). In 1875, he coauthored the Russian translation of the *chumash* (Hebrew Pentateuch) with Lev Levanda and Judah Leib Gordon. See *Evreiskaia entsiklopediia*, vol. 6, 428. Expert Jew Osip Gurvich compiled several Russian language textbooks in Jewish religion, biblical history, and ethics for Jewish schools. See Osip Gurvich, *Zakon evreiskoi very* (Grodno, 1870); Osip Gurvich, *Istoriia evreev v Bibleiskii period* (Vilna, 1871); Osip Gurvich, *Zhivaia moral' ili sokrovishchnitsa talmudicheskoi etiki* (Grodno, 1901); *Evreiskaia entsiklopediia*, vol. 6, 846. Gurvich extensively taught Jewish religion at various private and government-sponsored Jewish schools in Grodno and Minsk provinces. See RGIA, f. 821, op. 133, d. 701, ll. 4–9. In 1869, expert Jew Solomon Minor was co-opted into the leadership of the OPE (Society for the Spread of Enlightenment among Russian Jews), the first non-religious and non-official Jewish institution in Russia. See Eli Lederhendler, *The Road to Modern Jewish Politics: Political Tradition and Political Reconstruction in the Jewish Community of Tsarist Russia* (New York: Oxford University Press, 1989), 113. In the early 1890s, when the city governor of Moscow ordered the expulsion from the city of "thousands of Jews, [the government rabbi] Minor did a lot to protect his congregation." See *Evreiskaia entsiklopediia*, vol. 11, 77.

66. This biography of German Barats is almost entirely based on material collected by his son Leon in the 1930s. See YIVO, RG 309. Complementary sources are indicated by additional footnotes.

67. Freeze, *Jewish Marriage and Divorce in Imperial Russia*, 102. In 1859, Barats was twenty-four years old, while Rabbi Simeon Schwabacher, who won the elections, was thirty-nine.

68. Mikhail Morgulis, "K istorii obrazovaniia russkikh evreev," in *Voprosy evreiskoi zhizni* (St. Petersburg, 1889), 159, 321; Mikhail Morgulis, "Iz moikh vospominanii," *Voskhod* 6–7: 100.

69. *Evreiskaia entsiklopediia*, vol. 13, 233–34.

70. M. E. Mandel'shtam, "Ignat'evskaia komissiia v Kieve 1881 g," in *Perezhitoe*, vol. 4, 46–64.

71. Pavel Demidov San-Donato, *Evreiskii vopros v Rossii* (St. Petersburg, 1883).

72. Ivan Bliokh, *Sravnenie material'nogo byta i nravstvennogo sostoianiia naseleniia v Cherte osedlosti evreev i vne ee. Tsifrovye dannye i issledovaniia po otnosheniiu k evreiskomu voprosu* (St. Petersburg, 1889).

73. According to the contemporary account of professor V. Ikonnikov, in 1920, when Barats was upgraded by the Society to full membership status, he was completely satisfied and deeply touched by this acknowledgment of his contribution to scholarship. Barats's contribution to historiography was recognized by Jewish historians as well. Thus, in 1929, a study hall named after Barats was established at the YIVO Institute in Vilna with financial support from Barats's daughter and her husband. See YIVO, RG 309.

74. RGIA, f. 821, op. 133, d. 701, l. 195.

75. Three expert Jews born in the early 1850s to late 1860s.

76. Expert Jew Moisei Kreps organized rabbinical conventions, summoned by the MVD on a regular basis from the late 1890s. See RGIA, f. 821, op. 133, d. 701, ll. 185–88 ob. In the 1900s to the 1910s, Kreps was a member of the editorial board and edited many entries for the Russian Jewish encyclopedia. See RGIA, f. 821, op. 133, d. 701, ll. 185–88 ob. Expert Jew Gavriil Livshits served in the city administration of Odessa as a secretary of the Jewish division. See RGIA, f. 821, op. 133, d. 701, ll. 130–130 ob. Shmarya Levin, the government rabbi of Ekaterinoslav and expert Jew under the governor of Ekaterinoslav province, was a member of the State Duma. See RGIA, f. 821, op. 8, d. 437, ll. 100–100 ob.; Shmarya Levin, *Forward from Exile* (Philadelphia: Jewish Publication Society of America, 1967).

77. RGIA, f. 821, op. 133, d. 701, l. 185 ob.

78. Ibid.

79. Ibid., l. 186.

80. Ibid.

81. Ibid.

82. Ibid., l. 186 ob.

83. Ibid.

84. Ibid.; *Evreiskaia Entsiklopediia*, vol. 4, 678; V. N. Nikitin, *Evrei zem-ledel'tsy. Istoricheskoe, zakonodatel'noe, administrativnoe i bytovoe polozhenie kolonii so vremeni ikh vozniknoveniia do nashikh dnei. 1807–1887* (St. Petersburg, 1887), 640.

85. M. M. Shitiuk and V. V. Shchukin, *Evreis'ke naselennia Khersons'koi gubernii v XIX—na pochatku XX stolit'* (Nikolaev, 2008), 120.

86. RGIA, f. 821, op. 133, d. 701, l. 187.

87. Ibid.

88. Ibid., l. 188 ob.

89. Ibid.

90. Ibid., l. 186 ob.

91. Ibid., l. 187.

92. Ibid., l. 186 ob.

93. Ibid., l. 188 ob.

94. Ibid.; *Evreiskaia entsiklopediia*, vol. 13, 234.

95. That is, *Evreiskaia entsiklopediia*.

96. *Blokada 1941–1944. Leningrad. Kniga pamiati* (St. Petersburg, 1998–2006), http://www.visz.nlr.ru/search/lists/blkd/234_1343.html, accessed December 20, 2015.

97. RGIA, f. 821, op.133, d. 701, l. 185. After this point Kreps just disappeared like many of his fellow former servitors of the tsarist regime, seeking to become virtually invisible for the Bolshevik authorities, who ruthlessly pursued class enemies, such as tsarist bureaucrats, in order to execute them. I found nothing on Moisei Kreps and his whereabouts after 1917.

98. Freeze, *Jewish Marriage and Divorce*, 74; Paul Werth, *At the Margins of Orthodoxy: Mission, Governance, and Confessional Politics in Russia's Volga-Kama Region, 1827–1905* (Ithaca, N.Y.: Cornell University Press, 2002), 5–7, 177; Robert D. Crews, *For Prophet and Tsar: Islam and Empire in Russia and Central Asia* (Cambridge, Mass.: Harvard University Press, 2006), 23–24, 359–60.

99. Walter Pintner, "Civil Officialdom and the Nobility in the 1850s," in *Russian Officialdom: The Bureaucratization of Russian Society from the Seventeenth to the Twentieth Century*, ed. W. Pintner and D. Rowney (Chapel Hill: University of North Carolina Press, 1980), 242–47.

100. The Table of Ranks (*Tabel' o rangakh*) was a formal list of official positions in the military, government, and royal court of imperial Russia. The emperor Peter I introduced the system in 1722 as a means of modernization

of the Russian state. The Table linked loyal service to the state, embodied in the hierarchy of official ranks, to the social status of state servitors. The Bolshevik government of Soviet Russia abolished the Table of Ranks on November 11, 1917.

101. Expert Jews Perel'man and Gersh Cherner, entitled to the rank of VI class, collegiate councilor, were promoted to this rank due to their medical service, unrelated to their service as expert Jews. See RGIA, f. 821, op. 8, d. 456, ll. 85–87; RGIA, f. 821, op. 8, d. 449, ll. 156–57 ob.

102. H. A. Bennet, "Chiny, Ordena and Officialdom," in *Russian Official-dom*, 169, 172.

103. The government consistently raised this bar. Thus, the rank of the VIII class granted nobility until the 1850s; from the early 1850s, nobility was granted by rank of the V class; and from 1856, by rank of the IV class. Ranks of the X–XIV classes granted honorary citizenship. See Petr Zaionchkovskii, *Pravitel'stvennyi apparat samoderzhavnoi Rossii v XIX v.*, 42, 43.

104. Based on information about nineteen expert Jews, for whom data on their age, service appointments, and terms exist.

105. Service in the provinces presented fewer opportunities for growth for young talented and ambitious bureaucrats, especially in the early stages of their careers. In the 1850s, the majority of provincial Russian bureaucrats (60 percent) and only a small proportion (20 percent) of Russian bureaucrats in St. Petersburg started their service in the provinces. See Walter Pintner, "Civil Officialdom and the Nobility in the 1850s," in *Russian Officialdom*, 242–47.

106. Based on information about nineteen expert Jews, for whom data on their service appointments exist.

107. As represented by the service of acting expert Jews under the DDDII Moisei Berlin, Illarion Kaufman, and Iakov Brafman.

108. As represented by the service of the government rabbis of Riga and expert Jews under the governors of Kurland and Lifland provinces, Aaron Pumpianskii, Solomon Pukher, and Isidor Mikhel'son.

109. As represented by the service of government rabbis of St. Petersburg, Avraam Neiman and Avraam Drabkin.

110. As represented by the service of expert Jew under the DDDII Moisei Kreps.

111. Zaionchkovskii, *Pravitel'stvennyi apparat samoderzhavnoi Rossii v XIX v.*, 34.

112. From 1848 to 1873, the rabbinical seminaries in Vilna and Zhitomir produced 395 graduates, including 103 certified rabbis and 292 certified

teachers in total. The students who finished the course of study with only a certificate of secondary education are not counted here. See *Evreiskaia entsiklopediia*, vol. 13, 259, 261.

113. Vilna, Kovno, and Grodno provinces. See Freeze, *Jewish Marriage and Divorce*, 110–11.

114. Based on information about twenty-eight expert Jews, for whom data on their education exist.

115. Zaionchkovskii, *Pravitel'stvennyi apparat samoderzhavnoi Rossii v XIX v.*, 33.

116. Ibid., 34.

117. Based on information about thirty-eight expert Jews, for whom data on their compensation exist.

118. RGIA, f. 821, op. 8, d. 437, ll. 64–77.

119. RGIA, f. 821, op. 133, d. 701, ll. 152–54.

120. Ibid., ll. 1–1 ob.

121. Ibid., ll. 152–54.

122. A. I. Paperna, "Iz Nikolaevskoi epokhi," in *Evrei v Rossii: XIX vek*, ed. V. Kel'ner (Moscow: Novoe literaturnoe obozrenie, 2000), 166.

123. Ibid.

124. Information on the compensation of Russian bureaucrats based on data from Zaionchkovskii, *Pravitel'stvennyi apparat samoderzhavnoi Rossii v XIX v.*, 73–78, 86, 88, 90.

125. Expert Jews Moisei Berlin and Arnold Mandel'shtam received an annual travel allowance in the amount of 200 rubles each. See RGIA, f. 821, op. 8, d. 397, l. 62 ob.; RGIA, f. 821, op. 8, d. 397, ll. 126–27.

126. Zaionchkovskii, *Pravitel'stvennyi apparat samoderzhavnoi Rossii v XIX v.*, 80–86.

127. RGIA, f. 821, op. 8, d. 437, ll 7–10 ob.

128. Zaionchkovskii, *Pravitel'stvennyi apparat samoderzhavnoi Rossii v XIX v.*, 80–86.

129. RGIA, f. 821, op. 133, d. 701, ll. 1–1 ob.

130. Zaionchkovskii, *Pravitel'stvennyi apparat samoderzhavnoi Rossii v XIX v.*, 42, 43.

131. Bennet, "Chiny, Ordena and Officialdom," in *Russian Officialdom*, 174, 176, 179, 180.

132. Based on information about sixteen expert Jews, for whom data on honorary titles, awards, and ranks exist.

133. RGIA, f. 821, op. 133, d. 701, ll. 4–9.

134. RGIA, f. 821, op. 8, d. 437, ll. 62 ob.

135. RGIA, f. 821, op. 133, d. 701, l. 39 ob.

136. Ibid., ll. 4–9.

137. RGIA, f. 821, op. 8, d. 437, l. 62 ob.

138. Memorandum of D. N. Bludov and Ia. I. Rostovtsev, "On the Abrogation of the Regulation on the Accelerated Promotion of Educated Bureaucrats of 1834," cited in Petr Zaionchkovskii, *Pravitel'stvennyi apparat samoderzhavnoi Rossii v XIX v.*, 38.

139. Don Rowney, "Organizational Change and Social Adaptation: The Prerevolutionary Ministry of Internal Affairs," in *Russian Officialdom*, 299–314.

140. Based on information about ten expert Jews, for whom data on their family status and children exist.

141. As in the case of expert Jew Isaak Kaminer. See *Evreiskaia entsiklopediia*, vol. 9, 196.

142. As in the case of expert Jew Abram Tsuntser. See RGIA, f. 821, op. 133, d. 701, ll. 85–85 ob.

143. As in the case of expert Jew Boris Sheindel's. See ibid., l. 148 ob.

144. As in the case of expert Jews Moisei Berlin and German Barats. See *Evreiskaia entsiklopediia*, vol. 4, 271–72; YIVO, RG 309.

145. As in the case of Leon Barats and Fanni Berlin. See *Evreiskaia entsiklopediia*, vol. 4, 271–72; YIVO, RG 309.

146. As in the case of Faitel' Bliumenfel'd. See *Evreiskaia entsiklopediia*, vol. 4, 678–79. Isaak Kaminer's daughters, who married radical activists (including a non-Jew)—Nadezhda Akselrod, Anna Kalmanson, and Avgusta Tishchenko—were prominent among early Jewish socialist leaders. Kaminer's home in Kiev served as the center for a socialist group led by his son-in-law Pavel Akselrod in the 1870s. See Ben Halpern and Jehuda Reinharz, *Zionism and the Creation of a New Society* (New York: Oxford University Press, 1998), 125.

147. As in the case of Illarion Kaufman. See *Evreiskaia entsiklopediia*, vol. 9, 389.

148. Vladimir Fedorov and Iakov Brafman had converted to Christianity long before their appointment to the office of expert Jews, and for reasons unconnected to this specific career.

149. For example, the Hasidic denunciation of expert Jew Moisei Berlin claimed that he "completely lacked any piety." See Lurie and Zeltser, "Moses Berlin and Lubavich Hasidism," 48–49.

150. Of the twenty-eight expert Jews for whom data about their education exist, seventeen were educated at the Russian rabbinical seminaries, four

at traditional yeshivot, and one at a European Jewish theological seminary. The majority of expert Jews also received traditional *cheder* training; few of them were educated at home.

151. Of the thirty-four expert Jews for whom data on their service appointments exist, fifteen served as government rabbis.

152. G. B. Sliozberg, "Dela minuvshikh dnei," in *Evrei v Rossii: XIX vek*, 268–69.

153. Ibid., 269.

154. Ibid.

155. Ibid.

156. Dohrn, "Evreiskaia Riga," 247.

157. Ibid., 249.

158. Contemporaries defined the role of such rabbis in a similar manner. According to the contemporary Jewish press, expert Jew Solomon Minor "as the government rabbi of Moscow, i.e., the leader of the intelligentsia, saw it as his moral obligation to do his best for the protection and support of the major part of Russian Jewry." See B.V., "Zametka po povodu retsenzii g. L.L. na broshiuru Minora 'Rabbi Ippolit Liutostanskii'," *Russkii evrei* 7 (1879): 239–40.

159. Based on information about twenty-six expert Jews, for whom data on their extracurricular activities and occupations exist.

160. *Evreiskaia entsiklopediia*, vol. 6, 851; ibid., vol. 6, 851–52; RGIA, f. 821, op. 8, d. 456, ll. 38–40 ob.

161. *Evreiskaia entsiklopediia*, vol. 6, 428; ibid., vol. 11, 56; Dohrn, "Evreiskaia Riga," 243–53.

162. RGIA, f. 821, op. 8, d. 456, ll. 96–96 ob.

163. RGIA, f. 821, op. 133, d. 701, ll. 46–46 ob.

164. *Evreiskaia entsiklopediia*, vol. 4, 271–72; YIVO, RG 309. Kaminer was also a talented Hebrew poet. In 1888 he wrote a salutatory text that opened the first volume (1888) of Sholem Aleichem's *Di yidishe folks-bibliotek: A bukh fir literatur, kritik, un vissenshaft* (The Jewish Popular Library: A Book of Literature, Criticism, and Scholarship). See Gennady Estraikh, *In Harness: Yiddish Writers' Romance with Communism* (Syracuse, N.Y.: Syracuse University Press, 2005), 8.

165. YIVO, RG 309.

166. *Evreiskaia entsiklopediia*, vol. 9, 196.

Chapter 4

1. ChaeRan Freeze, *Jewish Marriage and Divorce in Imperial Russia* (Hanover, N.H.: University Press of New England, Brandeis University Press, 2002), 82.

2. Osip Lerner, *Evrei v Novorossiiskom krae: istoricheskie ocherki po dannym iz arkhiva byvshego Novorossiiskogo general-gubernatora* (Odessa, 1901), 73.

3. The survey is based on documents about the service of these expert Jews: Moisei Berlin and Litman Zeltser under the governor-general of Vitebsk, Mogilev, and Smolensk provinces (see RGIA, f. 821, op. 8, d. 397, ll. 60–69 ob.), Markus Gurovich under the governor-general of Novorossiia and Bessarabiia (see Lerner, *Evrei v Novorossiiskom krae*, 73–198; RGIA, f. 821, op. 8, d. 397, ll. 19–54) and Aaron Tseitlin under the governor of Poltava province (see RGIA, f. 821, op. 8, d. 437, ll. 7–10 ob), from 1851 to 1861.

4. For example, in 1859, in open violation of the "Secret regulation" clearly banning expert Jews from fiscal responsibilities, the governor of Poltava province assigned his expert Jew Aaron Tseitlin to supervise the collection of the *korobochnyi sbor* (excise tax on kosher meat). See RGIA, f. 821, op. 8, d. 437, ll. 7–10 ob.

5. The survey is based on documents about the service of these expert Jews: Aaron Tseitlin under the governor of Poltava province (see RGIA, f. 821, op. 8, d. 437, ll. 7–10 ob), Avraam Neiman under the *DDDII* (see RGIA, f. 821, op. 150, d. 362, ll. 32–36 ob., 85–88), German Barats under the governor-general of Kiev, Podolia, and Volhyn (see RGIA, f. 821, op. 150, d. 362, ll. 42–49a ob.), Simeon Schwabacher under the city governor of Odessa (Lerner, *Evrei v Novorossiiskom krae*, 228–29), Lazar' Genikes under the superintendent of Odessa educational district (see RGIA, f. 821, op. 150, d. 362, ll. 147–58 ob.), Sheftel' Kliachko under the governor-general of Vilna, Kovno, and Grodno (see RGIA, f. 821, op. 8, d. 152, ll. 8, 9, 15), and Osip Gurvich under the governor of Minsk province (see RGIA, f. 821, op. 8, d. 152, l. 31), from 1862 to 1871.

6. For examination of the commission's proceedings see Mikhail Dolbilov, "Russifying Bureaucracy and the Politics of Jewish Education in the Russian Empire's Northwest Region (1860s–1870s)," *Acta Slavica Iaponica* 24 (2006): 129. Dolbilov defines Jewish members of the commission—Iona Gershtein, Lev Levanda, and Asher Vol'—as "Russophile maskilim," without mentioning that two of them, Gershtein and Levanda, were incumbent expert Jews under the governor-general and sat on the commission in their official capacity.

7. RGIA, f. 821, op. 8, d. 437, ll. 7–10 ob.

8. The survey is based on documents about the service of these expert Jews: Samuil Katsenelenbogen, Osip Gurvich, and Boris Sheindel's under the governor of Minsk province (see RGIA, f. 821, op. 8, d. 449, ll. 8–8 ob., 28, 111; RGIA, f. 821, op. 133, d. 701, l. 25; RGIA, f. 821, op. 8, d. 152, l. 34 ob.; RGIA, f. 821, op. 133, d. 701, ll. 142–48), Filipp Keil'man under the Baltic governor-general (see RGIA, f. 821, op. 8, d. 437, ll. 56–58), Mikhail Vol'per, Sheftel' Kliachko, and Grigorii Shkliaver under the governor-general of Vilna, Kovno, and Grodno (see RGIA, f. 821, op. 8, d. 456, ll. 64–65), Lev Binshtok under the governor of Volhyn province (see RGIA, f. 821, op. 150, d. 362, ll. 82–85), Blavshtein under the governor of Podolia province (see RGIA, f. 821, op. 8, d. 532, ll. 12–12 ob.), Arnold Mandel'shtam under the governor of Mogilev province (see RGIA, f. 821, op. 8, d. 472, l. 23), Lev Zaidiner under the governor of Poltava province (see RGIA, f. 821, op. 8, d. 437, ll. 50–55, 64–77), Illarion Kaufman and Moisei Kreps under the DDDII (see RGIA, f. 821, op. 150, d. 362, ll. 90–97 ob.; RGIA, f. 821, op. 133, d. 701, ll. 185–88 ob.), and Efrem Freidin under the governor of Chernigov province (see RGIA, f. 821, op. 150, d. 362, ll. 158–60), from 1872 to 1917.

9. For the detailed account of the 1910 Rabbinical Congress in St. Petersburg by DDDII official Grigorii Bronnikovskii see RGIA, f. 821, op. 150, d. 393, ll. 1–41; for an analysis of the congress proceedings see Freeze, *Jewish Marriage and Divorce*, 260–70.

10. RGIA, f. 821, op. 8, d. 472, l. 23.

11. Daniel Orlovsky, *The Limits of Reform: The Ministry of Internal Affairs in Imperial Russia, 1802–1881* (Cambridge, Mass.: Harvard University Press, 1980), 37–41, 50–51.

12. RGIA, f. 821, op. 8, d. 456, ll. 159 ob.–160.

13. For the analysis of this process and its historical significance see the following essays in Walter Pintner and Don Rowney, eds., *Russian Officialdom: The Bureaucratization of Russian Society from the Seventeenth to the Twentieth Century* (Chapel Hill: University of North Carolina Press, 1980): Daniel Orlovsky, "High Officials in the Ministry of Internal Affairs, 1855–1881," 250–53; Walter Pintner, "Civil Officialdom and the Nobility in the 1850s," 227; Don Rowney, "Organizational Change and Social Adaptation: The Prerevolutionary Ministry of Internal Affairs," 283–84; and Walter Pintner and Don Rowney, "Officialdom and Bureaucratization: Conclusion," 369–77.

14. For example, the data reported by the governors included the lists of the official personnel of the Jewish communities. See Genrikh Deich, *Arkhivnye dokumenty po istorii i genealogii evreev v Rossii. Sinagogi, molitvennye*

doma i sostoiashchie pri nikh dolzhnostnye litsa v Cherte osedlosti i guberniiakh Kurliandskoi i Lifliandskoi Rossiiskoi imperii. 1853–1854 (New York, 1992).

15. The official communications and other documents of the provincial governors and the MVD testify that this obviously was the case. However, in 1886, the DDDII paradoxically concluded that the information provided by expert Jews was largely useless, since it "had the format of inspection reports on religious institutions and did not include any practical advice on the administration of the Jews in the provinces." See RGIA, f. 821, op. 8, d. 456, l. 161.

16. RGIA, f. 821, op. 8, d. 397, ll. 60–60 ob.

17. Ibid., ll. 61–61 ob.

18. Ibid., l. 61.

19. Ibid., l. 61 ob.

20. RGIA, f. 821, op. 8, d. 284, ll. 46 ob.–49.

21. RGIA, f. 821, op. 8, d. 152, l. 31.

22. RGIA, f. 821, op. 8, d. 397, l. 64.

23. Ibid., ll. 64–64 ob.

24. Ibid., ll. 66–66 ob.

25. *Polnoe sobranie zakonov Rossiiskoi imperii. Sobranie vtoroe. S 12 dekabria 1825 po 28 fevralia 1881 goda* (St. Petersburg, 1834), vol. 9, no. 1272.

26. RGIA, f. 821, op. 8, d. 397, l. 65 ob.

27. Ibid., l. 66.

28. Ibid.

29. Ibid., ll. 66 ob.–67.

30. Ibid., l. 65.

31. Ibid., ll. 66 ob.–67.

32. Ibid., l. 8 ob.

33. Ibid., ll. 26, 45.

34. Osip Lerner, *Evrei v Novorossiiskom krae*, 74.

35. Ibid.

36. RGIA, f. 821, op. 8, d. 397, ll. 17–17 ob.

37. Ibid., ll. 14–17.

38. Ibid., ll. 16, 39 ob.

39. Ibid., ll. 23 ob., 35 ob.–36, 43–43 ob.

40. Ibid., ll. 41–43.

41. Ibid., ll. 42 ob.–43.

42. Ibid., l. 48.

43. Lerner, *Evrei v Novorossiiskom krae*, 84, 88.

44. Ibid., 90.

45. RGIA, f. 821, op. 8, d. 397, l. 47.

46. Lerner, *Evrei v Novorossiiskom krae*, 85–86.

47. Ibid., 86.

48. Ibid., 82–83.

49. RGIA, f. 821, op. 8, d. 397, l. 8 ob.

50. Ibid., ll. 9–11 ob.

51. RGIA, f. 821, op. 8, d. 437, ll. 7–13 ob.

52. For a discussion of the role of inspection trips in the MVD's policy-making see W. Bruce Lincoln, *In the Vanguard of Reform: Russia's Enlightened Bureaucrats, 1825–1861* (DeKalb: Northern Illinois University Press, 1982), 42–51; Richard Wortman, *The Development of a Russian Legal Consciousness* (Chicago: University of Chicago Press, 1976), 207–34.

53. RGIA, f. 821, op. 8, d. 397, l. 62.

54. Ibid., ll. 62–62 ob.

55. Ibid., l. 62 ob.

56. Ibid.

57. RGIA, f. 821, op. 8, d. 437, ll. 12–13 ob.

58. RGIA, f. 821, op. 8, d. 503, ll. 1–13.

59. Ibid., l. 37.

60. Ibid., ll. 14–14 ob.

61. Ibid., ll. 14 ob.–17.

62. Ibid., l. 37 ob.

63. Ibid., l. 38.

64. In 1858, soliciting the MVD's approval for his appointment of Fedorov, Prince Vasil'chikov pointed out that he looked forward to using the expert Jew for such missions. See RGIA, f. 821, op. 8, d. 397, ll. 108–109 ob., 148–49.

65. RGIA, f. 821, op. 8, d. 437, ll. 12–13 ob.

66. Ibid.

67. Ibid., ll. 50–55, 64–77.

68. Ibid., ll. 56–58.

69. RGIA, f. 821, op. 8, d. 456, l. 159–60; Osip Lerner, *Evrei v Novorossiiskom krae*, 25, 26.

70. RGIA, f. 821, op. 8, d. 397, l. 68 ob.

71. RGIA, f. 821, op. 8, d. 456, l. 159.

72. RGIA, f. 821, op. 8, d. 397, l. 62 ob.

73. Ibid., l. 62 ob.–63.

74. See Ilia Lurie and Arkadii Zeltser, "Moses Berlin and Lubavich Hasidism: A Landmark in the Conflict between Haskalah and Hasidism," *Shvut* 5 (1997): 32–64.

75. RGIA, f. 821, op. 8, d. 397, l. 68 ob.

76. Ibid., l. 63.

77. See Vassili Schedrin, "Neizvestnaia istoriia khasidizma i drugie raboty Moiseia Berlina," *Arkhiv evreiskoi istorii* 1 (2004): 169–92.

78. RGIA, f. 821, op. 8, d. 284, l. 44 ob.

79. Ibid., l. 45.

80. Ibid.

81. See *Polnoe sobranie zakonov Rossiiskoi imperii. Sobranie vtoroe*, vol. 2, no. 788, 1271, 1273.

82. Lerner, *Evrei v Novorossiiskom krae*, 102.

83. Ibid., 102–7.

84. Ibid., 107.

85. Ibid., 109.

86. Benjamin Nathans, *Beyond the Pale: The Jewish Encounter with Late Imperial Russia* (Berkeley: University of California Press, 2002), 48, 56.

87. Already in 1853, the MVD challenged expert Jew Moisei Berlin under the governor-general of Vitebsk, Mogilev, and Smolensk provinces with a question: whether a sentenced Jewish convict should undergo the established procedure of confession before execution. See RGIA, f. 821, op. 8, d. 397, l. 63.

88. RGIA, f. 821, op. 150, d. 362, ll. 6–9.

89. Ibid.

90. Ibid., ll. 85–88.

91. Ibid., l. 88.

92. RGIA, f. 821, op. 8, d. 397, ll. 68–68 ob.

93. RGIA, f. 821, op. 150, d. 362, l. 29.

94. Ibid.

95. Ibid., l. 30 ob.

96. Ibid., ll. 42–49a ob.

97. Ibid., l. 43. Barats referred to the decision on the legitimacy of Jewish oaths by the Court of Appeals in Colmar on March 3, 1846, reported by the *Archives Israélites de France*.

98. RGIA, f. 821, op. 150, d. 362, l. 43 ob.

99. Ibid.

100. Ibid., l. 44.

101. Iakov Brafman, *Evreiskie bratstva, mestnye i vsemirnye* (Vilna, 1868), 109; Iakov Brafman, *Kniga Kagala* (Vilna, 1870), lxxxi.

102. For a comprehensive contemporary critical account of Brafman's expertise on Jewish oaths see Il'ia Shereshevskii, "Evreiskaia prisiaga i ee razreshenie," *Evreiskaia biblioteka: istoriko-literaturnyi sbornik* 5 (1875): 101–38.

103. RGIA, f. 821, op. 150, d. 362, ll. 81–82.

104. Ibid., l. 84.

105. Ibid., l. 85.

106. Ibid., l. 91 ob.

107. Ibid., ll. 92–92 ob.

108. Ibid., l. 92 ob.

109. Ibid., ll. 92 ob.–93.

110. Ibid., l. 93.

111. For a discussion of the evolution of imperial policy toward Russian Orthodoxy, Judaism, and Islam see Gregory Freeze, "Subversive Piety: Religion and the Political Crisis in Late Imperial Russia," *Journal of Modern History* 68 (1996): 308–50; ChaeRan Freeze, *Jewish Marriage and Divorce in Imperial Russia* (Hanover, N.H.: University Press of New England, Brandeis University Press, 2002), 244, 247–48; Paul Werth, *At the Margins of Orthodoxy: Mission, Governance, and Confessional Politics in Russia's Volga-Kama Region, 1827–1905* (Ithaca, N.Y.: Cornell University Press, 2002), 177; Elena Campbell, "The Muslim Question in Late Imperial Russia," in *Russian Empire: Space, People, Power, 1700–1930* (Bloomington: Indiana University Press, 2007), 328–31.

112. Werth, *At the Margins of Orthodoxy*, 124–25.

113. RGIA, f. 821, op. 8, d. 152, l. 34 ob.

114. Ibid., l. 35.

115. RGIA, f. 821, op. 8, d. 397, l. 61.

116. Lerner, *Evrei v Novorossiiskom krae*, 92.

117. Ibid., 94.

118. Ibid., 95. A similar opinion, independent of Gurovich's conclusions, was articulated by contemporary Russian bureaucrats. According to the acting governor of Kherson province Baron Ivan Osipovich Velio, the Jewish burial society established in Kherson in 1781 "pursued a benevolent agenda" and was "completely harmless for public order." See ibid., 93–94.

119. Ibid., 94.

120. Ibid., 92.

121. Ibid., 98.

122. RGIA, f. 821, op. 8, d. 284, l. 43 ob; *Evreiskaia entsiklopediia: svod znanii o evreistve i ego kul'ture v proshlom i nastoiashchem* (St. Petersburg, 1908–1913), vol. 13, 235.

123. RGIA, f. 821, op. 8, d. 152, ll. 8–9, 15.

124. Ibid., ll. 1–39.

125. Ibid., l. 34 ob.

126. Ibid., ll. 8–9, 15.

127. Ibid.

128. Ibid., l. 35.

129. Lerner, *Evrei v Novorossiiskom krae*, 216–17.

130. RGIA, f. 821, op. 133, d. 701, l. 187 ob.

131. Ibid., 188–188 ob.

132. Ibid.

133. RGIA, f. 821, op. 8, d. 437, ll. 12–13 ob.

134. Ibid.

135. RGIA, f. 821, op. 8, d. 152, l. 160.

136. Ibid.

137. Lerner, *Evrei v Novorossiiskom krae*, 194.

138. Ibid.

139. Ibid.

140. Ibid., 195.

141. Ibid., 196.

142. Ibid.

143. Ibid.

144. Ibid., 197–98.

145. Ibid., 218–19.

146. Ibid., 219.

147. Ibid.

148. *Cheder* (room in Hebrew) is a traditional Jewish school run by a melamed.

149. Lerner, *Evrei v Novorossiiskom krae*, 219–20.

150. Ibid., 222–23.

151. Ibid., 224.

152. Ibid.

153. Freeze, *Jewish Marriage and Divorce*, 86.

154. These were Avraam Neiman, Iankel' Barit, I. E. Landau, German Barats, Avraam Madievskii, and Ekutiel' Zisl Rapoport. See *Evreiskaia entsiklopediia*, vol. 13, 233–38.

155. Il'ia Zeiberling and Samuel Joseph Fuenn were coopted on the initiative of the Ministry of National Enlightenment; Moisei Berlin was coopted on the initiative of the MVD; Evzel' Gintsburg was coopted on the initiative of the emperor Alexander II. See *Evreiskaia entsiklopediia*, vol. 13, 233–38.

156. In 1863, Evzel' Gintsburg initiated the establishment of the OPE (Society for the Spread of Enlightenment among Russian Jews), the first non-religious and non-official Jewish institution in Russia. In order to get

official support for the new institution, Gintsburg recruited expert Jews Avraam Neiman, Zalkind Minor, Samuel Joseph Fuenn, and Simeon Schwabacher into the leadership of the OPE, as honorary members. Thus, the Society's leadership not only represented a who's who of Russian maskilim, as pointed out by Eli Lederhendler, but also a who's who of Russian Jewish bureaucracy. See Eli Lederhendler, *The Road to Modern Jewish Politics: Political Tradition and Political Reconstruction in the Jewish Community of Tsarist Russia* (New York: Oxford University Press, 1989), 113. On the emergence of the Russian Jewish economic elite as a spokesman for Russian Jews see Nathans, *Beyond the Pale*, 38–44.

157. RGIA, f. 821, op. 8, d. 284, ll. 27–49 ob.

158. Ibid., ll. 27–28 ob.

159. These questions included introduction of the universal ritual of Jewish worship services; ban of printed publications in Yiddish; introduction of a tax on the use Jewish public and ritual baths and on the annual rent of prayer spots in the synagogues; introduction of the ritual of confirmation for Jewish boys; examination of the traditional Jewish ritual of *eruv* and development of measures aimed at the elimination of this ritual; and examination of the ritual of *Kol Nidre* and of its significance among the Jews. See RGIA, f. 821, op. 8, d. 284, ll. 48–49.

160. These questions included institution of a permanent provincial religious administration for Jews; examination of the detrimental factors hampering the successful development of agriculture by Jewish farmers; and development of measures for elimination of these factors. See RGIA, f. 821, op. 8, d. 284, ll. 46 ob.–47 ob.

161. For comparison of the 1861 agenda with the agenda of the Commission's last session of 1910 see Freeze, *Jewish Marriage and Divorce*, 252, 260.

162. These questions included institution of a permanent provincial religious administration for Jews; principles of censorship of Jewish religious literature; preservation of the religious courts, *batei din*, in the Jewish communities; ban of printed publications in Yiddish; and introduction of a tax on the use of Jewish public and ritual baths and on the annual rental of prayer spots in the synagogues. See RGIA, f. 821, op. 8, d. 284, ll. 46 ob.–49.

163. These questions included introduction of the universal ritual of the Jewish worship services; introduction of the ritual of confirmation for Jewish boys; examination of the traditional Jewish ritual of *eruv* and development of measures aimed at elimination of this ritual; and examination of the ritual

of *Kol Nidre* and its significance among the Jews. See RGIA, f. 821, op. 8, d. 284, ll. 46 ob.–49.

164. These questions included the divorce case of Feiga Gelenfonova; examination of detrimental factors (especially early marriages between Jews) hampering the successful development of agriculture by Jewish farmers; and development of measures for elimination of these factors. See RGIA, f. 821, op. 8, d. 284, ll. 46 ob.–49.

165. These questions included introduction of a universal curriculum for education of Jewish youth and development of a special program of Jewish religious subjects for official examination of candidates for the rabbinate. See RGIA, f. 821, op. 8, d. 284, ll. 46 ob.–49.

166. Expert Jews Markus Gurovich, under the governor-general of Novorossiia and Bessarabiia, Moisei Berlin, under the MVD, and Arnold Mandel'shtam, under the governor of Mogilev province, were among the most prolific contributors to the agenda and deliberations of the Commission's session of 1861.

167. RGIA, f. 821, op. 8, d. 284, ll. 40 ob.–46 ob.

168. This goal was fully shared by contemporary unofficial Jewish public opinion, which also envisioned an important role for Jewish bureaucracy and its institutions like the Rabbinical Commission. Assessing the decisions of the Rabbinical Commission of 1861, a contemporary account by Mikhail Morgulis pointed out that the government, by using the Rabbinical Commission for the regulation of marital issues of the Jews, could "release a whole class of people from personal whim." See Freeze, *Jewish Marriage and Divorce*, 94–95.

169. Orlovsky, *The Limits of Reform*, 3–6.

170. These recommendations included introduction of a universal curriculum for education of Jewish youth, introduction of an official qualifying examination for candidates for the government rabbinate, instituting a permanent provincial religious administration for Jews. See RGIA, f. 821, op. 8, d. 284, ll. 48–49; *Evreiskaia entsiklopediia*, vol. 13, 235.

171. Thus, in some cases the solutions recommended by the Rabbinical Commission, upon their selective implementation and assessment of the results by the authorities, became part of official policy as administrative precedents. See Freeze, *Jewish Marriage and Divorce*, 247.

172. For a well-documented discussion of this policy see Vladimir Levin, "Orthodox Jewry and the Russian Government: An Attempt at Rapprochement, 1907–1914," *East European Jewish Affairs* 2 (2009): 187–204.

173. RGIA, f. 821, op. 8, d. 331, ll. 99–100 ob.

174. Ibid., ll. 95–98 ob.

175. Ibid.

176. Ibid., ll. 101–101 ob.

177. Ibid., ll. 95–98 ob.

178. Vera Lebedeva-Kaplan, "Evrei Petrograda v 1917 g.," *Vestnik Evreis-kogo universiteta v Moskve*, 2 (1993): 4.

179. RGIA, f. 821, op. 8, d. 397, ll. 62–62 ob.

180. Ibid., ll. 67–67 ob.

181. Ibid., l. 69.

182. RGIA, f. 821, op. 133, d. 701, l. 188 ob.

183. RGIA, f. 821, op. 8, d. 472, l. 23.

184. Ibid.

185. Ibid., l. 23 ob.

186. Expert Jew Markus Gurovich started his career in 1852. However, his first documented mission was assigned to him by the governor-general in 1854. See *Evreiskaia entsiklopediia*, vol. 6, 851; RGIA, f. 821, op. 150, d. 362, l. 147.

187. Osip Lerner, *Evrei v Novorossiiskom krae*, 138–39.

188. Ibid., 140–41.

189. Ibid., 145–47.

190. Ibid., 110–19.

191. Ibid., 183–91.

192. RGIA, f. 821, op. 150, d. 362, l. 115.

193. Lerner, *Evrei v Novorossiiskom krae*, 216–18.

194. For examination of bureaucratic policies toward the Jews in this region see Mikhail Dolbilov, "Russifying Bureaucracy," 112–43, and *Russkii krai, chuzhaia vera: Etnokonfessional'naia politika imperii v Litve i Belorussii pri Aleksandre II* (Moscow: Novoe literaturnoe obozrenie, 2010).

195. RGIA, f. 821, op. 8, d. 456, l. 161.

196. RGIA, f. 821, op. 8, d. 397, ll. 60–69 ob.

197. RGIA, f. 821, op. 150, d. 362, ll. 114–15.

198. Ibid., ll. 90–97 ob.

199. Ibid., ll. 85–88.

200. Robert Crews makes a similar point about the effect of the Russian religious administration for the Muslims. See Robert D. Crews, *For Prophet and Tsar: Islam and Empire in Russia and Central Asia* (Cambridge, Mass.: Harvard University Press, 2006), 359–60.

201. Shmarya Levin, *Forward from Exile* (Philadelphia: Jewish Publication Society of America, 1967), 370.

202. For data on the governors see Petr Zaionchkovskii, *Pravitel'stvennyi apparat samoderzhavnoi Rossii v XIX v.* (Moscow, 1978), 144–45; for data on the expert Jews see Table 6 in Appendix.

203. RGIA, f. 821, op. 8, d. 397, ll. 126–27.

204. RGIA, f. 821, op. 133, d. 701, l. 33.

205. Ibid.

Chapter 5

1. Elise Kimerling Wirtschafter, *Structures of Society: Imperial Russia's "People of Various Ranks"* (DeKalb: Northern Illinois University Press, 1994), 6, 12, 16.

2. Likewise, in the 1830s–1840s, Russian enlightened Jews—maskilim—emerged as an influential secular Jewish sub-culture, the Russian Jewish intelligentsia, a self-proclaimed elite devoted to the modernization of traditional Russian Jews. However, beyond this basic common goal, the maskilic intelligentsia was dramatically fragmented with different visions of paths leading to modernization, including a wide spectrum of cultural, linguistic, religious, and political approaches. See Michael Stanislawski, *For Whom Do I Toil? Judah Leib Gordon and the Crisis of Russian Jewry* (New York: Oxford University Press, 1988), 18–19, 26.

3. W. Bruce Lincoln, *In the Vanguard of Reform: Russia's Enlightened Bureaucrats, 1825–1861* (DeKalb: Northern Illinois University Press, 1982), 67–70.

4. Ibid., 144–67. Lincoln used the term "artificial publicity" to describe this phenomenon. However, in my opinion, "false transparency" better conveys the meaning of Russian expression *iskusstvennaia glasnost'*. I would like to thank Annette Ezekiel Kogan for drawing my attention to this issue.

5. Ibid., 102–38.

6. Iona Gurliand, *K istorii bedstvii izrail'skikh* (Yaroslaw-Krakow, 1888). In 1871 Iona Khaimovich Gurliand (1843–1890), graduate of Vilna Rabbinical Seminary (1860) and of the Oriental faculty of St. Petersburg Imperial University (1863), applied for the position of expert Jew under governor-general of Kiev, Podolia, and Volhyn provinces but was rejected. In the 1870s, he was appointed superintendent of the Jewish Teachers' Institute (former Rabbinic Seminary) in Zhitomir. In the 1880s, he served as the government rabbi of Odessa.

7. *Voskhod* 4 (1889): 31–35.

8. RGIA, f. 821, op. 8, d. 456, ll. 156–84.

9. The selection was made on the basis of 205 publications by expert Jews, appearing in the press from 1860 to 1927.

10. For more information on this periodical and its publisher see Verena Dohrn, "Evreiskaia Riga," in *Evrei v meniaiushchemsia mire: materialy chetvertoi mezhdunarodnoi konferentsii: Riga, 20–22 noiabria 2001 g.* (Riga: Fond "Shamir" im. M. Dubina, 2002), 249–50.

11. G. M. Brarats, "Zakrytie Ravvinskoi komissii," *Sion* 42 (1862): 660–61.

12. I. G. Gershtein, "Kratkoe izvestie ob ispytaniiakh i vypuske uchenikov 1864–1865 uchebnogo goda Ravvinskogo i prochikh evreiskikh uchilishch v Vil'ne," *Gakarmel* 39 (1865): 69–71.

13. A. Pumpianskii, "Izvlechenie iz vedomostei ob okonchatel'nykh i perevodnykh ispytaniiakh v Zhitomirskom Ravvinskom uchilishche 1867/8 Uch. G.," *Kievlianin* 114 (1868).

14. A. Pumpianskii, "Pis'mo v redaktsiiu," *Vestnik russkikh evreev* 39 (1871): 1208–10.

15. G. M. Barats, "K voprosu o tsenzure," *Prilozhenie k Gakarmeliu* 10 (1862): 33–36.

16. S. Minor, "Neskol'ko slov o Ravvinskoi komissii," *Vestnik russkikh evreev* 12 (1872): 365–67.

17. A. Pumpianskii, "K ravvinskomu voprosu," *Nedel'naia khronika Voskhoda* 23 (1887): 589–90.

18. L. Binshtok, "Ob obnarodovanii otchetov po molitvennym domam," *Sion* 22 (1861): 349–50.

19. Z. Minor, "Publichnaia biblioteka pri Minskom evreiskom obshchestve," *Sion* 39 (1862): 621–22.

20. A. Pumpianskii, "Pis'mo v redaktsiiu," *Gakarmel* 39 (1869): 154–55.

21. O. Gurvich, "Neskol'ko slov o napravlenii sovremennogo iudaizma v Zapadnoi Evrope i v Rossii," *Vilenskii vestnik* 16 (1867).

22. G. M. Barats, "Ob obiazatel'nom obrazovanii dlia evreev," *Rassvet* 33 (1861): 526–31.

23. Ibid.; O. Gurvich, "Zametki evreiskogo pedagoga," *Vilenskii vestnik* 7 (1864).

24. Ibid.

25. L. Binshtok, "Sovremennyi vopros. Na sud molodogo evreiskogo pokoleniia," *Sovremennaia letopis'* 16 (1864): 10–14.

26. O. Gurvich, "Zametki evreiskogo pedagoga."

27. A. Pumpianskii, "Rech', proiznesennaia v Ponevezhskom kazennom evreiskom uchilishche 17 apr. 1867 g.," *Severnaia pochta* 122 (1867); F. Bliumenfel'd, "O russkikh shkolakh v evreiskikh koloniiakh Khersonskogo

uezda dlia detei oboego pola evreev-zemledel'tsev," *Russkii evrei* 12 (1879): 427–32; O. Ia. Gurvich, "O neobkhodimosti vvedeniia prepodavaniia zakona evreiskoi very v muzhskikh gimnaziiakh," *Russkii evrei* 13 (1879): 461–62.

28. Z. Minor, *Rechi po-russki, proiznesennye v evreiskom molitvennom dome v Moskve* (Moscow, 1875), vol. 1.

29. R. I. Shnitkind, "K voprosu ob otbyvanii evreiiami voinskoi povinnosti," *Russkii evrei* 13 (1879): 470–71.

30. R. I. Shnitkind, "Pis'mo v redaktsiiu," *Nedel'naia khronika Voskhoda* 42 (1887): 1052–53.

31. S. Schwabacher, *Zapiska o prichinakh besporiadkov na iuge Rossii, predstavlennaia Ego Siiatel'stvu Grafu Kutaisovu* (Odessa, 1881).

32. S. Schwabacher, *Tri prizraka. Sovremennyi vopros* (Odessa: I. Sychevskii, 1879); S. Schwabacher, *Zapiska o prichinakh besporiadkov na iuge Rossii.*

33. Schwabacher, *Zapiska o prichinakh besporiadkov na iuge Rossii.*

34. Ibid.

35. Z. Minor, *Posle pogromov ili tri glavy o evreiskom voprose. Glava 1. Storona politiko-ekonomicheskaia* (Moscow, 1882).

36. E. Freidin, *Vozzvanie k evreiam* (Chernigov, 1881).

37. Schwabacher, *Zapiska o prichinakh besporiadkov na iuge Rossii.*

38. Minor, *Posle pogromov.*

39. I. Kulisher, "Statisticheskii ocherk smertnosti evreev v 16-tiletnii period s 1851 g. po 1866 vkliuchitel'no," *Volynskie gubernskie vedomosti* 35–36 (1867).

40. F. Bliumenfel'd, "Evreiskie kolonii Ekaterinoslavskoi gubernii: statisticheski etiudy," *Russkii evrei* 3 (1881): 85–87.

41. R. I. Shnitkind, "Evrei-remeslenniki v Kovenskoi gubernii v 1887 g.," *Voskhod* 6 (1889): 1–6.

42. M. El'kan, *Rukovodstvo k prepodavaniiu istorii evreiskogo naroda ot samykh drevnikh do noveishego vremeni s kratkim ocherkom geografii Palestiny. Per. s nem. i dop. kratkim istoricheskim ocherkom o evreiakh v Pol'she, Litve i Rossii Z. Minora* (Moscow, 1881) (to be discussed further in this chapter).

43. A. Pumpianskii, "Evrei v Lifliandskoi i Kurliandskoi guberniiakh," *Rizhskii vestnik* 135, 142, 151–53 (1875); Verena Dohrn, "Evreiskaia Riga," 250–51.

44. Osip Lerner, *Evrei v Novorossiiskom krae: istoricheskie ocherki po dannym iz arkhiva byvshego Novorossiiskogo general-gubernatora* (Odessa, 1901), 196.

45. Ibid., 195–96.

46. Aleksei Miller, *"Ukrainskii vopros" v politike vlastei i russkom obshchestvennom mnenii (vtoraia polovina XIX veka)* (Moscow, 2002).

47. A. Pumpianskii, *Psalmy Davida (dlia evreev). Evreiskii tekst s russkim perevodom i novym kommentariem na evreiskom iazyke* (Warsaw, 1872).

48. O. Gurvich, *Evreiskii molitvoslov, vpervye perevedennyi na russkii iazyk* (Vilna, 1870).

49. *Kievlianin* 64 (1870).

50. Lincoln, *In the Vanguard of Reform*, 42–51, 70.

51. Ilia Lurie and Arkadii Zeltser, "Moses Berlin and Lubavich Hasidism: A Landmark in the Conflict Between Haskalah and Hasidism," *Shvut* 5 (1997): 45.

52. Leopold Zunz, *Etwas uber die rabbinische litteratur* (Berlin, 1818).

53. Ismar Schorsch, *From Text to Context: The Turn to History in Modern Judaism* (Hanover, N.H.: Brandeis University Press, University Press of New England, 1994), 347.

54. See Leopold Zunz's *Die Synagogale Poesie des Mittelalters* (1855), *Die Ritus des sinagogalen Gottesdienstes geschichtlich entwickelt* (1859), *Literaturgeschichte der synagogalen Poesie* (1865), and *Nachtrag zur Literaturgeschichte der synagogalen Poesie* (1867).

55. See Heinrich Graetz's *Geschichte der Juden von den Anfängen bis auf die Gegenwart* (1853–1875), Abraham Geiger's *Urschrift und uebersetzungen der Bibel in ihrer abhängigkeit von der innern entwickelung des Judenthums* (1857), and Zecharias Frankel's *Darkhei ha-Mishnah* (1859).

56. See Isaak Markus Jost's *Geschichte des Judenthums und seiner Sekten* (1857–1859), Peter Beer's *Geschichte, Lehren und Meinungen aller bestandenen und noch bestehenden religiösen Sekten der Juden und der Geheimlehre oder Cabbalah* (1822–1823), and Julius Furst's *Geschichte des Karäerthums* (1862–1869).

57. See Moritz Steinschneider's *Die Hebräischen Übersetzungen des Mittelalters und die Juden als Dolmetscher* (1893).

58. This phenomenon was studied in detail in the following works by Verena Dohrn, *Jüdische Eliten im Russischen Reich. Aufklärung und Integration im 19. Jahrhundert* (Köln, 2008); "Rabbinical Seminaries as Instruments of Socialization," *Polin* 14 (2001): 87–104; "Russkoe v evreiskom," *Vestnik Evreiskogo universiteta v Moskve* 4 (2000): 71–86; and "Evreiskaia Riga," in *Evrei v meniaiushchemsia mire: materialy chetvertoi mezhdunarodnoi konferentsii: Riga, 20–22 noiabria 2001 g.* (Riga: Fond "Shamir" im. M. Dubina, 2002), 243–53.

59. Abraham Harkavy (1835–1919) had a traditional Jewish education and completed the full course of study at the rabbinical seminary in Vilna. From 1863 to 1868, he studied Oriental languages at the Imperial University of St. Petersburg and graduated with an award-winning master's thesis in history. In 1872, upon commencement of his graduate studies at the University of

Berlin and at the Sorbonne in Paris, Harkavy was awarded a doctorate. In 1877, Harkavy received the prestigious appointment of Orientalia librarian at the Imperial Public library in St. Petersburg, and made a distinguished career for himself as an outstanding scholar in the fields of Jewish and Oriental studies. Harkavy's extensive list of publications testifies to his significant contribution to Russian Wissenschaft, as well as to his effort to disseminate the classics of German Wissenschaft des Judentums on Russian soil. See Abraham Harkavy, "Istoricheskie ocherki Sinoda chetyrekh stran," *Voskhod* 2 (1884): 1–15, 4; (1884): 9–27; Harkavy, *Ob iazyke evreev, zhivshikh v drevnee vrema na Rusi i o slavianskikh slovakh, vstrechaemykh u evreiskikh pisatelei. Iz issledovanii ob istorii evreev v Rossii* (St. Petersburg: Imperatorskaia Akademiia nauk, 1865). Harkavy annotated and commented Russian translations of Heinrich Graetz's *History of the Jews* (St. Petersburg, 1889–1902) and of Gustav Karpeles's *History of Jewish Literature* (St. Petersburg, 1889–1890), and the Hebrew translation of Graetz's *History* (Warsaw, 1893–1899).

60. Betsalel Shtern, "Evrei-Karaimy," *Zhurnal Ministerstva Vnutrennikh Del* 1 (1843): 263–84; Abraham Firkovich, *O proiskhozhdenii sekty karaimov* (St. Petersburg: 2e Otd. E.I.V. Kantseliarii, 1859); Moisei Berlin, *Ocherk etnografii evreiskogo narodonaseleniia v Rossii* (St. Petersburg, 1861).

61. RGIA, f. 821, op. 8, d. 397, l. 63. Berlin's memorandum, including its background and sources, is discussed in detail in Vassili Schedrin, "Neizvestnaia istoriia khasidizma i drugie raboty Moiseia Berlina" (Unknown History of Hasidism and Other Works of Moisei Berlin), *Arkhiv evreiskoi istorii* 1 (2004): 169–92.

62. RGIA, f. 821, op. 8, d. 397, l. 64 ob.

63. Ibid., l. 56. Berlin's "essay on Kabbalah" was evidently based on study of Jewish sects—"The History, Teachings and Views of All Former and Present Jewish Sects, Including the Secret Teachings or Kabbala"—by Peter Beer (1758–1838), Bohemian Jewish educator, historian, and religious reformer. See Peter Beer, *Geschichte, Lehren und Meinungen aller bestandenen und noch bestehenden religiösen Sekten der Juden und der Geheimlehre oder Cabbalah* (Brunn, 1822–1823). For more on Beer as historian and on his relationship to Wissenschaft des Judentums see Ismar Schorsch, *From Text to Context*, 304; and especially Michael Brenner, "Between Haskala and Kabbalah: Peter Beer's History of Jewish Sects," in *Jewish History and Jewish Memory*, ed. Elisheva Carlebach, John M. Efron, and David N. Myers (Hanover, N.H.: Brandeis University Press, 1998), 389–404. For analysis of other maskilic histories of Hasidism see Israel Bartal, "The Imprint of

Haskalah Literature on the Historiography of Hasidism," In *Hasidism Reappraised*, ed. Ada Rapoport-Albert (London: Valentine Mitchell, 1992), 367–75.

64. RGIA, f. 821, op. 8, d. 397, ll. 62–62 ob.

65. Ibid.

66. RGIA, f. 821, op. 8, d. 331, ll. 21 ob.–22 ob.

67. Ibid., ll. 25 ob.–27.

68. Ibid., l. 39.

69. Ibid., l. 65 ob.

70. Moisei Berlin, *Ocherk etnografii*, viii, 76.

71. Ibid., 57.

72. Simon Dubnow, "Ob izuchenii istorii russkikh evreev i ob uchrezhdenii russko-evreiskogo istoricheskogo obshchestva," *Voskhod* (April–September 1891): 1–91.

73. Moisei Berlin, *Ocherk etnografii*, xi.

74. RGIA, f. 821, op. 8, d. 246, ll. 68 ob., 86 ob., 94 ob.

75. Ibid., ll. 68–68 ob.

76. Ibid., l. 164.

77. Ibid.

78. Ibid., l. 216 ob.

79. Ibid., l. 46.

80. Ibid., ll. 48 ob.–49.

81. Ibid., l. 49. According to Eliyana R. Adler, as early as in the 1870s, a vision such as Gintsburg's was realized in creation of a "new genre"—Russian language textbooks about Judaism—that sought "to reformulate Judaism in a delimited, structured, and comprehensible idiom for [its] students." Adler also notes that due to the negative perception of the Talmud by the Russian government, the textbook authors tended to avoid including talmudic texts among other study materials. See Eliyana R. Adler, "Reinventing Religion," *Journal of Jewish Education* 77 (2011): 142, 152.

82. Examples of such works include I. G. Orshanskii, *Russkoe zakonodatel'stvo o evreiakh*; Moisei Berlin, *Ocherk etnografii*; and Abraham Harkavy, *Ob iazyke evreev*.

83. Mark Nemzer, *Istoriia evreiskogo naroda (ot pereseleniia evreev v Vavilon do razrusheniia vtorogo khrama) dlia obuchaiushchikhsia Zakonu evreiskoi very v gimnaziiakh i evreiskikh kazennykh uchilishchakh* (Vilna: A.G. Syrkin, 1880).

84. Nemzer applied for the position in 1906 but was rejected by the DDDII because it was not yet vacant. See RGIA, f. 821, op. 8, d. 472, ll. 9–11 ob.

85. Heinrich Graetz, *Istoriia evreev ot zakliucheniia Talmuda do prots-vetaniia evreisko-ispanskoi kul'tury* (Moscow: M.Ia. Khashkes, 1880).

86. Ibid., i–ii.

87. Ibid., iv.

88. Ibid.

89. Nemzer, *Istoriia evreiskogo naroda*, 18–20, 95–101.

90. Ibid., 44–46, 106–14.

91. Ibid., 34–36, 89–95.

92. Ibid., 136.

93. Ibid., 147.

94. Ibid., 147–52.

95. A. Vol', "Plagiator," *Vilenskii vestnik* 206, 210 (October 1, 7, 1880).

96. Mark Nemzer, "Otvet na klevety," *Vilenskii vestnik* 230, 233, 238, 245 (October 31, November 4, 10, 11, 19, 1880).

97. See examples of using Talmud as historical source in Nemzer, *Istoriia evreiskogo naroda*, 92–93, 98.

98. See examples of using contemporary scholarship by Samuel Joseph Fuenn and by Daniel Chwolson in ibid., 42, 69, 78.

99. M. Elkan, *Rukovodstvo k prepodavaniiu istorii evreiskogo naroda ot samykh drevnikh do noveishego vremeni s kratkim ocherkom geografii Palestiny dlia evreiskikh uchilishch. Kratkii istoricheskii ocherk o evreiakh v Pol'she, Litve i Rossii*, trans., ed., and amended Solomon Minor (Moscow: N. N. Kushnerev and Co., 1881).

100. RGIA, f. 821, op. 8, d. 397, ll. 99–102 ob., 120–120 ob., 134 ob.

101. *Evreiskaia entsiklopediia: svod znanii o evreistve i ego kul'ture v pro-shlom i nastoiashchem* (St. Petersburg, 1908–1913), vol. 11, 77; Z. Minor, *Rechi po-russki*.

102. See, for example, the following by Solomon Minor: *Posle pogromov; Rabbi Ippolit Liutostanskii i ego 'Talmud i evrei'* (Moscow, 1889); and *Bibliia ob upotreblenii vina* (Moscow, 1899). For analysis of Minor's publications see Azriel Schochat, "The Assimilatory Views of Zalkind Minor, 'Crown Rabbi' of Moscow," *Zion* 44 (1979): 303–20.

103. M. Elkan, *Leitfaden beim Unterricht in der Geschichte der Israeliten, von den fruhesten Zeiten bis auf unsere Tage: nebst einem furzen Abriss der Ge-ographie Palastina's, fur israelitische Schulen* (Minden: F. Essmann, 1845).

104. M. Elkan, *Rukovodstvo k prepodavaniiu*, 83, 88.

105. Ibid., 86.

106. Ibid., translator's foreword to the second edition, s.p.

107. I was unable to locate this edition in bibliographies and libraries.

108. M. Elkan, *Rukovodstvo k prepodavaniiu*, translator's foreword to the second edition, s.p.

109. Ibid.

110. For example, see ibid., 114.

111. Ibid., 130–58.

112. Ibid., 159–61.

113. Ibid., translator's foreword to the second edition, s.p.

114. Ibid., 22 (second pagination).

115. Ibid., 125–26.

116. Ibid., 65 (second pagination).

117. Ibid., 67 (second pagination).

118. Ibid., 102–3.

119. Ibid., 120.

120. Mevakker, "M. Elkan, Rukovodstvo k prepodavaniiu istorii evreisk-ogo naroda ot samykh drevnikh do noveishego vremeni s kratkim ocherkom geografii Palestiny dlia evreiskikh uchilishch. Kratkii istoricheskii ocherk o evreiakh v Pol'she, Litve i Rossii. Per s nem. i dop. Z. Minor. Moskva, 1881," *Voskhod* 5 (1881): 60–68 (second pagination). Mevakker was one of pen names used by Hebrew poet Judah Leib Gordon (1830–1892).

121. Z. Minor, "Otvet g. Mevakkeru," *Voskhod* 6 (1881): 21–25 (second pagination).

122. M.R., "O zapadno-russkikh evreiakh," *Prilozhenie k Gakarmeliu* 11 (1866). M.R. was Minor's pen name, meaning "M[insk].R[abbi]." See M. Elkan, *Rukovodstvo k prepodavaniiu*, 4 (second pagination).

123. Alexander Krauszar, *Historya Zydow w Polsce* (Warsaw, 1865). See M. Elkan, *Rukovodstvo k prepodavaniiu*, 16 (second pagination).

124. *Akty, otnosiashchiesia k istorii Iuzhnoi i Zapadnoi Rossii* (St. Petersburg: Arkhograficheskaia komissiia, 1846) and others. See M. Elkan, *Rukovodstvo k prepodavaniiu*, 8 (second pagination).

125. Tadeusz Czacki, *Rozprawa o zydach* (Vilna, 1807).

Conclusion

1. RGIA, f. 821, op. 150, d. 371, l. 2.

2. Yohanan Petrovsky-Shtern, *Golden Age Shtetl: A New History of Jewish Life in East Europe* (Princeton, N.J.: Princeton University Press, 2014), 329.

3. Eli Lederhendler, *The Road to Modern Jewish Politics: Political Tradition and Political Reconstruction in the Jewish Community of Tsarist Russia* (New York: Oxford University Press, 1989), 88.

4. Moisei Berlin, *Ocherk etnografii evreiskogo narodonaseleniia v Rossii* (St. Petersburg, 1861), v.

Epilogue

1. Nochum Shtif, "German Barats," *Jewish Morning Journal*, January 31, 1926.

2. Boris Gurevich, "Genrikh Markovich Barats kak uchenyi," *Rassvet*, March 6, 1932.

3. Moisei Mazor, "Vospominaiia o Germane Markoviche Baratse," manuscript, YIVO, RG 309.

4. Boris Gurevich, ibid.

5. Simon Dubnow, "German Barats," *Rul'*, May 20, 1925.

6. Ibid.

7. Nochum Shtif, ibid.

Works Cited

Unpublished Primary Sources

Departament Dukhovnykh Del Inostrannykh Ispovedanii. Fond 821. Rossiiskii Gosudarstvennyi Istoricheskii Arkhiv (RGIA). St. Petersburg, Russia.

Leon Baratz. RG 309. YIVO Institute for Jewish Research, New York.

Published Primary Sources

Akty, otnosiashchiesia k istorii Iuzhnoi i Zapadnoi Rossii. St. Petersburg: Arkhograficheskaaia komissiia, 1846.

Aleichem, Sholem. "S iarmarki." *Sobranie sochinenii*. Moscow: Gosudarstvennoe izdatel'stvo khudozhestvennoi literatury, 1960.

Blokada 1941–1944. Leningrad. Kniga pamiati (St. Petersburg, 1998–2006).

B.V. "Zametka po povodu retsenzii g. L.L. na broshiuru Minora 'Rabbi Ippolit Liutostanskii'." *Russkii evrei* 7 (1879): 239–40.

Barats, G. M. "K voprosu o tsenzure." *Prilozhenie k Gakarmeliu* 10 (1862): 33–36.

Barats, G. M. "Ob obiazatel'nom obrazovanii dlia evreev." *Rassvet* 33 (1861): 526–31.

Barats, G. M. "Zakrytie Ravvinskoi komissii." *Sion* 42 (1862): 660–61.

"Bedstiviia vremen. V pamiat' bedstvii, postigshikh evreev v 1648 i 1649 godakh v Ukraine, Podolii, Litve i Belorussii ot soedinennykh buntovshchikov pod nachal'stvom Bogdana Khmel'nitskogo. Sostavleno Egoshieiu, synom L'vovskogo ravvina, pravednika Davida iz Zamost'ia.

Pechatano v Venetsii v 1656 godu. Perevedeno M. Berlinym." *Chteniia Obshchestva istorii i drevnostei rossiiskikh* 1 (1859).

Beer, Peter. *Geschichte, Lehren und Meinungen aller bestandenen und noch bestehenden religiosen Sekten der Juden und der Geheimlehre oder Cabbalah.* Brunn, 1822–1823.

Berlin, Moisei. *Ocherk etnografii evreiskogo narodonaseleniia v Rossii.* St. Petersburg, 1861.

Binshtok, L. "Ob obnarodovanii otchetov po molitvennym domam." *Sion* 22 (1861): 349–50.

Binshtok, L. "Sovremennyi vopros. Na sud molodogo evreiskogo pokoleniia." *Sovremennaia letopis'* 16 (1864): 10–14.

Bliokh, Ivan. *Sravnenie material'nogo byta i nravstvennogo sostoianiia naseleniia v Cherte osedlosti evreev i vne ee. Tsifrovye dannye i issledovaniia po otnosheniiu k evreiskomu voprosu.* St. Petersburg, 1889.

Bliumenfel'd, F. "Evreiskie kolonii Ekaterinoslavskoi gubernii: statisticheski etiudy." *Russkii evrei* 3 (1881): 85–87.

Bliumenfel'd, F. "O russkikh shkolakh v evreiskikh koloniiakh Khersonskogo uezda dlia detei oboego pola evreev-zemledel'tsev." *Russkii evrei* 12 (1879): 427–32.

Brafman, Iakov. *Evreiskie bratstva, mestnye i vsemirnye.* Vilna, 1868.

Brafman, Iakov. *Kniga Kagala.* Vilna, 1870.

Czacki, Tadeusz. *Rozprawa o Zydach.* Vilna, 1807.

Deich, Genrikh. *Arkhivnye dokumenty po istorii i genealogii evreev v Rossii. Sinagogi, molitvennye doma i sostoiashchie pri nikh dolzhnostnye litsa v Cherte osedlosti i guberniiakh Kurliandskoi i Lifliandskoi Rossiiskoi imperii. 1853–1854.* New York, 1992.

Demidov San-Donato, Pavel. *Evreiskii vopros v Rossii.* St. Petersburg, 1883.

Dontsova, Dar'ia. *Striptiz Zhar-ptitsy.* Moscow: Eksmo: 2012.

Dubnow, Simon. "German Barats." *Rul'* (May 20, 1925).

Dubnow, Simon. *Kniga zhizni.* Riga, 1934.

Dubnow, Simon. "Ob izuchenii istorii russkikh evreev i ob uchrezhdenii russko-evreiskogo istoricheskogo obshchestva." *Voskhod* (April–September, 1891): 1–91.

Dubnow, Simon. "Vozniknovenie khasidizma." *Voskhod* 6–8, 10 (1888).

El'kan, M. *Rukovodstvo k prepodavaniiu istorii evreiskogo naroda ot samykh drevnikh do noveishego vremeni s kratkim ocherkom geografii Palestiny.*

Per. s nem. i dop. kratkim istoricheskim ocherkom o evreiakh v Pol'she, Litve i Rossii Z.Minora. Moscow, 1881.

Firkovich, Abraham. *O proiskhozhdenii sekty karaimov.* St. Petersburg: 2e Otd. E.I.V. Kantseliarii, 1859.

Freidin, E. *Vozzvanie k evreiam.* Chernigov, 1881.

Gershtein, I. G. "Kratkoe izvestie ob ispytaniiakh i vypuske uchenikov 1864–1865 uchebnogo goda Ravvinskogo i prochikh evreiskikh uchilishch v Vil'ne." *Gakarmel* 39 (1865): 69–71.

Gershtein, Iona. *Pervye uroki russkoi gramoty.* Vilna, 1866.

Giliarov-Platonov, N. P. *Evreiskii vopros v Rossii: sostavleno na osnovanii statei i pisem Giliarova-Platonova.* St. Petersburg, 1906.

Gradovskii, Nikolai. *Otnoshenie k evreiam v drevnei i sovremennoi Rusi.* St. Petersburg: Tipo-litografiia A.E. Landau, 1891.

Graetz, Heinrich. *Istoriia evreev ot zakliucheniia Talmuda do protsvetaniisa evreisko-ispanskoi kul'tury.* Moscow: M.Ia. Khashkes, 1880.

Gurevich, Boris. "Genrikh Markovich Barats kak uchenyi." *Rassvet* (March 6, 1932).

Gurliand, Iona. *K istorii bedstvii izrail'skikh.* Yaroslaw-Krakow, 1888.

Gurvich, O. *Evreiskii molitvoslov, vprevye perevedennyi na russkii iazyk.* Vilna, 1870.

Gurvich, O. "Neskol'ko slov o napravlenii sovremennogo iudaizma v Zapadnoi Evrope i v Rossii." *Vilenskii vestnik* 16 (1867).

Gurvich, O. "Zametki evreiskogo pedagoga." *Vilenskii vestnik* 7 (1864).

Gurvich, O. Ia. "O neobkhodimosti vvedeniia prepodavaniia zakona evreiskoi very v muzhskikh gimnaziiakh." *Russkii evrei* 13 (1879): 461–62.

Gurvich, Osip. *Istoriia evreev v bibleiskii period.* Vilna, 1871.

Gurvich, Osip. *Zakon evreiskoi very.* Grodno, 1870.

Gurvich, Osip. *Zhivaia moral' ili sokrovishchnitsa talmudicheskoi etiki.* Grodno, 1901.

Harkavy, Abraham. "Istoricheskie ocherki Sinoda chetyrekh stran." *Voskhod* 2 (1884): 1–15, 4 (1884): 9–27.

Harkavy, Abraham. *Ob iazyke evreev, zhivshikh v drevnee vrema na Rusi i o slavianskikh slovakh, vstrechaemykh u evreiskikh pisatelei. Iz issledovanii ob istorii evreev v Rossii.* St. Petersburg: Imperatorskaia Akademiia nauk, 1865.

Kanovich, Grigorii. *I net rabam raia.* Moscow: Sovetskii pisatel', 1989.

Kanovich, Grigorii. *Slezy i molitvy durakov.* Vilnius: Vaga, 1987.

Kiselev, Pavel. "Ob ustroistve evreiskogo naroda v Rossii." *Voskhod* 4, 5 (1901): 25–40, 3–21.

Krauszar, Alexander. *Historya Zydow w Polsce.* Warsaw, 1865.

Kulisher, I. "Statisticheskii ocherk smertnosti evreev v 16-tiletnii period s 1851 g. po 1866 g. vkliuchitel'no." *Volynskie gubernskie vedomosti* 35–36 (1867).

Lerner, Osip. *Evrei v Novorossiiskom krae: istoricheskie ocherki po dannym iz arkhiva byvshego Novorossiiskogo general-gubernatora.* Odessa, 1901.

Levin, Shmarya. *Forward from Exile.* Philadelphia: Jewish Publication Society of America, 1967.

Mandel'shtam, M. E. "Ignat'evskaia komissiia v Kieve 1881 g." In *Perezhitoe: sbornik, posviashchennyi obshchestvennoi i kulturnoi istorii evreev v Rossii* (St. Petersburg: Brokgauz-Efron, 1908–1913), vol. 4, 46–64.

Marek, Pesakh. "Krizis evreiskogo samoupravleniia i khasidizm." *Evreiskaia starina* 12 (1928).

Mazor, Moisei. *Vospominaiia o Germane Markoviche Baratse.* Manuscript.

Mevakker [Gordon, Judah Leib]. "M. Elkan, Rukovodstvo k prepodavaniiu istorii evreiskogo naroda ot samykh drevnikh do noveishego vremeni s kratkim ocherkom geografii Palestiny dlia evreiskikh uchilishch. Kratkii istoricheskii ocherk o evreiakh v Pol'she, Litve i Rossii. Per s nem. i dop. Z. Minor. Moskva, 1881." *Voskhod* 5 (1881): 60–68 (second pagination).

Minor, S. "Neskol'ko slov o Ravvinskoi komissii." *Vestnik russkikh evreev* 12 (1872): 365–67.

Minor, Z. "Otvet g. Mevakkeru." *Voskhod* 6 (1881): 21–25 (second pagination).

Minor, Z. *Posle pogromov ili tri glavy o evreiskom voprose. Glava 1. Storona politiko-ekonomicheskaia.* Moscow, 1882.

Minor, Z. "Publichnaia biblioteka pri Minskom evreiskom obshchestve." *Sion* 39 (1862): 621–22.

Minor, Z. *Rechi po-russki, proiznesennye v evreiskom molitvennom dome v Moskve.* Moscow, 1875.

Morgulis, Mikhail. "Iz moikh vospominanii." *Voskhod* 6–7.

Morgulis, Mikhail. "K istorii obrazovaniia russkikh evreev." *Voprosy evreiskoi zhizni* (1889).

M.R. [Minor, Solomon]. "O zapadno-russkikh evreiakh." *Prilozhenie k Gakarmeliu* 11 (1866).

Works Cited

Paperna, A. I. "Iz Nikolaevskoi epokhi." In *Evrei v Rossii: XIX Vek*, ed. V. Kel'ner. Moscow: Novoe literaturnoe obozrenie, 2000.

Pumpianskii, A. "Evrei v Lifliandskoi i Kurliandskoi guberniiakh." *Rizhskii vestnik* 135, 142, 151–53 (1875).

Pumpianskii, A. "Izvlechenie iz vedomostei ob okonchatel'nykh i perevodnykh ispytaniiakh v Zhitomirskom Ravvinskom uchilishche 1867/8 uch. G." *Kievlianin* 114 (1868).

Pumpianskii, A. "K ravvinskomu voprosu." *Nedel'naia khronika Voskhoda* 23 (1887): 589–90.

Pumpianskii, A. "Pis'mo v redaktsiiu." *Gakarmel* 39 (1869): 154–55.

Pumpianskii, A. "Pis'mo v redaktsiiu." *Vestnik russkikh Evreev* 39 (1871): 1208–10.

Pumpianskii, A. "Rech', proiznesennaia v Ponevezhskom kazennom evreiskom uchilishche 17 apr. 1867 g." *Severnaia pochta* 122 (1867).

Pumpianskii, A. *Psalmy Davida (dlia evreev). Evreiskii tekst s russkim perevodom i novym kommentariem na evreiskom iazyke.* Warsaw, 1872.

Pumpianskii, Aaron. "Evrei v Lifliandskoi i Kurliandskoi guberniiakh. Istoricheskii ocherk." *Evreiskie zapiski* 1–6 (1881).

"Rech' S.M. Dubnowa na sobranii Evreiskogo istoriko-etnograficheskogo obshchestva 21 fevralia 1910 g." *Evreiskaia starina* 1 (1910): 157–58.

Schwabacher, S. *Tri prizraka. Sovremennyi vopros.* Odessa: I. Sychevskii, 1879.

Schwabacher, S. *Zapiska o prichinakh besporiadkov na iuge Rossii, predstavlennaia Ego Siiatel'stvu Grafu Kutaisovu.* Odessa, 1881.

Shereshevskii, Il'ia. "Evreiskaia prisiaga i ee razreshenie." *Evreiskaia biblioteka: istoriko-literaturnyi sbornik* 5 (1875): 101–38.

Shnitkind, R. I. "Evrei-remeslenniki v Kovenskoi gubernii v 1887 g." *Voskhod* 6 (1889): 1–6.

Shnitkind, R. I. "K voprosu ob otbyvanii evreiiami voinskoi povinnosti." *Russkii evrei* 13 (1879): 470–71.

Shnitkind, R. I. "Pis'mo v redaktsiiu." *Nedel'naia khronika Voskhoda* 42 (1887): 1052–53.

Shtern, Betsalel. "Evrei-Karaimy." *Zhurnal Ministerstva Vnutrennikh Del* 1 (1843): 263–84.

Shtif, Nochum. "German Barats." *Jewish Morning Journal* (January 31, 1926).

Sliozberg, G. B. "Dela minuvshikh dnei." In *Evrei v Rossii: XIX vek*, ed. V. Kel'ner. Moscow: Novoe literaturnoe obozrenie, 2000.

Tolstoy, Leo. *Anna Karenina*. Petrozavodsk: Gosudarstvennoe izdatel'stvo, 1960.
Trudy Gubernskikh komissii po evreiskomu voprosu. St. Petersburg, 1884.
Vol', Asher. "Plagiator." *Vilenskii vestnik* 206, 210 (October 1, 7, 1880).

Encyclopedias, Reference Works, Legal Compendiums

Dal', Vladimir. *Tolkovyi slovar' zhivogo velikorusskogo iazyka*. St. Petersburg, 1880–1882.
Evreiskaia entsiklopediia: svod znanii o evreistve i ego kul'ture v proshlom i nastoiashchem. St. Petersburg, 1908–1913.
Orshanskii, Il'ia. *Russkoe zakonodatel'stvo o evreiakh*. St. Petersburg, 1877.
Polnoe sobranie zakonov Rossiiskoi imperii. Sobranie pervoe. S 1649 po 12 dekabria 1825 goda. St. Petersburg, 1830.
Polnoe sobranie zakonov Rossiiskoi imperii. Sobranie vtoroe. S 12 dekabria 1825 po 28 fevralia 1881 goda. St. Petersburg, 1850.
Polnoe sobranie zakonov Rossiiskoi imperii. St. Petersburg, 1891.
Polovtsov, Aleksandr, ed. *Russkii biograficheskii slovar'*. St. Petersburg: Tipografiia I.N. Skorokhodova, 1896–1918.

Secondary Literature

Abramson, Henry. *A Prayer for the Government: Ukrainians and Jews in Revolutionary Times, 1917–1920*. Cambridge, Mass.: Harvard University Press, 1999.
Adler, Eliyana R. "Reinventing Religion." *Journal of Jewish Education* 77 (2011): 77–141.
Albert, Phyllis. *The Modernization of French Jewry: Consistory and Community in the Nineteenth Century*. Waltham, Mass.: Brandeis University Press; Hanover, N.H.: University Press of New England, 1977.
Avrutin, Eugene. *Jews and the Imperial State: Identification Politics in Tsarist Russia*. Ithaca, N.Y.: Cornell University Press, 2010.
Avrutin, Eugene. "The Politics of Jewish Legibility: Documentation Practices and Reform During the Reign of Nicholas I." *Jewish Social Studies* 11, no. 2 (2005): 136–69.

Bartal, Israel. "The Imprint of Haskalah Literature on the Historiography of Hasidism." In *Hasidism Reappraised*, ed. Ada Rapoport-Albert, 367–75. London: Valentine Mitchell, 1992.

Bennet, H. A. "Chiny, Ordena and Officialdom." In *Russian Officialdom: The Bureaucratization of Russian Society from the Seventeenth to the Twentieth Century*, ed. W. Pintner and D. Rowney. Chapel Hill: University of North Carolina Press, 1980.

Brenner, Michael. "Between Haskala and Kabbalah: Peter Beer's History of Jewish Sects." In *Jewish History and Jewish Memory*, ed. Elisheva Carlebach, John M. Efron, and David N. Myers, 389–404. Hanover, N.H.: Brandeis University Press, 1998.

Bugai, N. F. "1920e–1930e gody: pereseleniia i deportatsii evreiskogo naseleniia v SSSR." *Otechestvennaia istoriia* 4 (1993).

Campbell, Elena. "The Autocracy and the Muslim Clergy in the Russian Empire (1850s–1917)." *Russian Studies in History* 44, no. 2 (2005): 8–29.

Campbell, Elena. "The Muslim Question in Late Imperial Russia." In *Russian Empire: Space, People, Power, 1700–1930*, 321–51. Bloomington: Indiana University Press, 2007.

Crews, Robert D. *For Prophet and Tsar: Islam and Empire in Russia and Central Asia*. Cambridge, Mass.: Harvard University Press, 2006.

Dohrn, Verena. "Evreiskaia Riga." In *Evrei v meniaiushchemsia mire: materialy chetvertoi mezhdunarodnoi konferentsii: Riga, 20–22 noiabria 2001 g.*, 243–53. Riga: Fond "Shamir" im. M. Dubina, 2002.

Dohrn, Verena. *Judische Eliten im Russischen Reich. Aufklarung und Integration im 19 Jahrhundert*. Koln, 2008.

Dohrn, Verena. "Rabbinical Schools as Instruments of Socialization." *Polin* 14 (2001): 87–104.

Dohrn, Verena. "Russkoe v evreiskom." *Vestnik Evreiskogo universiteta v Moskve* 4 (2000): 71–86.

Dolbilov, Mikhail. "Russifying Bureaucracy and the Politics of Jewish Education in the Russian Empire's Northwest Region (1860s–1870s)." *Acta Slavica Iaponica* 24 (2006): 112–43.

Dolbilov, Mikhail. *Russkii krai, chuzhaia vera: Etnokonfessional'naia politika imperii v Litve i Belorussii pri Aleksandre II*. Moscow: Novoe literaturnoe obozrenie, 2010.

Dubnow, Simon. "Evrei v Rossii v epokhu evropeiskoi reaktsii (1815–1848)." *Evreiskaia starina* 5 (1912): 274–89; 6 (1913): 23–50, 308–24.

Dubnow, Simon. "Sud'by evreev v Rossii v epokhu zapadnoi pervoi ema-sipatsii (1789–1815)." *Evreiskaia starina* 5 (1912): 3–25, 113–43.

Eroshkin, Nikolai. *Istoriia gosudarstvennykh uchrezhdenii dorevoliutsionnoi Rossii.* Moscow, 1983.

Eroshkin, Nikolai. *Ministerstva Rossii pervoi poloviny XIX veka-fondoobrazovateli tsentral'nykh gosudarstvennykh arkhivov SSSR.* Moscow, 1980.

Estraikh, Gennady. *In Harness: Yiddish Writers' Romance with Communism.* Syracuse, N.Y.: Syracuse University Press, 2005.

Fishman, David. *Russia's First Modern Jews: The Jews of Shklov.* New York: New York University Press, 1995.

Frankel, Jonathan. *Prophecy and Politics: Socialism, Nationalism, and the Russian Jews, 1862–1917.* Cambridge: Cambridge University Press, 1981.

Freeze, ChaeRan. *Jewish Marriage and Divorce in Imperial Russia.* Hanover, N.H.: University Press of New England, Brandeis University Press, 2002.

Freeze, Gregory. "Handmaiden of the State? The Orthodox Church in Imperial Russia Reconsidered." *Journal of Ecclesiastical History* 36 (1985): 82–102.

Freeze, Gregory. "The Soslovie (Estate) Paradigm and Russian Social History." *American Historical Review* 91 (1986): 11–36.

Freeze, Gregory. "Subversive Piety: Religion and the Political Crisis in Late Imperial Russia." *Journal of Modern History* 68 (1996): 308–50.

Gassenschmidt, Christoph. *Jewish Liberal Politics in Tsarist Russia, 1900–1914: The Modernization of Russian Jewry.* New York: New York University Press, 1995.

Gerasimov, Ilya. *Modernism and Public Reform in Late Imperial Russia. Rural Professionals and Self-Organization, 1905–30.* London: Palgrave Macmillan, 2009.

Gessen, Iulii. "Deputaty evreiskogo naroda pri Aleksandre I." *Evreiskaia starina* 3 (1909).

Gessen, Iulii. *Istoriia evreev v Rossii.* St. Petersburg, 1914. Vol. 1.

Gessen, Iulii. *Istoriia evreev v Rossii.* Leningrad, 1926. Vol. 2.

Gitelman, Zvi. *Jewish Nationality and Soviet Politics. The Jewish Sections of the CPSU, 1917–1930.* Princeton, N.J.: Princeton University Press, 1972.

Halpern, Ben, and Jehuda Reinharz. *Zionism and the Creation of a New Society.* New York: Oxford University Press, 1998.

Kappeler, Andreas. *The Russian Empire: Ethnicity and Nationalism.* Harlow: Longman, 2001.

Kefeli, Agnes. *Becoming Muslim in Imperial Russia: Conversion, Apostasy, and Literacy.* Ithaca, N.Y.: Cornell University Press, 2014.

Khalid, Adeeb. *The Politics of Muslim Cultural Reform: Jadidism in Central Asia.* Berkeley: University of California Press, 1999.

Kimerling Wirtschafter, Elise. *Structures of Society: Imperial Russia's "People of Various Ranks."* DeKalb: Northern Illinois University Press, 1994.

Klier, John. *Russia Gathers Her Jews: The Origins of the "Jewish Question" in Russia, 1772–1825.* DeKalb: Northern Illinois University Press, 1986.

Kostyrchenko, Gennadii. *V plenu u krasnogo faraona: politicheskie presledovaniia evreev v SSSR v poslednee stalinskoe desiatiletie: dokumental'noe issledovanie.* Moscow, 1994.

Kotkov, Viacheslav. *Voennoe dukhovenstvo Rossii.* St. Petersburg, 2004.

Kotsonis, Yanni. *States of Obligation: Taxes and Citizenship in the Russian Empire and Early Soviet Republic.* Toronto: University of Toronto Press, 2014.

Lebedeva-Kaplan, Vera. "Evrei Petrograda v 1917 g." *Vestnik Evreiskogo universiteta v Moskve* 2 (1993).

Lederhendler, Eli. *The Road to Modern Jewish Politics: Political Tradition and Political Reconstruction in the Jewish Community of Tsarist Russia.* New York: Oxford University Press, 1989.

Levin, Vladimir. "Orthodox Jewry and the Russian Government: An Attempt at Rapprochement, 1907–1914." *East European Jewish Affairs* 2 (2009): 187–204.

Lincoln, W. Bruce. *In the Vanguard of Reform: Russia's Enlightened Bureaucrats, 1825–1861.* DeKalb: Northern Illinois University Press, 1982.

Litvak, Olga. *Conscription and the Search for Modern Russian Jewry.* Bloomington: Indiana University Press, 2006.

Lowenstein, Steven. "Governmental Jewish Policies in Early Nineteenth Century Germany and Russia: A Comparison." *Jewish Social Studies* 46–3/4 (1984): 303–15.

Lurie, Ilia, and Arkadii Zeltser. "Moses Berlin and Lubavich Hasidism: A Landmark in the Conflict Between Haskalah and Hasidism." *Shvut* 5 (1997): 32–64.

Marek, Pesach. "Bor'ba dvukh vospitanii. Iz istorii prosveshcheniia evreev v Rossii (1864–1873)." In *Perezhitoe*. St. Petersburg, 1909, vol. 1, 106–43.

Miller, Aleksei. *The Ukrainian Question. The Russian Empire and Nationalism in the 19th Century*. Budapest: Central European University Press, 2003.

Miller, Aleksei. *"Ukrainskii vopros" v politike vlastei i russkom obshchestvennom mnenii (vtoraia polovina XIX veka)*. Moscow, 2002.

Nathans, Benjamin. *Beyond the Pale: The Jewish Encounter with Late Imperial Russia*. Berkeley: University of California Press, 2002.

Nikitin, V. N. *Evrei zemledel'tsy. Istoricheskoe, zakonodatel'noe, administrativnoe i bytovoe polozhenie kolonii so vremeni ikh vozniknoveniia do nashikh dnei. 1807–1887*. St. Petersburg, 1887.

Orlovsky, Daniel. "High Officials in the Ministry of Internal Affairs. 1855–1881." In *Russian Officialdom: The Bureaucratization of Russian Society from the Seventeenth to the Twentieth Century*, ed. W. Pintner and D. Rowney. Chapel Hill: University of North Carolina Press, 1980.

Orlovsky, Daniel. *The Limits of Reform: The Ministry of Internal Affairs in Imperial Russia, 1802–1881*. Cambridge, Mass.: Harvard University Press, 1980.

Pen, S. "Deputatsiia evreiskogo naroda. K istorii evreev v Rossii v epokhu Aleksandra I." *Knizhki Voskhoda* 30–31 (1905).

Petrovsky-Shtern, Yohanan. *Golden Age Shtetl: A New History of Jewish Life in East Europe*. Princeton, N.J.: Princeton University Press, 2014.

Petrovsky-Shtern, Yohanan. *Jews in the Russian Army, 1827–1917: Drafted into Modernity*. Cambridge: Cambridge University Press, 2009.

Pintner, W. M. "Civil Officialdom and the Nobility in the 1850s." In *Russian Officialdom: The Bureaucratization of Russian Society from the Seventeenth to the Twentieth Century*, ed. W. Pintner and D. Rowney. Chapel Hill: University of North Carolina Press, 1980.

Pintner, W. M. "The Evolution of the Civil Officialdom, 1755–1855." In *Russian Officialdom: The Bureaucratization of Russian Society from the Seventeenth to the Twentieth Century*, ed. W. Pintner and D. Rowney. Chapel Hill: University of North Carolina Press, 1980.

Pintner, W. M., and D. K. Rowney. "Officialdom and Bureaucratization: Conclusion." In *Russian Officialdom: The Bureaucratization of Russian Society from the Seventeenth to the Twentieth Century*, ed. W. Pintner and D. Rowney. Chapel Hill: University of North Carolina Press, 1980.

Polonsky, Antony. *The Jews in Poland and Russia*. Oxford: Littman Library of Jewish Civilization, 2010.

Pulzer, Peter. *Jews and the German State: The Political History of a Minority, 1848–1933*. Oxford: Blackwell, 1992.

Reyfman, Irina. *Rank and Style: Russians in State Service, Life, and Literature*. Brighton, Mass.: Academic Studies Press, 2012.

Rodrigue, Aron. *French Jews, Turkish Jews: The Alliance israelite universelle and the Politics of Jewish Schooling in Turkey, 1860–1925*. Bloomington: Indiana University Press, 1990.

Rogger, Hans. *Jewish Policies and Right-Wing Politics in Imperial Russia*. Berkeley: University of California Press, 1986.

Rowney, D. K. "Organizational Change and Social Adaptation: The Pre-revolutionary Ministry of Internal Affairs." In *Russian Officialdom: The Bureaucratization of Russian Society from the Seventeenth to the Twentieth Century*, ed. W. Pintner and D. Rowney. Chapel Hill: University of North Carolina Press, 1980.

Schedrin, Vassili. "Neizvestnaia istoriia khasidizma i drugie raboty Moiseia Berlina." *Arkhiv evreiskoi istorii* 1 (2004): 169–92.

Schochat, Azriel. "The Assimilatory Views of Zalkind Minor, 'Crown Rabbi' of Moscow." *Zion* 44 (1979): 303–20.

Schorsch, Ismar. *From Text to Context: The Turn to History in Modern Judaism*. Hanover, N.H.: Brandeis University Press, University Press of New England, 1994.

Shitiuk, M. M., and V. V. Shchukin. *Evreis'ke naselennia Khersons'koi gubernii v XIX-na pochatku XX stolit'*. Nikolaev, 2008.

Slocum, John W. "Who, and When, Were the Inorodtsy? The Evolution of the Category of 'Aliens' in Imperial Russia." *Russian Review* 57 (1998): 173–90.

Slutsky, Judah. "Beit ha-Midrash le-Rabbanim be-Vilna." *He'avar* 7 (1960): 29–48.

Soifer, Paul. "The Bespectacled Cossak: S. A. Bershadskii (1850–1896) and the Development of Russo-Jewish Historiography." Ph.D. diss., Pennsylvania State University, 1975.

Sorkin, David. *The Transformation of German Jewry, 1780–1840*. New York: Oxford University Press, 1987.

Sosis, Israel. "Obshchestvennye nastroeniia epokhi Velikikh reform." *Evreiskaia starina* 7 (1914): 21–41, 182–97, 342–64.

Staliunas, Darius. *Making Russians: Meaning and Practice of Russification in Lithuania and Belarus after 1863*. Amsterdam-New York: Rodopi, 2007.

Stanislawski, Michael. *For Whom Do I Toil? Judah Leib Gordon and the Crisis of Russian Jewry*. New York: Oxford University Press, 1988.

Stanislawski, Michael. *Tsar Nicholas I and the Jews: The Transformation of Jewish Society in Russia, 1825–1855*. Philadelphia: Jewish Publication Society of America, 1983.

Stein, Sarah Abrevaya. *Making Jews Modern: The Yiddish and Ladino Press in the Russian and Ottoman Empires*. Bloomington: Indiana University Press, 2004.

Trunk, Isaiah. "Istoriki russkogo evreistva." In *Kniga o russkom evreistve*. New York, 1960.

Tsinberg, Israel. "Isaak Ber Levinzon i ego vremia." *Evreiskaia starina* 3 (1910): 505–41.

Varadinov, Nikolai. *Istoriia Ministerstva vnutrennikh del*. St. Petersburg, 1858–1863.

Vitenberg, Maiia. "Vlast', obshchestvo i evreiskii vopros v Rossii v 80-e gody XIX veka." Ph.D. diss., St. Petersburg Institute of History, Russian Academy of Sciences, 2009.

Wcislo, Francis. *Reforming Rural Russia: State, Local Society and National Politics, 1855–1914*. Princeton, N.J.: Princeton University Press, 1990.

Wcislo, Francis. *Tales of Imperial Russia: The Life and Times of Sergei Witte, 1849–1915*. Oxford: Oxford University Press, 2011.

Werth, Paul. *At the Margins of Orthodoxy: Mission, Governance, and Confessional Politics in Russia's Volga-Kama Region, 1827–1905*. Ithaca, N.Y.: Cornell University Press, 2002.

Werth, Paul. *The Tsar's Foreign Faiths: Toleration and the Fate of Religious Freedom in Imperial Russia*. Oxford: Oxford University Press, 2014.

Whittaker, Cynthia. *The Origins of Modern Russian Education: An Intellectual Biography of Count Sergei Uvarov, 1786–1855*. DeKalb: Northern Illinois University Press, 1984.

Wortman, Richard. *The Development of a Russian Legal Consciousness*. Chicago: University of Chicago Press, 1976.

Wortman, Richard. *Scenarios of Power: Myth and Ceremony in Russian Monarchy, Volume One: From Peter the Great to the Death of Nicholas I.* Princeton, N.J.: Princeton University Press, 1995.

Zaionchkovskii, Petr. *Pravitel'stvennyi apparat samoderzhavnoi Rossii v XIX v.* Moscow, 1978.

Zalkin, Mordechai. "The Vilna Rabbinical Seminary: Image and Reality." *Gal-Ed* 14 (1995): 59–72.

Zipperstein, Steven. *The Jews of Odessa: A Cultural History, 1794–1881.* Stanford, Calif.: Stanford University Press, 1985.

Index

Index

Poltava, Chernigov, and Kharkov governor-generalship, 73
Poltava province, 64, 67, 73, 75, 76, 94–96, 98, 118, 124, 131, 142, 143, 145, 161, 212, 218, 234n65, 248n3–5, 249n8. *See also* Poltava, Chernigov, and Kharkov governor-generalship
Poltavskie gubernskie vedomosti (newspaper), 142
Potapov, Aleksandr L'vovich, 158
Pototzki, Severin, 33
Priluki, 98
Protestant (Evangelical Lutheran) Christianity, 24, 26–30, 38, 40, 236n91
Provincial Commissions on Jewish Question (1881), 79, 105
Provisional Government, 84, 113, 114
Prussia, 6, 36, 37
Psalms of David, 184
Pukher, Solomon, 56, 71, 211, 213, 214, 217, 219, 221, 244n108
Pumpianskii, Aaron: as government rabbi, 124, 244n108; as scholar, 183, 241n65; biography and career of, 56, 211, 213, 214, 218, 219, 221; non-official pursuits of, 125, 180

rabbinate: "double", 132, 137; "spiritual" (*dukhovnyi*), 55, 58, 109, 112, 128, 132, 137, 138, 141, 180, 239n47; district (*uezdnyi*), 17, 18, 32, 42, 46, 48, 52, 55, 70, 75, 111, 128, 130, 145, 160, 172, 201, 202, 234n57; government (*kazennyi*), 52, 55, 56, 85, 93, 95, 124, 150, 151, 162, 164, 234n57; provincial (*gubernskii*), 17, 18, 36, 45–48, 69–72; traditional, 41, 43, 47, 51, 112, 180, 190, 239n47
Rabbinical Commission: 37, 56, 66, 69, 208; as Jewish religious supreme court of appeals, 145; as state institution, 6, 8, 10, 18, 20, 43, 48, 75, 78, 201, 202, 234n57, 256n171; expert Jews' membership in, 80, 97, 105, 107, 161, 176, 202, 216, 217, 237n7; of 1861, 72, 130, 136, 158, 165–67, 180, 256n168; of 1879, 152; of 1909, 113, 132. *See also beit din*; censorship; *halacha*, fanaticism; Jewish oath; synagogue
rabbinical congress: in Nikolaev (1901), 112; in St. Petersburg (1910), 56, 112, 113, 132, 249n9

rabbinical seminaries: 181, 218; and education of expert Jews, 57, 65, 67, 69, 91–94, 103, 107, 109 113, 117, 118, 246n150; curriculum of, 47, 239n20; European experience, 37, 40. *See also* Metz Rabbinical Seminary; Vilna Rabbinical Seminary; Zhitomir Jewish Teacher's Institute; Zhitomir Rabbinical Seminary
Rabinovich, Osip, 162
raison d'état, 4, 9, 226n26
Rapoport, Ekutiel' Zisl, 245n154
Rapoport, Kiev merchant, 145
rapprochement (*sblizhenie*): 11, 74, 92, 150, 162, 184, 223n12; and religion, 17, 26; and service of expert Jews, 43, 60, 80, 103, 201; and secret international Jewish government, 78. *See also* Fanaticism; Jewish education
Rassvet (journal), 105, 161, 162, 179, 183
recognized religions, 23–25, 27, 30, 38, 42
Red Cross society, 122
regeneration, 7, 8, 39, 50, 70
Règlement of 1806. *See* French Jewish consistories
religious boards (*dukhovnye pravleniia*): as general religious institution controlled by the Department of Spiritual Affairs, 28; as governing body of Jewish prayer assemblies, 54, 128, 138, 150; as institutional supplement to provincial rabbinate, 17, 46, 70, 232n1
religious indifference, policy of, 27, 29
Riga, 50, 56, 98, 124, 125, 146, 180, 183, 217, 218, 241n65, 244n108. *See also* Baltic governor-generalship
Rikhter, Aleksandr Borisovich, 37
Rogger, Hans, 226n26
Roman Catholic Christianity, 24, 26–30, 38
Romanovka, 111
Rosh Hashana, 3, 154, 156
Rostovtsev, Iakov Ivanovich, 122
Russian Bible Society (RBO), 28, 29, 230n30
Russian Civil War, 209
Russian-Japanese War, 122
Russian Jewish historiography, 8, 14, 183, 186, 188, 200
Russian language: 1; and term "expert Jew," 54; as means of social transformation, 162, 181; expert Jews and proficiency in,

CPSIA information can be obtained
at www.ICGtesting.com
Printed in the USA
LVOW04*1113291016
510415LV00007B/19/P